PENGUIN BOOKS
C.V. RAMAN

Uma Parameswaran was born in Chennai, and educated in Jabalpur and Nagpur, where her father was a professor of physics. In 1966, she emigrated to Canada with her husband. She earned her PhD from Michigan State University in 1972 and recently retired as professor of English from the University of Winnipeg. She has published extensively in the field of postcolonial literatures and is the author of several works of fiction, poetry and drama, including the award-winning collection *What Was Always Hers* and a recent novel, *A Cycle of the Moon*.

D1784677

C.V. Raman
A Biography

UMA PARAMESWARAN

PENGUIN BOOKS

PENGUIN BOOKS

USA | Canada | UK | Ireland | Australia
New Zealand | India | South Africa | China

Penguin Books is part of the Penguin Random House group of companies
whose addresses can be found at global.penguinrandomhouse.com

Published by Penguin Random House India Pvt. Ltd
7th Floor, Infinity Tower C, DLF Cyber City,
Gurgaon 122 002, Haryana, India

Penguin
Random House
India

First published by Penguin Books India 2011

ISBN 9780143066897

Typeset in Minion by Eleven Arts, Delhi

Printed at Repro Knowledgecast Limited, India

www.penguin.co.in

To my parents, A.S. Ganesan and Rajalakshmi Ganesan

To my parents, A.S. Sachan and R. Lakshmi Ganesan

Contents

Author's Note

The scientific life of C.V. Raman has been documented in various ways. All of his scientific papers were presented in a series of six volumes in time for Raman's birth centenary—that was also the Diamond Jubilee year of the Raman Effect—in 1988 and much of the works by Raman and about him were digitized and made available at the Raman Research Institute in Bangalore. His science is great and well documented but perhaps his personal vision, idiosyncrasies and struggles would be even more fascinating for the average reader. Alas, most of those who knew him personally have also died by now. This volume is an attempt to record his life and to trace the influences and events that made him the interesting man and scientist that he was.

I am indebted to several individuals and books in the writing of this biography. For incidents related to Raman's early life, I acknowledge the data included in a family history written by his elder brother, C. Subrahmanya Ayyar (1885–1960). Written in 1946, it records family genealogy and main events. Throughout the book, I have generally followed a style of reconstructing the events with conversations and narrations while adhering to facts.

I acknowledge, too, the work done by Sivaraj Ramaseshan in preserving the scientific works of Raman and for freely sharing personal and professional experiences of his relationship with

Raman, through narrated anecdotes and published articles. He has done more than any other single person to perpetuate Raman's legacy.

There are three excellent biographies of Raman's scientific life: *Journey into Light*, written by G. Venkataraman (1988), *Professor C.V. Raman: Scientific Work at Calcutta* by S.N. Sen (1988) and *Nobel Laureate C.V. Raman's Work on Light Scattering: Historical Contributions to a Scientific Biography* by Rajinder Singh (2004). Rajinder Singh's volume is a very useful compilation of records of Raman's scientific life, complete with direct references to reports of organizations ranging from the Indian Association for the Cultivation of Science in Calcutta to the Nobel archives in Stockholm, letters to and from Raman, Raman's contacts and correspondence with scientists within India and from Europe and the United States and a host of details about Raman's working life. Another book on Raman's scientific life is *Raman and His Effect* (1980) by G.H. Keswani.

One can glean the person behind the scientist from memoirs and biographical sketches written by his students and associates— P. Krishnamurti (1938), S. Bhagavantam (1971), P.R. Pisharoty (1982), A. Jayaraman (1989).

I had the pleasant experience of the wonders of cyberspace when I found that nearly every individual I contacted by e-mail promptly responded with the information I sought from them.

In particular, I would like to specially acknowledge:

the late Lokasundari Raman, who shared many stories about her life and times with me during the 1970s when I started writing a biography of her early life and times;

the late Sivaraj Ramaseshan, for valuable information about Raman, given to me during our informal meetings;

Rajinder Singh, whose book, and especially e-mails about sources, have been extremely useful;

Raman Research Institute for providing me open access to digitized material and library resources;

Mr G. Madhavan for photographs from the Indian Academy of Sciences;

Dr Y.M. Patil, librarian, Raman Research Institute; and

Mr Manjunatha for copying photographs from the archives of the Raman Research Institute.

The Man, the Scientist, the Legacy

Look at the resplendent colours on the soap bubbles!
Why is the sea blue?
What makes diamonds glitter?
Ask the right questions, and nature will open the doors to her secrets.

~

'I have planted a papaya tree today. I will not be here when it bears fruit, but there will be others to enjoy them.'

Chandrasekhara Venkata Raman (1888–1970) responded to beauty in nature and in art with all his senses. He was at all times a scientist, breathing and living science throughout his life, giving all he had—material, intellectual, spiritual—to the cause of science. He made the Indian Association for the Cultivation of Science in Calcutta everything that its founder, Mahendralal Sircar, had dreamt it would be. At the Indian Academy of Sciences that he founded in Bangalore, he continued to shape as per his own vision a space where scientists could pursue their research without bureaucratic interference, where journals would publish research results expeditiously and where the physical environment was set against nature's unfailing beauty. The truest part of education, he maintained, was to cultivate 'a love of the Beautiful'.[1]

He often spoke about the links between art, aesthetics and science. The man of science, he once said, 'seeks to resolve her [nature's] infinite complexities into a few simple principles or elements of action which he calls the laws of nature. In doing this, the man of science, like the exponents of other forms of art, subjects himself to a rigorous discipline, the rules of which he had laid down for himself and which he calls logic. . . . Science . . . is a fusion of man's aesthetic and intellectual functions devoted to the representations of nature. It is therefore the highest form of creative art'.[2]

Raman won the Nobel Prize for Physics in 1930 for his observation of a phenomenon of light scattering, which was to be one of the most convincing proofs of the quantum theory. It was the culmination of seven years of work. During his sea voyage to England in 1921, he had wondered about the blueness of the Mediterranean Sea. Unable to accept Lord Rayleigh's explanation that the colour of the sea was just a reflection of the colour of the sky, Raman speculated that it was the result of the scattering of sunlight by the water molecules. He published his speculation right away but it was another seven years before he could experimentally prove the details of the phenomenon. The Raman Effect was discovered in February 1928.

Raman's love for his country was clear in his actions throughout his life. When Raman was a physically immature but an intellectually precocious sixteen-year-old student at Presidency College, Madras, noting his academic potential, his professors suggested he go to England for further studies. But the civil surgeon of Madras declared him too frail to withstand the rigours of the English climate. In later years, Raman often said he was very glad at the turn of events for it had made him realize that since a scientist studied nature, India had everything any scientist needed and one did not have to go West.

When Raman was forty-two, and rose to receive the Nobel Prize from King Gustav in Stockholm on 10 December 1930, he broke down in tears because 'when I turned round and saw the British Union Jack under which I had been sitting . . . I realised that my poor country, India, did not even have a flag of her own—and it was this that triggered off my complete breakdown'.[3]

Raman was passionate about two things—that the individual scientist should be able to do his work unhindered by bureaucracy and that scientific inquiry should be directed towards the welfare of humanity and never towards any form of destruction. He regretted that the powers of science had unleashed the horrors of Hiroshima and Nagasaki and repeatedly pleaded that the scientists of the world unite in ensuring that such an event never takes place again.

If one were to look for a word that characterized Raman's life and work, it would be 'consistency'. His ideas and attitudes developed and evolved but always in a consistent manner. Consistency does not mean a refusal to change or accept one's errors. As he said, 'We should learn that no one is infallible. New knowledge may . . . completely throw out what has been done before.'

His core values were straightforward: he to whom much has been given must in his turn give much. Simple as this sounds, like the simple edicts of the Sermon on the Mount, it is very difficult to practise, but Raman never wavered from this edict and gave freely of his time and talents to research, training of students and to the cultivation of science in India.

He based his life on a set of principles that remained consistent all through his life. Foremost of these was that nature was a source of beauty and was to be valued and enjoyed at all times. He saw hidden worlds of beauty such as most of us have never noticed. He had a childlike love for colours and shapes and for simple pleasures such as walks around his eucalyptus grove and rose bushes. Wherever he lived, he ensured the presence of nature's beauty around himself. When he accepted the directorship of the Indian Institute of Science, one of the first things he did was to have saplings planted on the campus, which later became beautiful avenues of trees. Shortly before he died, he planted a papaya tree, known for the sweetness of its fruit.

Next was Raman's loyalty to his country. His patriotism was not the proselytizing or banner-waving kind that sought to convert others, but one that rooted his own actions firmly within the context of India's past and potential greatness, and faith that development and applications of scientific research would improve the quality of life in India and make India a recognized leader in the comity of nations. Love of country for him did not constitute loyalty to the ruling government but 'love of the earth that bore us, feeds us and sustains us'.[4]

Science was his religion, his godhead. Krishna says in the Bhagavad Gita (VII:3): 'From among thousands one seeks Me, and of the thousands who seek Me one finds Me.' Raman recognized that scientific achievement can come to a nation only if there is a widespread base of researchers, from among whom a few might be genuine seekers, and a select handful might actually find some basic truths about the workings of nature. He sought to build a strong scientific community in the country, one that consisted not only of individual talent and well-equipped centres, but had forums such as meetings and journals that would bring scientists together and showcase their achievements with national pride.

Raman drew his personal inspiration from his childhood reading of Edwin Arnold's *Light of Asia*, about Buddha's life, that one must focus on the search even if it means renunciation of life's pleasures. He never spared himself and he expected his students to be totally focused as well. In the course of forty years, about five hundred students passed through his direct mentorship and wrote a total of 1500 papers on experiments they had done under his direction. He himself published about 450 papers. Within the first ten years of his affiliation with the Indian Association for the Cultivation of Science in Calcutta, he established a centre of scientific activity that produced students who went on to lead the modern renaissance of science in India.

Self-discipline was another strong trait. He lived a simple life and did not hanker after novelty or variety in his lifestyle, clothes, food or daily routine. He treasured the gold-brocaded coat and shawl that came with the title of 'Rajasabha Bhushana' conferred on him by the maharaja of Mysore and loved the photograph of himself in the durbar regalia, but cared little for the insignia of robes and medal that came with the knighthood conferred on him by the British. However, he was proud of his knighthood and bore the title throughout his life. Many other Indians gave up the title, some before Independence and some after, but Raman kept the title. He claimed it was a distinction he had received for his scientific contribution and political lines of demarcation were not relevant to science. He liked to be called Sir C.V. Raman, and his wife was addressed as Lady Raman.

His sense of humour enlivened all his public lectures and always drew a crowd. Many of his speeches were masterpieces of extemporaneous orations, which have come to us only through newspaper summaries and oral anecdotes. The attention and mentoring he gave his students seem phenomenal, considering the number of students who worked with him at any given time. One of his students in the 1930s, P.R. Pisharoty (1909–2002), who is also one of his biographers, relates an anecdote about Raman's wit. Once when Pisharoty was working on an experiment, Raman asked him why he was looking so dejected. Pisharoty replied that a British scientist might leave him behind in completing the experiment, owing to the five-kilowatt X-ray tube he had at his disposal, instead of the one-kilowatt tube Pisharoty was using. 'There is a very simple solution,' pat came Raman's reply. 'Put a ten-kilowatt brain on the problem.'

Raman had the ability to identify promising students at the first meeting; most of the 500 students who researched under his supervision went on to distinguish themselves. He was also said to be an egotist and blunt in his criticism of ideas that did not meet with his approval. But with students he was nurturing, Pisharoty says, he would first compliment the student for the work done and then point out what was wrong. 'His initial encouragement so much boosted up the student's morale' that the student would willingly repeat the experiment over and over again until he got it right.

Another principle that drove Raman's life was a love of autonomy that verged on a fierce independence which brooked no interference in the fair pursuit of his goals—a quality that was the source of many of his later problems with politicians and everything political.

Two early examples of his insistence on autonomy were his decision to choose his own life partner at a time when arranged marriages were the norm and his decision to take up a government job so as to be free from financial constraints in his pursuit of science. Another instance was when Sir Asutosh Mookerjee offered him the Palit Professorship in 1914; he countered the offer with a request, among other things, that he would be 'in the sole executive charge of all laboratory arrangements'.[5] This was not given to him at that time, but he held fast to this concept of absolute autonomy all his life. A few days before his death in 1970, addressing the future of the Raman Research Institute, he said, 'Any person who assumes the responsibility of running the Institute must have full control of the laboratories, libraries, workshops and other facilities. He must be empowered to acquire and dispense money in the name of the Institute.'[6] Of course we can see that this autonomy is dangerous unless it comes with the self-discipline and honesty that Raman himself had, and which he assumed everyone would have.

Examples of autonomy in his later life often led his actions to be misconstrued because of the way he asserted his view on the matter. Those who were close to him have numerous stories of the way he brushed off politicians and potential government funds. The dictum 'Do unto others as you would have them do unto you' underlay many of the problems he had in his later life. Political expediency often demands that you do unto others as *they* would have you do unto them, and this was abhorrent to him.

Raman had strong views on the incompatibility of politics and science, politics and patriotism, politics and independence, and he expressed his views without mincing words. He paid a price and he paid it willingly. He did not accept government grants during his lifetime. But as he lay dying, he relieved his successors of his own ideology. 'I strongly believe that fundamental science cannot be driven by instructional, industrial, governmental or military pressures. This was the reason why I decided, as far as possible, not to accept money from the government. I am a practical man, and I am practical enough to see that it would not be possible for others to run or grow a good institution without funds. . . . I therefore will not put it as a condition that no government funds should be accepted by the Institute.'[7]

Politics and science should not mix, Raman declared unequivocally in his speeches, but his life was often impacted by the force of politics. Provincial politics drove him out of Calcutta, a city he loved as his own, and followed him to his new post as director of Indian Institute of Science in Bangalore. The politics of scientific rivalry pursued him in his post-Nobel Prize years. Raman had a lot to say about the intrusive way in which politics toxicized life and a scientific career. None of what he said endeared him to peers and politicians, but he was steady in his pursuit of scientific inquiry and relied on his own intellectual and financial resources, achieving spectacular results in a long life dedicated to his vision.

His scientific work was in physics, in the fields of acoustics, optics and light scattering, ultrasonics and crystallography, vibrations of crystal lattices in diamond and other gems, optics of minerals and the physiology of vision. Even a cursory look at these and other subjects reveals his love of everyday wonders: the colours of leaves, bird plumage, shells and seawater, the shapes of soap bubbles, the intricacies of musical instruments, the facets of gems and diamonds, the marvels of vision and sound and so on.

Raman made his major discovery in February 1928 at the laboratories of the Indian Association for the Cultivation of Science. The Raman Effect is the inelastic scattering of a photon. It questioned the phenomenon known as Rayleigh Scattering, which states that when light is scattered from a molecule most photons are elastically scattered. According to Rayleigh's principle, the scattered photons have the same frequency and, therefore, wavelength, as the incident photons. However, Raman found that a small fraction of light scattered by liquids consists of photons with energies different from (and usually lower than) that of the incident photons. Since differences in energy are equivalent to differences in wavelengths, these lines show up as distinct features in the scattered spectrum. Each molecule has a unique Raman spectrum. Since no two compounds have the same Raman spectrum, and since the intensity of a Raman line of a substance is proportional to its concentration, Raman spectroscopy can be used extensively in qualitative and quantitative analysis of substances, in the calculation of thermodynamic properties and in the study of molecular structures.

The conclusive experiments were carried out during the first two weeks of February 1928, and a one-page paper titled 'A New Type of Secondary Radiation' was published in *Nature* on 31 March 1928. Raman sent a further note to *Nature*, published on 21 April. On 16 March 1928, he spoke before the scientific community in Bangalore about his findings. The lecture was published on 31 March in the *Indian Journal of Physics* and copies were mailed out throughout the world. Raman and his associate, K.S. Krishnan, sent yet another note to *Nature* on 'Optical Analogue of the Compton Effect' that was published on 5 May 1928. Raman's promptness in recognizing the importance of the discovery gave him an edge over two Russian scientists who had arrived at similar results but did not seek the publication of their results till later.

Within a year of the discovery, 150 papers had mentioned his discovery. By 1970, about ten thousand scientific papers had been published on the Raman Effect. In May 2009 Google listed about 5,30,000 scholarly articles on the applications of Raman Effect and another search engine, Lycos, 57,000. By June 2011 the numbers were 86,70,000 and 4,50,000 respectively (though the high numbers may owe to the repetition in statistics collected through search engines).

In the 1980s commercial FT Raman spectrometers built using the Fourier Transform technique, coupled with the sophistication of computer technology for handling data, was only one of the many uses that led to resurgence in the application of the Raman Effect. In 1998 the Raman Effect was designated an ACS (American Chemical Society) National Historical Chemical Landmark in recognition of its significance as a tool for analysing the composition of liquids, gases and solids.

As professor of physics at the Indian Institute of Science (1933–48), Raman went on to research other scientific phenomena and, more importantly, to discover and mentor a whole generation of scientists. Those who worked with him in Calcutta and Bangalore carried the torch to other parts of the country, holding high administrative and research positions. After retiring from the Indian Institute in 1948, Raman opened his own Raman Research Institute in Bangalore and engaged in his scientific interests until his death in 1970.

The Raman Research Institute is now a flourishing research centre, a living monument to Raman's legacy.

Family background and early years

When a journalist assumed C.V. Raman had been born with a silver spoon in his mouth, Raman, with his usual loud laugh, said it was a copper spoon, for at the time of his birth his father was earning the princely sum of ten rupees per month.

C.V. Raman's family origins have been traced to the second quarter of the eighteenth century.[1] The earliest name we have is of Pethar Seshadry, who lived sometime between 1730 and 1800 in Vaigalathur, a village near Thanjavur. His son, Ayyamuthian (a nickname for the given name of 'Muthuswami') was Raman's great-great-great-grandfather. Ayyamuthian is said to have gone to Malabar, on the west coast, to seek his fortune. He came back with enough money to purchase 200 acres of agricultural land in the villages of Mangudi and Porasakudi, in the Papanasam taluk of Thanjavur district. He and his wife Ananda Lakshmi had two sons, Vengappan and Adimurti. Vengappan and his wife Laxmi had two sons, the elder of whom was named Subrahmanya and called Amritham or Amridappan. The younger son, Kailasam, was given away in adoption to a *sagotra*, a relative of the paternal line of descent, who did not have any son of his own. It was the custom in those days for members in an extended family to allow a cousin who did not have a son to adopt one of their sons since a son plays a key role in certain practices and rituals of Hinduism.

Since an adopted son got all the rights and responsibilities of a birth-son, he lost the claim to those within his birth family. This percolated into the legal context of property rights and so Amridappan's brother, having been adopted, would have lost his share of his father's property. However, Amridappan decided that sons born to the same parents should not deprive one another of their inheritance. He kept only half of their father's land, which had grown to a total of 104 acres since his grandfather's time. Amridappan and his wife Rangammal had four sons. The youngest, born in 1837, was named Ramanathan.

Ramanathan's first wife died before their marriage was consummated. In those days, it was customary for girls to be married off before they attained puberty. They usually continued to live with their parents until they reached puberty, after which there was a second religious ceremony, *shanti kalyanam*, in which the families came together again and the couple and their parents reiterated many of the prayers and vows. This was followed by the young woman moving into her in-laws' home.

Ramanathan was a famous bamboo-fencer in the village. He regularly trained at the *talimkhana* (gymnasium) and led others to train likewise. In a society where each caste was associated with a particular kind of profession, the Brahmins were custodians of religious and philosophical knowledge. Their training was, therefore, oriented towards intellectual contexts. They did not usually train in actual physical attack or defence tactics. However, when the times demand change, changes take place. The Kallars (literally, Robbers), who lived in nearby villages, were a group of people who took to aggressive means to sustain themselves. They stole crops, both from fields at harvest time and from storage bins in other seasons. Threshing season was their favourite time for they could carry large amounts of grain right off the threshing floor. If the landowners or peasants chased them as they ran with their loot, rather than leave the bags and flee, they would selfishly strew the grain on to the ground so no one could use it. To protect themselves from these raiders, Brahmins took to the art of bamboo-fencing.

Ramanathan's father had once outmanoeuvred a Kallar raid by organizing his peasant helpers to surround them and tie their hands and feet; he then extracted a promise from the leader that he would not raid Porasakudi village in his lifetime. The Kallars had their own code of honour and the chieftain kept his word. But once he died, the raids started again. Ramanathan, who like his father, took care to be very physically fit, organized physical training classes for both Brahmins and peasants so that they would be ready to resist the Kallars during such raids.

Ramanathan knew by rote the standard Sanskrit slokas required in daily worship, but he could read only Tamil. He regularly read from the *Bhagavatham* and the Puranas in Tamil. His puja room had *vigraha*s of all the standard deities but his deity of special preference was Subrahmanya. He frequently went to worship at the Subrahmanya temple at Swamimalai, near Kumbakonam.

Ramanathan and his second wife, named Sitalakshmi but called Muthuchipi, had five children in all. The first, a son, died at the age of two. The second, a son, was born in September 1866 and was named Chandrasekharan. Next came three daughters, Gnanam, Rangam and Sundaram. Gnanam was widowed at the age of fourteen and lived in her parental home all her life, first with her parents, then with her brother, and still later with her nephew, Subrahmanya. Rangam was married to Vaidyanatha Iyer, a schoolteacher. Sundaram was married to Sivananda Subrahmanya Sastri, a *bhagavathar* who won awards from the durbar of the Travancore king for his performances. A bhagavathar is one who retells stories from the scriptures in a combination of songs (often accompanied by music) and narrative.

About the time his second daughter was born, Ramanathan moved from Mangudi village to the adjacent village of Porasakudi, his lands spanning both villages. Soon his actual income from his fields diminished considerably as he mortgaged various segments of his land from time to time to meet the expenses of his fast-growing extended family.

Though Ramanathan had no knowledge of English he, like the Brahmin community around him, saw that the new system of education under the British offered prospects of progress and prosperity. When Chandrasekharan was about ten years old, Ramanathan enrolled him at the high school in Kumbakonam, a town that was about twelve miles from the village. He set up a second household, with his mother-in-law's mother in charge. Bullock carts were the mode of transportation and he would make the journey every few weeks, carrying rice and other kitchen provisions required to run a household. Chandrasekharan matriculated in 1881.

About the time he was graduating from school, he was married to Parvathi, who was two years younger to him. She was the fifth child of Saptarishi Sastriar of Tiruvanaikkaval, a temple town near Trichinopoly (Tiruchirappalli or Trichy). Saptarishi had been adventurous as a young man, who seems to have taken rather literally one of the prescribed marriage rituals, Kashi yatra, where the bridegroom symbolically goes to Kashi (Varanasi) to study the scriptures before settling down to wedded life. Soon after his wedding and before the shanti kalyanam that took place two years later, Saptarishi ran away from home and walked north, all the way to Bengal, where he spent some time studying *navya nyaya*, which provides the logical base for Hindu sciences. There is a story that when he was leaving Bengal, a group that periodically offered human sacrifice to Goddess Kali, captured him but he managed to escape. He then returned to his wife and led a normal life, dutifully discharging his family responsibilities, and was respected by all for the knowledge he had gained.

Parvathi was scarcely literate at the time of her wedding, but Chandrasekharan quickly made sure that she learnt to read and write in Tamil, and also taught her many of the songs that he had learnt from his music teacher.

Chandrasekharan went on to enrol for a BA degree at Madras Christian College, in 1884, staying with his cousin Visvam. He took as his subjects English, mathematics and Tamil. Though he did well in the first two, he failed in Tamil. Since the rule was that one had to pass all three subjects in the same attempt, his failure in Tamil set him back. His readings in Herbert Spencer's philosophy and his leanings towards agnosticism (he avidly read R.G. Ingersoll—the American political leader, and Charles Bradlaugh—the English founder of the National Secular Society) and mainly his lack of money to repeat the courses, led him back to the village. He started teaching at a secondary school at Thiruvadamaruthur, near Kumbakonam. His first son, Subrahmanya (C. Subrahmanya Ayyar, hereafter referred to as CS), was born on 8 October 1885. His second son, Venkata Raman (C.V. Raman) was born on 7 November 1888, which according to the Tamil calendar was in the year Sarvadhari, on the twenty-fourth day of the month of Aippassi, at twenty-seven naligais (night hours) of Wednesday, second padam of Purada, Tulam lagnam. For both confinements, Parvathi went back to her parental home in Tiruvanaikkaval near Trichy.

At the time of Raman's birth, Chandrasekharan, or Chandrasekhara Aiyar as he came to be known, was a student-teacher at the high school attached to SPG College (run by the Society for the Propagation of the Gospels) in Trichinopoly, on a salary of ten rupees a month. Parvathi's father helped them out by adding another ten rupees each month. Chandrasekhara Aiyar accepted it as a loan and paid him back once he had a better job.

Soon after this, examination rules changed in his favour and he could take each subject one by one rather than concurrently. He chose Physics instead of Tamil. Over the course of the next few years, 1889–92, while he worked full-time as a teacher at SPG College, he got his bachelor's degree in English, physics and mathematics. He augmented his income by tutoring sons of the rich. There is a story on record that to satiate his love of reading he borrowed a volume of the *Encyclopedia Britannica* from the father of one of these boys and the volume got accidentally soaked in oil. He had to pay Rs 25 to replace that volume, a huge sum for him at the time.

In 1892, having got his BA degree, Chandrasekharan was appointed to teach at Mrs. A.V.N. College in Vizagapatam (now Visakhapatnam), or Waltair, as the British section was called. By now he had three children. He left his older son with his parents and took his wife, Raman and baby daughter Mangalam (born 1891) with him. It took a journey of more than two weeks to go from Trichy to Waltair. The first lap, from Madras to Bezwada and on to Guntakal, was by regular train. The railway tracks beyond were still in the process of being laid, and the family took construction trains and then canal boats to Rajahmundry. There they transferred to bullock carts and finally reached their destination. The tracks were completed soon after, and when he returned next year to bring back his older son, the journey was much shorter. Five more children were born to him between 1894 and 1907: Skandan (Kumaraswamy was his given name) 1894–1914; Sundaram 1898–1907; Sitalaxmi 1901–1972; Meena 1903–1912; and Ramaswamy 1907–1991.

Chandrasekhara Aiyar got his yen for physical fitness from his father. Even as a student in Trichy, he had trained assiduously at bodybuilding and would swim across the Kaveri every day. There is a story that when he was on his way to Vizagapatam to join his teaching job, his fellow passenger, noting his physique, assumed he was going to teach 'gym', as physical education was then called. He had a following among the youth, and many young men trained with him, at daily exercises as well as at the arts of wielding the *karla*, a heavy club, and lifting the *santhula*, a circular granite rock with a handle at the top.

Chandrasekhara transmitted his enthusiasm for athletics to his students at the college, where he coached them in cricket and football and insisted they also train in long jump and other field sports. However, he was unable to enthuse his sons into his idea of a rounded education, that one should be good at all three: academics, music and athletics. The boys were certainly not interested in anything athletic. Nor did they share their father's interest in the violin to learn it at the time, but in later life, both took to the violin, one to play and the other to study vibrations and sound waves. They both had a good ear for music, but did not spend any time learning to sing. Chandrasekhara Aiyar himself was an extrovert, who enjoyed bringing people together by initiating group activities such as starting a Tamil association in his Telugu-speaking environment and organizing music sessions, but his sons preferred to be alone. However, they excelled at their school studies. Both boys voraciously read books written in English. Chandrasekhara Aiyar had a modest collection of books, and he brought more from the college library for them to read. While CS read the European and British classics and books related to literature, Raman was fascinated by science books, even if they were mostly just textbooks used in senior classes that his father had acquired in the pursuit of his own aspirations.

Raman went through his elementary and secondary grades in Vizagapatam. He was always ahead of the class, despite being the youngest student, and aced at every subject. He would complete his schoolwork quickly in order to read something new.

In the summer of 1897, when CS was nearing twelve and Raman nearing nine, their grandfather decided it was time for the boys' *upanayanam* ceremony. This is an initiation ceremony, where the Brahmin boy begins to wear the sacred thread across his chest. Their father had become an agnostic as a student in Madras, but at home, due to the influence of the older generation, Hinduism was a presence that had its ways. The grandfather arranged for a *paal-kaavadi* ceremony at the Swamimalai temple prior to the upanayanam.

The ceremony consists of each of the initiates, in this case CS and Raman, carrying a *kaavadi* to the temple. The kaavadi is in the shape of a weighing scale; the sturdy wooden bar is carried on the shoulder and there is a pot or a basket on either side, hung from ropes. The pots are filled with rice or milk (paal) or fruit, depending on what the devotee has undertaken to offer to God Subrahmanya. Brass bells adorn the wooden stick and announce the coming of the kaavadi bearer, who sometimes observes the vow of silence as he walks to the shrine. Traditionally, the bearer is supposed to start with empty pots and beg for them to be filled; alternately, the pots are filled by his family. Later the sanctified offering is distributed to devotees at the temple.

At the upanayanam, Raman was initiated into the sacred words of the *gayatri mantra* by his grandfather and his older brother, by his father. Throughout life, Raman cared little for religious rituals and always referred to the beauty and creativity of nature when asked about his faith, but, strangely enough, there were a few external manifestations of Brahminism that he followed. He sported a tuft—a few strands of uncut hair usually tied into a topknot—that was seldom seen because he always wore a turban. He wore his sacred thread, or *poonal*. He remained a vegetarian; and he said his *pariseshanam* at every meal taken at home. The pariseshanam is a short ritual where one pours water on the palm of one's right hand, sprinkles a few drops around the leaf or plate on which the food is served, and drinks what remains, intoning prescribed words of prayer. But Raman clearly inherited his desire to keep away from the dogmas of the faith from his father.

Even though Raman's father had spent some time in his student days trying to prove that Madame Blavatsky—the co-founder of the Theosophical Society—was not a genuine philosopher, and that theosophy was a hoax, Chandrasekharan took to theosophy in his later days, perhaps through his neighbours, Babu Govind Das and Babu Bhagvan Das. Govind Das would come with his family from Banaras to spend the winter in Vizagapatam's more salubrious climate, and their house was close to Chandrasekhara Aiyar's. They spent many hours discussing theosophy and India's future and what needed to be done to improve the educational system. There was an intellectual rapport between the three men; their sons too became good friends and the families stayed in touch over the years. Govind Das and Bhagvan Das were at Raman's side several years later when he received news of his father's death, and their presence was comforting at that difficult time.

Raman matriculated at the age of twelve at the end of 1900 and joined Mrs. A.V.N. College where his father taught physics, mathematics and geography. In those days the school year corresponded to the calendar year. Raman went through all the texts much before classes started—Radhakrishnan's *Algebra*, Smith and Bryant's *Geometry*, Hall and Steven's *Trigonometry*—and read the texts prescribed for literature and the Greek classics even though he did not need them for the intermediate courses.

Raman's need for new books to read seemed to never end. He devoured standard texts used in high school and college, such as S.L. Loney's *Plane Trigonometry*, Benjamin Williamson's *Elementary Treatise on Differential Calculus*, Forsythe's *Differential Equations* and a new edition of George Salmon's 1848 text, *A Treatise on Conic Sections*. He was upset that his father's college library did not have a copy of Salmon's later works, *A Treatise on Higher Plane Curves* (1852) and *A Treatise on the Analytic Geometry of Three Dimensions* (1862).

When he was in middle school, Chandrasekharan, noting how

interested Raman was in experiments, took him to the college laboratory. On seeing the real experiments, where he could directly observe the reactions of the chemicals in the test tube, Raman was thrilled. There was magic in the Leyden jar, where you could store what could not be seen. A jar, some tin foil, a tight-fitting lid and abracadabra—a spark, energy out of the air as it were. Soon after, when he fell ill, Raman asked his father to bring home a Leyden jar. Just how did things happen in that jar?

Now, as he spent the holidays waiting for classes to begin, Raman wanted more books. Way up on the topmost shelf of his father's almirah were books that drew his attention. His father was excited. He talked to Raman about the basics of physics; electricity, electromagnetism, magnetic fields. Chandrasekharan himself had hoped to do his master's degree in physics and had bought those books, planning to get help from Ramalinga Iyer, of the Government College at Rajahmundry, during his vacations. But it had proved impractical, and the tomes had lain untouched for several years. Now he took the books down and Raman was instantly glued to Maxwell's *A Dynamical Theory of the Electromagnetic Field*. His father had hoped to explain the concepts further when he returned from work, but there was no need. Instead, Raman animatedly talked about the initial chapters of the book that evening, having spent the day poring over it.

The advanced physics and mathematics books were brought down, and Raman read them all, over the course of the next few months. He was particularly taken up with Edward Routh's books, *A Treatise on Dynamics of Rigid Bodies*, *A Treatise on Analytic Statistics* and the just published *A Treatise on Dynamics of a Particle*. He glanced at George Boole's books and put them away for the future.

Raman completed his intermediate courses in December 1902 and left for Madras in January 1903 to do his BA. His older brother had already moved to Madras the previous year.

Chandrasekhara Aiyar was not happy sending away his second son, especially to a hostel. Raman was so young, so inexperienced, so unaware of the world and its ways that he was concerned about the boy and often thought of him with tears in his eyes. But he took comfort in the thought that his elder son was by Raman's side. Then, when the boys came home in the summer of 1903, he noticed how thin Raman had grown, and how little he ate. Raman laughed it away. Hostel food, he said, was enough to destroy the hugest appetite and to contract the stomach's capacity to half its original. But his father was concerned. He took steps to rent a house in Madras and set up a household to be run by his parents and his sister, Gnanam, who lived with them. He wrote to friends and relatives in Madras to find a suitable place. Throughout the time Raman was with them that summer, Chandrasekharan watched his son for symptoms of ill health.

Raman, however, was in high spirits. He talked to his family about Madras, the iridescent shells on the beach, the colour of sunrise above the eastern horizon of the sea, the hustle and bustle of the streets, the sight of fishermen pushing their catamarans into the sea early morning, the smell of fish on the beach on his evening walks. He laughingly told them about how people were always surprised to see a little schoolboy—which they thought he was because of his slim, small frame—walking the corridors of Presidency College. At his first English class, Professor E.H. Elliott assumed he had walked into the classroom by mistake and was surprised to learn that this fourteen-year-old boy was indeed a student.

Raman's younger siblings were enthusiastic listeners. 'Presidency College' sounded so important, so awesome. Sitalaxmi, just two and lisping her first sentences, liked the name and tried saying it: 'Presidency, am going to Presidency College.' Sundaram, five, was too young to understand what all this talk was about, but Skandan, now nine, listened eagerly to what his brother had to say about this new world of science. He wanted to know why seashells came in so many different kinds and shapes and sizes.

Raman explained what he knew of this. Shells are essentially common chalk, or calcium carbonate. When this is burnt, it quickly converts to quicklime, which is used in everyday life. Quicklime is used on the soil to get rid of some of the acidity; it is used by potters and in the making of mortar and plaster to hasten the hardening of the clay and make it adhere better so the pot, or wall, doesn't fall apart.

But what did all this have to do with the shapes and colours of the shells, Skandan asked.

Sorry, Raman said, I'd got carried away by my class notes. The creature within the shell secretes this chalk and deposits it on itself every day till the shell is built up so the creature is safe inside it and cannot be attacked and eaten up. While the shell is being formed, chalk, with the help of the sticky secretion, forms crystals, thin layers and layers of it, which reflect sunlight and give rise to colours just as the rainbow is formed by refraction and reflection when sunlight hits molecules of water. Colours, nature's most wonderful magic! Raman could not have enough of colours.

Raman made a bowl of soap bubbles to show the colours of the rainbow, and thereafter, blowing soap bubbles became a favourite game for the siblings. Sundaram loved the bubbles when they were all stuck together. Sometimes they burst, but sometimes two bubbles became one, and he loved that. Bubbles were always round, but here the bubbles stuck together. How did that happen, he wanted to know. Why was the bubble round anyway? How did a bubble start out long and thin and eventually become round? Raman explained that the surface tension gives the layer a kind of elasticity, and the soap causes the surface tension to increase, so the bubble lasts longer; and that bubbles always end up spherical because for a given volume, the sphere had the smallest possible surface area.

Raman's language had already become hybrid, with many nouns in English and a few Tamil verbs and adjectives holding sentences together. While Sundaram was happy to repeat the English words into a sing-song chant, Skandan paid keen attention, asking more questions. He practised the tricks Raman showed them: how to make a coin disappear from the bottom of a tumbler by adding more water to the tumbler, how to make a stick appear to break underwater—simple tricks of refraction of light.

When the newspaper published a report about the progress of the hydroelectric project at Sivasamudram, and that the power station was transmitting three megawatts of electricity all the way to the Kolar gold mines ninety miles away, Raman remembered his fascination with the Leyden jar and replicated some of the experiments for the delight of his younger brothers. There are gold and diamond mines underground, under the rivers, he said, and one day we'll bring all the treasures up, and bask in the beauty of the gems' colours. Like in Ali Baba's cave? Skandan asked.

His grandmother had questions too. She wanted to know how often he washed his hair, that it was so grimy and in strings instead of hanging glossily down his back. It is the weather, Raman sought an excuse. Hair does not dry easily in the humid air of the sea coast. That is the reason then, she said, why you have become so thin, always with a cough, a cold. Don't you know that wet hair bundled under that cap of yours affects the lungs? Cut off your hair; why does a boy need long hair? Just cut it off and oil your hair every day.

But I do. I oil it every day, he said in his defence.

No wonder it was in such straggly clumps: to oil your hair without taking off the excess with *shikakai*, no wonder your hair is such a mess all knotted up under your cap.

Raman's grandmother took her seat on the stone bench in the back veranda and made him sit on the floor at her feet. She rubbed hot oil into his hair, massaging and combing, while he sat back enjoying the massage. Great gobs of hair-knots came off on the comb. She sent him off for a warm bath. Get it cropped really short, she said; short hair is good enough for boys. What do boys know about taking care of long, beautiful hair?

Raman loved talking to grandmother Muthuchipi because she was so quick to grasp what he said. Mother was always busy, and pregnant. But Paati had time. She always seemed to finish her work fast, whether it was cutting vegetables or cooking or doing her puja. She attended to Grandfather's needs but did not interfere with Mother's running of the household. Raman spoke to her about his readings. He talked about the Buddha, having just read Sir Edwin Arnold's *Light of Asia*. One has to renounce the world if one is to do anything worthwhile, he said, and quoted:

One even as I,
Who ache not, lack not, grieve not, save with griefs
Which are not mine, except as I am man;
If such a one, having so much to give,
Gave all, laying it down for love of men.
And thenceforth spent himself to search for truth,
Wringing the secret of deliverance forth,
Whether it lurk in hells or hide in heavens,
Or hover, unrevealed, nigh unto all:
Surely at last, far off, sometime, somewhere,
The veil would lift for his deep-searching eyes,
The road would open for his painful feet,
That should be won for which he lost the world,
And Death might find him, conqueror of death.
. . .
Wife! Child! Father! and people, ye must share
A little while the anguish of this hour
That light may break and all flesh learn the Law.

I don't have the vocabulary to translate it for you, Paati, he said. But what Prince Siddhartha says is that when the call comes, and we don't know from where it comes, but when it comes you have to give up everything and not rest until truth is found. One must be prepared to give up everything: wife, child, kingdom, people.

Muthuchipi told him to read Ramakrishna Paramahamsa's teachings; he says one should be like a boat—it should stay on water but water should not be in the boat. I don't know much of what else he said, but this I know for myself: Live here in the world, with the world, if you want to do anything for the world. Those who renounce the world save only their own souls. Be like a boat, my child.

I can't argue philosophy with you, Paati, I'll stick to science, where questions have only one answer, Raman said.

Raman talked at length to his father about his excitement at the books available at the university library. True, there were far more books on the European classics and on philosophy and English literature than on science, but he read those too. It was so much easier to read on his own than have to listen to the lectures. But the teachers were good, especially those who taught literature and classics. Maybe it was the classroom—a big lecture hall overlooking the sea, where he could look at the sea, instead of having his back to it as in the other rooms, and watch the waves endlessly lashing against the shore. A good environment was most definitely important to inspire students to study, work and enjoy.

The Greeks knew it: just look at the amphitheatres they carved on the hillside, on the height of Taormina from which they could watch the waves of the Ionian Sea washing the coast of Sicily, and see the glittering heights of Mount Etna. There were no hills to look at from Presidency College, but the sea was always there, like the music of languages, singing to the students in Sanskrit or Tamil or Latin or English, beating against the sands.

Don't spend so much time on books, my son, his father said. Do you listen to music? Do you take long walks by the sea? Living in the hostel, with your library and classes close by, has not been good for you. Look at the way your shirt hangs on you, as from a scarecrow. Look at what your teachers have said about your work—brilliant, great alertness of mind, quick to grasp even difficult concepts—but what use is a brain if you let your body starve? Souls are said to live forever, but brains are no use at all if you don't have a body to house it in.

Raman had missed watching his father play the violin, but he had heard it in his head all along, and his inquisitive mind had played with questions—what role did friction play when the bow ran over the strings of the violin? The movement of the fingers of the left hand were so important because they had to press on the wire just right, at exactly the right spot; what mathematical connections were there between the length of the wire and the frequency of the sound? Helmholtz would have the answer, he thought, Helmholtz the demigod who knew that scientific progress was the yardstick of civilization.

His grandmother would probably say the answer was in the ancient sciences of Hindu culture. Perhaps it was. After all, one could see examples of the ancients' knowledge in the architectural splendours of the temples, the ruins of palaces and forts of old, in herbal medicine and the arts of massage therapy. Yes, the ancients had probably mapped out a great many territories. But he had cast his die, or it had been cast for him by his father, who had opted for an English education. Raman could read thirty pages in English in the time it took him to understand one page of Tamil or Sanskrit. So it had to be Helmholtz and Euclid who could give him the answers. He wished he had access to all of Helmholtz's writings, instead of just to his *Sensations of Tone*. But there was time. He had all the time in the world to read every book in the science library of the university, and then there was the Connemara Library.

His father, in the meantime, arranged to set up a household in Madras: 8, Iswaradoss Lala Street was in Triplicane, a crowded walk through lanes and streets if one took the shortest route to the college, but a pleasant walk along the beach to and from the college if one enjoyed walking. In July 1903, at the end of the summer vacation, the grandparents and Aunt Gnanam moved with Raman and CS to Madras, and Muthuchipi took complete charge. She discouraged Raman from reading for long stretches in dim light and made sure he went to bed early. She got him into the habit of rising early too.

Love the sun, make maximum use of sunlight, she said, the sun is the only thing you can always count on, sunlight the only treasure you need, to do whatever you want to do with all those books you carry all the time. Sunlight and mathematics and observation, Raman used to say, that's all I need to get nature to reveal her secrets.

Muthuchipi fed the boys rice *kanji* early in the morning, popping mustard in hot oil and adding a pinch of salt to the previous evening's leftover rice that had been soaking all night in water. She packed a nutritious tiffin for them, rice mixed with curds garnished with one or the other pickle, or idli layered with chutney or chilli-lentil powder, and insisted they carry a *kooja* (jug) of diluted buttermilk. She wished Raman had his father's physique, but at least he had a good head—too big for his body but she was going to nag him into making his body catch up with the size of his head.

On weekends, she listened to him reciting from Homer or from Tennyson or whatever he was reading at the time, and to his long descriptions of what scientists were doing in Germany, France and Britain. He left Adolphe Ganot's book on natural philosophy with her during the day so she could look at all the illustrations when he was away at college. They laughed together as they went over the illustrations in the evenings, Raman explaining the scientific component, and then both offering their own annotations to the curious pictures. She was enthusiastic about the balloonist and the parachute. That is what we read of in the epics, she said, Lord Rama flying back to Ayodhya in his aerial chariot; maybe our ancients knew all this eons ago and we lost it over time.

After an early lunch that consisted of three courses of rice, mixed with sambhar or *kootu*, with rasam and with curds, Raman spent the day at the college and returned in the evening, always with some journal or book, which he read by lantern light till Muthuchipi ordered him to bed. Having home-cooked meals completed Raman's idea of an Edenic existence. Throughout his life, he ate whatever was placed before him, provided it was vegetarian, but he often joked about how the south Indian staple of rice mixed with rasam or with curds was the ultimate necessity to keep the brain working full steam.

College education

At the end of 1903 the Madras household was kept running just to take care of Raman. His brother, CS, had completed his BA and gone back to Vizagapatam to study for the entrance examination to Civil Engineering College. Taking long walks along the beach proved good for Raman's health. He would walk, or cycle even greater distances. Papers in the journals he read referred to other journals that were not available at the university library. He asked his professors if they had any copies of those journals. After all, they went home to England often enough to have picked up journals in which significant discoveries were reported. But they did not have too many. It was the Connemara Library that helped Raman most. Formally opened at the end of 1896, it was planned on the lines of the British Museum: that a copy of every new book published in the country should be placed in it, and it should also acquire books published in the past. It had received hundreds of books from Haileybury College in England, where Indians were trained for the civil service, and Raman found himself diverted into reading a lot that was outside his research focus.

He frequented Moore Market, where second-hand stalls stood cheek by jowl, books stacked up to the ceiling in random clusters. There were old magazines, women's weeklies by the scores and copies of *Punch* left by English administrators and soldiers going back to Britain or to another colony after their stint in India. There were also science journals and books, many of which were almost new, sold by English government officers who had moved on.

Between Connemara Library and Moore Market, Raman found several issues of the *Philosophical Magazine*, which, he decided, was where he would send his papers once he wrote them. It was the leading journal for all scientists. Started in 1798, it had a series of brilliant scientists as editors. Later, he told his professors about the journal, saying it was a shame the university did not subscribe to it. The university library started subscribing to the journal in 1908, after Raman had left for Calcutta.

He had a great many ideas and he tinkered around the physics lab conducting experiments. The questions came to him faster than he could jot them down on paper. The possible answers to some of the questions also came to him, but there was a roadblock when it came to working on them. What was the point of working at getting the experimental proof if it had already been done in Europe? He did not have the resources of journals or contacts to find out what was happening there. But soon he would get to all that, he told himself. First he had to complete his BA degree.

He did exceptionally well in his studies, winning the English and physics gold medals and getting top rank in the final examinations. His professors, all British, suggested that he go to England. But the civil surgeon of Madras decided his health was not good enough to withstand the British climate. Later, Raman was to often express his gratitude to the civil surgeon as at the time he was too young to know what he knew later—that he would much rather do what he wanted to do in India and prove to the world that India was as good a place as any European centre for learning.

January 1905 saw Raman back at Presidency College, this time enrolled for a master's degree in physics. His elder brother had spent almost all of 1904 in Vizagapatam, studying on his own, preparing to join the engineering courses. In November, CS returned to Madras. The family shifted to another house nearby, to the rear portion of 52, Pycrofts Road.

Raman was totally focused on his research. By now, the professors, some of whom had exempted him from attending classes even when he was in his BA programme, knew who he was and of his potential. They also knew he was already far ahead of the other students and perhaps beyond the parameters of their own knowledge. Professor R. Llewellyn Jones, under whom Raman was to study, had given him carte blanche to miss classes during his BA, and now he gave him permission to work in the labs any time he wanted. Years later, Raman would gratefully record: 'I enjoyed a measure of academic freedom which seems almost incredible.'

However, once he came home in the evening, he could not escape his brother's worries. CS shared his worries with his brother in small doses. Staying at home in Vizagapatam for ten months, CS had learnt of the family's financial troubles, which they had never known as children. One day CS told Raman of how their father had sold most of his science books to the SPG College in Trichy. He had asked CS to make a list of the books and to pack them up. CS salvaged some of the books that he wanted and some that he thought Raman might like to have, and the rest had been sent to Trichy. Raman was shocked. Why would Appa do that? Those books were precious, and what amount would they have fetched anyway? Every little paisa counts, CS said. Raman could not believe they were this hard-pressed for money.

What about the land and its produce? CS said only six and a half acres were really in Grandfather's possession, the rest being heavily mortgaged. Grandfather had taken a series of loans at usurious rates of interest and had no way of paying anything into the redemption. Once, Grandfather had felt he had to sell some of the land to pay for Paati's brother's wedding celebrations. Knowing it would break the old man's heart if the land were sold, Father took another loan. Often the interest on the loans was

18 per cent compounded and, at one time, the interest, which had accrued over the years because due payments had not been made, amounted to 500 rupees.

Another day, CS referred to Babu Govind Das. Remember how Appa would help his sons with their studies whenever he went to their house? It was not, as we had thought, the kind of free, occasional help one offers to the sons of neighbours and friends, but regular, paid tutoring, which he did because we needed money. So it was with the Roman Catholic lady who lived near the station. Her name, if I recall correctly, was Blanche Paulie. She aspired to complete her college degree but was weak in mathematics; Appa tutored her, going to the convent to give the lessons. Only with the Naidu boys who came every morning did the others know it was paid tutoring that Appa was engaged in. CS did not know how many others he tutored.

One day, after listening to yet another string of stories about family finances, Raman told his brother that he worried unduly. CS retorted that someone had to worry, Raman and their father and grandfather being what they were. Did Raman know that their upanayanam had cost 500 rupees? Raman was astounded. Five hundred rupees to walk through the town carrying that milk kaavadi? Good lord! And Appa didn't even believe in all that hocus-pocus! What was Appa's salary? CS answered that as vice principal he was now on a pay scale of Rs 125 to Rs 175 per month. Back in 1897 he was on a pay scale of 80–120 rupees. Raman whistled his incredulity. Six months' salary to have us carry that paal-kaavadi, whew!

When CS told him that 1400 rupees had been spent on their sister, Mangalam's wedding four years ago, Raman was dismayed. Here they were, so happy that they were getting a scholarship of fifteen and twenty rupees a month, and Appa had taken a debt of god knows how much. CS explained that some of the social changes taking place had also contributed to this. When their parents were married, Appa had paid *vara-sulka*, bride-money, to his father-in-law, as was the custom. But social reformers had been bickering about how this custom degraded women, as though the parents were selling their daughters for money, and so the opposite movement was gaining ground now. Appa had to pay dowry to get their daughters married.

Raman scoffed: Here, please, take away my daughter, I will give you 1400 rupees to take her off my hands, please, please say you will marry her. Some reform, this mumbo jumbo.

CS, always precise, said: Only 300 rupees were given as cash, the rest was for the jewellery and celebrations.

Raman said: This whole conversation makes me ill. I didn't think Appa would give in to such hocus-pocus.

CS hotly replied: Appa won't take a paisa of dowry for his sons. But daughters have to be married in due time, and what can fathers do when social expectations decree this, that and the other? This dowry plague is totally new. When Father got married, he paid vara-sulka, less than twenty-five years ago. And those gifts were not as exorbitant as the current dowry demands. How quickly customs change!

CS announced one day that he was thinking of dropping out of his engineering programme. It took too long and, at the end of it, no job would bring in much money anyway. Instead, he would take the financial service examination and enter the administrative service. One had to go to England to take the civil service exam but one could write the financial civil service exam in India. The pay was excellent; the British paid their servants handsomely to do the daily routine of running the Empire. The British were here to stay and, to give them due credit, they knew what good education was and what it could do to get the country moving.

Raman listened to the soliloquy quietly.

CS mused that he would become a government officer and would repay all the loans. He would learn to avoid what their grandfather and father had done—he would never take loans. Money, one needed crass lucre to survive in this world, and he would earn enough to support the family, which was growing every year.

Raman snorted: Yes, let both of them learn that too—not to have so many children.

CS snapped back that yes, he knew that, which was why he [CS] had not started living with his wife yet. She had come of age and her father wanted to have the shanti kalyanam but he knew that children came fast upon that ceremony. He would have children, no doubt about that, many of them too, but he would wait till he had completed his education. He would not saddle his sons with debts. He would educate them and expect nothing from them for himself. Nothing. He would give and give, not ask anything of them except that they lead moral lives. They would have no debts, no obligations, no expectations from his side. They would be free, to make or break their own lives. All this he would do in due time. First thing was to get a good job.

But one has to like the job too, Raman said. Appa loves his job.

CS was impatient by now. You keep talking about teaching and research, he said, but what will you do with the master's degree that you plan to get? A teaching job with a measly pay scale? You think you will get a university professorship? Hah. The British will never do that—small colleges in outposts of the Empire, sure they will give you that, but a plum university job in Madras? Dream on. Remember the case of Anandamohan Bose, the first Indian to be admitted to Cambridge? Bose could not get a job at Presidency College in his native Calcutta. Sometime later, Jagadish Chandra Bose did, but at one-third the salary of his British predecessor. And this was just ten years ago. Nothing has changed.

Raman said softly: All I want is a life where I can concentrate on my science.

Well then, said CS, get into government service, render unto Caesar what is Caesar's from ten o'clock to five, and then with all the money you get, build yourself a place where you can work the rest of the time.

Look, Raman said, science doesn't need much money. I am working on an experiment studying the diffraction bands that appear when light enters through an aperture and all I am using are a thin sheet of zinc and basic instruments such as a collimator, prism, telescope and spectrometer.

CS interrupted: What's new? Want to show Huygens's principle over again?

No, said Raman patiently, not about the secondary waves either, though I still have to work on that. I am looking at the *unsymmetrical* bands that appear when the light is incident *obliquely*. He went on to explain further.

CS nodded. Good luck, but I think I shall take the exam and get into government service.

I too just might have to do that, Raman said. Man does not live by bread alone, but one's daily curd-rice is an absolute basic if one is to do anything in science, he laughed. They can talk all they want about artists in garrets but my science needs a regular routine of food in addition to study habits.

Sometime later, when the brothers sat as usual in the rear veranda before their evening meal, when Raman talked excitedly about his experiments, CS said that maybe Raman should go into teaching after all. Maybe teaching was in their blood. Appa was such a fine teacher, as CS personally knew, having been in his class three years running. Did Raman remember how Appa took them to Dolphin's Nose so often just to look at the beauty of the sea and to the Borra Caves to teach them about stalactites and stalagmites? He did not stop with theory, but took his students on walking tours during his physiography class. He did not make his students learn by rote but insisted they understand the concepts;

the questions he asked always fooled those who learnt by rote
and gave an edge to those who thought the concepts through. CS
himself was sure that he wanted to get an officer's position in the
government, but maybe Raman could pursue his dream of being
a university professor.

And what about family debts, which had no doubt increased
by now? Raman asked.

CS laughed and said: Do you remember the Gosthani in the
Borra Caves where Appa used to take us when the tide was low?
Stones in the shape of udders that devotees worshipped as those
of Kamadhenu, the giver of perpetual food? Government service
is our Kamadhenu, and I am taking my exams soon. There will
be enough money once I start working and time too to do other
things. Did you know that married officers get an allowance of 150
rupees over and above their salary? I want to read all the classics of
the West and of India. There's so much literature to read, one life
isn't enough. I want to go to Europe, to Greece, Italy, to the Alps,
there's so much to see.

Raman forgot about family finances once he was at the
college. Professor Jones ambled to the lab every day, talked about
miscellaneous topics, said he was impressed with Raman's ideas
and left it at that. He knew the boy had intellectual acumen that
cut to the core of every concept but he himself did not know how
to help the boy advance. He allowed him to do whatever he wanted
at the lab and requisitioned any lab equipment the boy asked for.
More, he could not do. Too bad the civil surgeon only had thumbs
down on the boy's ability to live in Britain. Maybe he would change
his verdict now—the boy had certainly grown taller and put on
some weight. There was no doubt he looked at home in the college
now. Even Elliott would have to agree, Jones thought, for the story
about Elliott's question on Raman's first day at the English class
had now become a familiar one, to be repeated every time Raman
carried off one of the book prizes for class work.

Marriage and government service

In January 1906, the grandparents went back to their village. Mother came from Vizagapatam with the younger children, to keep house for the two brothers. They moved from Pycrofts Road to Tank Square in Triplicane, just south of the temple *mandapam*. Raman focused on his research, staying long hours at the college and university library. All he now needed were lenses to study Newton's polarized rings. Two recent texts—Thomas Preston's 'Theory of Light' and Edwin Edser's 'Light'—had it wrong. Both editions were dated, five and four years old respectively, and for all he knew, others had already talked about the error.

Though his younger brothers still looked up to him adoringly, he felt crowded in the house and he missed his grandmother.

He was already getting the results he needed on his next major experiment: soap bubbles. His fascination with bubbles and drops had led him to Lord Kelvin's *Popular Lectures and Addresses*. He had neatly written the title of his paper in his notebook—'The curvature method of determining the surface tension of liquids'—but the experimental proofs were not panning out as easily as he had hoped. He was dealing with drops of liquid, and a drop would not stay long enough on the tip of the capillary for him to take the measurements. He would have to figure out how to use photography to get his experimental data.

Soon, home became a busier place than ever. The whole family got together as arrangements were being made for CS's shanti kalyanam. CS was twenty-one years old, he had been married four years already, his wife Seetha had long come of age and her parents were anxious to see her duly join her husband's family.

After the celebrations, in July 1906, Father and Grandfather left for Vizagapatam right away. After a few days, Mother and the younger siblings also left. They took Seetha with them to introduce her to their family and friends. Muthuchipi Paati and Aunt Gnanam stayed back to keep house for the boys.

Raman was focused on his research. The laboratories, even of this premier institution, were equipped only for basic experiments. The physics lab had an assortment of lenses, desk telescopes, prisms, a sonometer, a spectrometer and a few other basic pieces of equipment. But Raman did not need much. Ask the right questions, and nature will reveal her secrets. He had already written his paper on 'Unsymmetrical diffraction bands due to a rectangular aperture observed when light is reflected very obliquely at the face of a prism'. He gave a copy to Professor Jones for his comments, but the professor kept it for weeks without responding. Raman then decided to send it directly to the *Philosophical Magazine*. He took out his copy, on which he had made a few marginal notes, and set about making a clean copy. Paati came to his room as he was recopying. She looked at the diagrams and noted he had no pictures of people in top hats and boots as in Ganot. He laughed and said that maybe he should put people with a tuft and a *veshti*, like himself, to make it realistic, though the editors who read this in England may not like that.

One day you will go there, child, she said, with your *kudumi* (tuft) and poonal and all, and make them listen to you.

He said: But first they have to read what I send them; it seems even my professor has not bothered to read it, and I don't know if I should send it directly without consulting him.

She asked: Would it be wrong to do so?

No, he said, there's nothing that says one has to go only through one's professor.

She touched the sheets he had on the table and said: Then go ahead and send it off, child; you have a lot going on in that head of yours. You will do well.

Raman sent his paper. It was five pages long, and he had identified himself at the end of the paper: 'Demonstrator in Physics at Presidency College, Madras'. The paper was duly published in November 1906.

Grandfather fell ill shortly after. Mother brought Seetha to Madras and left with Paati and Gnanam. Grandfather died in September, but that short period with his son gave him great happiness. Father took a loan of Rs 800 to cover the expenses of the funeral ceremonies and the travel of those few months.

Early in the New Year, the family, which now consisted of just CS, his wife and Raman, moved to 25, Venkatachala Chetty Street nearby, in Triplicane. Both young men wrote their financial civil service examination. The examination to enter the Indian Civil Service was held only in England—a British ploy that ensured that only those with an English education could enter the service. Only after 1922 it began to be held in India. The Indian Financial Service exam, however, could be written in India, and most of the academically brilliant students did this as a matter of course. It made no difference to Raman, as he continued his usual fast pace of work, spending his days at the lab or the library. He had already completed his second paper and sent it off to the *Philosophical Magazine*. When it was published, Lord Rayleigh, the eminent scientist, noticed both papers and wrote to him, addressing him as 'Professor Raman', not knowing that a boy of eighteen was the author of the papers.

Raman had written the civil service examination simply because many of his classmates at college were writing it. But the results

meant a lot to CS, who was eager to start his life, and he waited
impatiently for the results. Both were notified of their success
and next they waited for their postings. It could be anywhere in
the country and they had to be prepared to report at their post at
short notice. Father wanted to visit them to share the grief he felt
for his father, but work kept him from coming. Moreover, Mother
was again pregnant.

~

Meanwhile, the brothers came across a very interesting
person—Ramaswami Sivan. He was from the second generation
of English-educated youth. University education had become
far more common among Brahmins than in Chandrasekhara
Aiyar's student days. A youthful intelligentsia cropped up all
over the country. They drank deep of the founts of knowledge
and were intoxicated with the philosophy of men such as John
Stuart Mill and Swami Vivekananda. They questioned entrenched
traditions and reopened long-closed issues of social conscience.
This intelligentsia both absorbed and emanated the wind of
transformation that swept over the subcontinent. Sivan had strong
opinions on social reform and he orated to all he met, and he met
many people because he loved to interact with people.

Born Varadaraja Sarma on 15 November 1871, he earned his
name, Ramaswami Sivan, for his part in what may be called the
'Hindu renaissance' of the late nineteenth century. His academic
brilliance had won him a scholarship, and he had enrolled at St
Joseph's College in Trichy. He lived in a hostel attached to the
college. An incident that took place during his final year reveals
the spirit of the times and the background against which Sivan's
radicalism was nurtured.

Trichinopoly was a major centre of the Jesuit Mission in India.
The college and the missionaries' residence were located on the
cathedral premises, in Clive House. This area is at the foot of

the hill on which stands the Rock Temple, one of the foremost pilgrimage centres. Atop a massive rock, about 300 feet above the ground, stand the shrines of Ganesha and of Siva-Parvati. Faith has hewn the stone beams of the temple; faith has carved the 437 steps that lead to the shrine of Ganesha. Clive House, standing east of the temple tank, at the foot of the rock, fell on the route of all temple processions. The car festival, when Lord Ganesha is carried in the temple car of incredibly intricate woodwork, is a spectacular procession, and people from the town and nearby villages would throng to it. Even on ordinary days, it is a popular shrine, for the deity atop the rock is considered especially powerful and beneficent.

The missionaries at Clive House had complained to the collector that their sleep was often disturbed by the temple processions. They asked that the temple authorities be told not to stop any procession in front of the small Ganesha shrine that was to the south of Clive House. It was the custom of all processions to halt there to make an offering, as it was the start of the hike up the hill.

As expected, the Jesuits' demand was taken up favourably by the British collector, who was the local representative of the British Crown. The collector requested the *devasthanam* (temple trust) officials to ensure that the car was not stopped at the shrine. They agreed, for a request by a collector, stripped of its formality, was nothing less than an order. When the Hindu students of St Joseph's and of SPG College came to know of this, they were furious. They put forward an organized and orderly demonstration. They stopped the temple car opposite the Ganesha shrine and lined up with their offering. As the custom is to never refuse to conduct an offering, the priest accepted a coconut from each student by turn, sanctified the offering with prayers and chants, broke the coconut before the deity and returned the *prasadam* (sanctified offering). One by one the students came up and the line seemed endless. Meanwhile, the devotees and priests in the procession sang songs of worship as is the custom from the start to the finish of a procession.

A halt that would have normally taken five minutes was prolonged for more than an hour. The students were so peaceful, so orderly, that the police could not crack down on them. But they noted the identity of those they thought were the leaders of the protest. They tried to apprehend one person whom they were sure was a leader—Chandrasekhara Aiyar, a student-tutor at SPG College. Chandrasekhara Aiyar was a tall, well-built man and as he stood under the lamp, wielding his karla, no one dared approach him.

Varadaraja noted this with deep appreciation. This incident inspired him to take up the cause of religious independence. But even before he could begin any rebel action, he was barred from writing the BA examination because he had doubly violated the code. As a scholarship-holder, he was bound to stay away from riots and as a hostel resident he was bound to stay within the hostel after sunset. Proud to be branded a rebel, soon Varadaraja was seen in every group that went around the town singing *thevaaram*s (religious songs).

He came to be called Ramaswami Sivan, 'Sivan' being a title conferred on ardent Saivites.

Sivan was a radical in more ways than one. Ready to fight for Hinduism against the British, he was equally willing to take up the cudgels against Hinduism if he felt there was injustice in a custom or belief. He was a champion of women's rights. Raman knew of Sivan because the group of educated young men in Madras was small enough for them to know each other by name; they frequently ran into each other at lectures and music get-togethers. Sivan was known for talking about the need for abolishing barriers between castes, abolishing the new dowry curse and improving educational opportunities for everyone. He urged young men to change society through action and to first educate and influence people in their own lives.

Practising what he preached about women's abject slavery in the kitchen, Sivan insisted that his wife, Lakshmi, cook only once a day, and he arranged to have their breakfast and dinner brought in from an eatery. This was unheard of in those times. The Brahmin streets were full of scandalous reactions to his actions. One could wink at a Brahmin who had snacks at the coffee shops that were multiplying on street corners, but making it a daily habit to get meals from outside was going too far. And then to make his wife do likewise! What kind of a Brahmin was he who made his wife partake of food cooked by alien and inevitably polluted hands?

Sivan's home was a meeting place for radicals and reformers. He invited them to his home, and the front veranda became the site of heated discussions about social reform and ways of transforming society. Among his friends were Englishwomen who wanted to change life and values for the women of the new century; there were also young men who were attracted by Sivan's energy; and there were some of his contemporaries who had grown up with the same ardour for reform.

When Sivan heard that the sons of his hero, Chandrasekhara Aiyar, were in Madras, he tracked them down. It was not difficult to reach them through the Brahmin network, meshed by word-of-mouth communication, and Raman was already a name that was familiar in the circle, due to the prizes he had won. Sivan was an intelligent listener as well and was soon discussing Raman's experiments with the same confidence with which he lectured on his own philosophies.

At this time, Sivan was on the lookout for a suitable bridegroom for his wife's youngest sister, Lokasundari. Lokam, as she was called, had been in his charge for more than nine years, her parents having sent her with Lakshmi when she was hardly three years old so that Lakshmi would not feel isolated in the big city. The child's presence did indeed help everyone, including Lakshmi—and her children, when they arrived. Sivan had enthusiastically welcomed the prospect of shaping a child after his ideals; he quickly made sure Lokam went to school, learnt English, studied music and followed his every edict.

Lokam usually stayed with the Sivans for eight months of each year and spent the other four with her parents. Her father, Krishnaswamy Aiyar, had recently taken early retirement from the customs service and settled in his ancestral house in Madurai. He was anxious to get her married before she came of age, as was the custom. He and his wife had hoped to have a double wedding, Lokam's and their older son's. The process was stalled as the son, Kalyanasankaran, suddenly died. Lokam was now past thirteen. Sivan joined the search with his usual gusto. He told his friends too to be on the lookout. He arranged for several such meetings where an eligible bachelor formally meets an eligible young woman's family and gets a glimpse of the girl.

Meanwhile, Chandrasekhara Aiyar had asked his cousin Visvam to be on the lookout for an appropriate match for Raman. The procedure was fairly standard—the young man came with his parents or relatives to the girl's home, where her accomplishments were showcased and her eligibility determined; usually the girl's accomplishments comprised musical talent of some sort. A day or two later, the young man's family conveyed their impression to the girl's family through an intermediary. If both parties felt positively, more talks took place, and if all went well, a *muhurtham* date was set in consultation with the family priest. Visvam arranged several such meetings, but Raman did not agree to any of the matches.

It so happened that one day Raman and his friend[1] came by to see Sivan at his house, which was in the Agricultural College premises in Saidapet, where he was assistant bailiff. As they neared the house, the sound of the veena drifted towards them. Since one of the prerequisites for an eligible bride was musical skill, Sivan and Lakshmi had ensured that Lokam had a basic proficiency in playing the veena and Lokam practised her music with painstaking conscientiousness.

The tune she was playing that particular day was one of the few in her small repertoire. It was a Tyagaraja *kriti*: *Raama nee samana evaro* (Rama, is there anyone equal to you?). The serendipitous choice of the song, in addition to the coincidence that Lokam was playing at all, has become part of the legend of how Raman fell for the girl who was strumming the veena. Sivan was not at home and the young men went away.

From my conversations with Lokam in 1972, who told me about this visit, I speculate that Raman had been approached by Sivan about his sister-in-law and that Raman had come intending to explore the matter himself instead of waiting for protocol. This would be quite consistent with Raman's modus operandi of immediate action once an idea had struck him, and also in line with Raman's later references to how he himself chose whom he would marry.

Sivan soon arranged a formal meeting with Raman, who was accompanied by CS and the same friend. After the formalities of being served snacks and beverage, and listening to Lokam playing the veena, Raman's friend left and Sivan called for a *jutka* for Raman and CS. CS paid off the jutka-driver as they neared San Thome beach and told his brother they needed to talk. He was uneasy about having gone to see a girl without telling their father first. Before CS could say anything, Raman said he thought this girl was the one for him. Once he had made a decision, he believed in acting on it promptly. He said he planned to write to Sivan to tell him he was agreeable to the match.

CS demurred. He insisted that Appa must know about this just as he knew about the other formal visits to prospective brides. Raman shrugged him off. According to Raman, Sivan talked too much but he was a talented and decent man, and so the girl's background and upbringing would surely be acceptable. She herself had something about her, a combination of shyness and defiance, that was appealing. In any case, Raman declared, he had made up his mind and Father would of course trust his judgement and be happy he would not be alone in Calcutta.

CS remonstrated him on his unseemly haste. As Raman's joining orders had come, and he had to leave for Calcutta in a matter of days, it was just not enough time to think things through.

Raman was pragmatic. He had to marry at some time, so why not now? He had seen the girl and was satisfied, so why should he wait? 'And, besides, you remember the Married Officer allowance? You should be happy I am being so practical!' Raman laughed. He said he would postpone his departure by a few days, even by a fortnight. He need not leave until the end of the month. There was enough time to find a good muhurtham day.

CS said, 'But Father . . .'

Raman impatiently cut him off. 'Of course Father always means well, but I wouldn't want him to promise me off to some friend's daughter whom I have never seen.'

The comment stung CS to the quick. In the summer of 1902, when he had gone back from Madras during his first year of studies, his father had announced that he was now betrothed to Seetha, the second daughter of his friend Dewan Balakrishna Iyer of Pudukkottai. CS, a spirited romantic at heart despite being a worrier for the family, was dismayed that he was now bound to someone he had never even seen, leave alone known to any degree. He had stormed in anguish all that summer.

But Raman's words were no taunt. 'You worry too much, brother,' he said, 'but you are the one who has told me often enough to learn from others' advice and experience, and I have. I will render unto Caesar what is Caesar's. I will help clear Appa's debts and never take a loan; I will not have children for a long time and since abstinence is the only way to do that, I will abstain. And I will follow my star, which is and will always be a life in science.'

He continued, 'But right now I would like to eat some spicy groundnuts, and so let us look for a vendor. Do you have some change?'

CS said, 'How is it you never ever have ready change but must always empty my pockets?'

'Because I went to Moore Market yesterday and picked up two issues of *Nature*, two years old, but worth it anyway. First let us get drenched in ocean spray and then look for the peanut seller. Just feel the sand under your bare feet, it is so wonderful a sensation, and the salt in the air, aah!' Raman proceeded towards the water, footwear in hand.

The face-to-face meeting with Lokasundari confirmed to Raman that his choice was a good one, and he wanted to hasten the arrangements so that he could take his wife with him on his posting. Calcutta, the capital of British India, was where he was hopeful of finding resources by way of laboratory, journals and like-minded people, who could see that science was the one unifying element in a world that was getting both smaller and more contentious by the day.

He wrote to Sivan on 18 May that he was postponing his departure for Calcutta, originally scheduled for the end of the month, by a 'week, if not a fortnight'. He wrote that Sivan should get Lokam's consent to the match and also invite Raman for a longer visit so that he and Lokam could confirm for themselves what he felt would be a mutually satisfactory marriage.

Sivan diplomatically diverted Raman's unconventional request for a stay as their house guest and responded that he would expeditiously fix the wedding date. They decided they would notify Raman's and Lokam's parents as soon as the priest advised them of a suitable date, which turned out to be 28 May.

Raman's father was in Vizagapatam, a long train journey away; Lokam's father was in Madurai. What the parents did not know was that the prospective bride and groom were of different sub-sects. Among Brahmins, there are several sub-sects, *brahacharanam* and *vadama* being two major ones, and matrimonial alliances were made only within the sub-sect. Raman was brahacharanam and Lokam was vadama. Sivan, with his penchant for defying traditions in order to make social changes, did not mention this detail to his father-in-law. Raman and CS had not bothered about such details at all, and so their father too was unaware of this fact.

Though both sets of parents were upset at not having been part of the decision-making, they had set out immediately on hearing that the wedding date had been fixed. However, once in Madras, when they came to know of the sub-sect difference between the families, they were taken aback. Chandrasekhara Aiyar very quickly came round, for he was after all a liberal thinker who endorsed social changes. But Lokam's father, Krishnaswamy Aiyar, was not appeased. He refused to give away his daughter. The wedding did not take place on the scheduled date, for Chandrasekhara Aiyar rejected Sivan's proposal that Sivan himself would give away the bride. He wanted to be assured the couple would have the unconditional blessings of all parents.

Guests were notified, the pandal was taken down, the cooks sent back.

Sivan knew most of the Brahmin dignitaries in Madras, but he was already considered a rebel to tradition. His wife's uncle, Anantanarayana Iyer, who was more pacific in his demeanour than Sivan, led the conciliation process. He and Sivan approached respected Brahmins in the city, many of whom were in high government or social positions. Among them were Mani Iyer (a cousin of Krishnaswamy who later became a judge), T. Sadasiva Iyer (who too became a judge) and A.C. Pranaharthihara Iyer, who were cousins of Chandrasekhara Aiyar, and G. Subramania Iyer, the editor of *Swadesamitran*.

These dignitaries interceded and brought Krishnaswamy Aiyar around with assurances that the inner circle of Brahmin society would not ostracize him for permitting an inter-sub-sect alliance. They promised to be there in person to bless the bridal couple. The wedding was performed on Sunday, 2 June 1907. The *Hindu* of 6 June carried the following report, with the dateline of 3 June.

An inter-sectal marriage was celebrated yesterday at the Maharajah of Vizianagaram Girls' School premises, Triplicane. The bridegroom, Mr. C. Venkataraman, M.A., recently appointed on the enrolled list in the Finance Department of the Govt. of India, is the son of Mr. R. Chandrasekhara Aiyar, B.A., Vice Principal, A.V.N. College, Vizagapatam, and is of the Brahacharanam sect. The bride is the daughter of Mr. S. Krishnaswamy Aiyar, late of the Customs Dept. Pamban, and the sister-in-law of Mr. M.R. Ramaswamy Sivan B.A., of the Agricultural College, Saidapet. The bride belongs to the Vadama sect. This Marriage is of great importance from the Social Reformer's point of view, as being the first of its kind. Though according to the Shastras such inter-sectal alliances are not prohibited, yet no families till now initiated them. Great credit is due to Mr. Krishnaswamy Aiyar especially, who, in spite of his old age had the courage to help forward the cause of reform in this most desirable and practical manner. A large number of guests of different sects attended the wedding and thus evinced their sympathy for the cause.

'You have come at last.'

Within the week, the whole family, except for Seetha and CS who were left to wind down the household, left for Vizagapatam by train. By now CS knew that he too was posted to Calcutta and had to join by mid-August. From Vizagapatam, Mother and the new couple, along with the girls, Meena and Sitalaxmi, who could not be left behind, went on to Calcutta in time for Raman to join duty.

Even though Calcutta was so far away from Madras, there were already a fair number of south Indians working in different government departments. Chandrasekhara Aiyar knew some of them, and Raman had already written to a friend, T.K. Rajagopalan.

They arrived in the morning and were met at the station by Rajagopalan, who took them to his house. Rajagopalan had scouted a few houses in advance, and after lunch Raman and he went out and decided on one. The address was 26/4 Scott's Lane. That very evening, they moved into the new location. Mother, with her experience, soon gave the house a feel of home.

Raman joined his post as assistant accountant general in the middle of June 1907. When his mother asked him about his place of work, Raman said, Excellent. The British certainly knew how to build. He liked the large windows and marble flooring and stone pillars. He liked the feel of vast space that government buildings had, with their high ceilings and sweeping stairways, and gardens and trees. He would take them around, he said, so they could see the avenues and domes for themselves.

That Saturday afternoon, Raman hired a phaeton and took the family for a drive around the city. Sitalaxmi and Meena were delighted at the big black horses that snorted as they paced at a sedate pace. All were duly impressed at the country's capital—the dome of the post office, the minarets on Dharamtolla Street, the shuttered windows of the Municipal Market, the vast façades of the Great Eastern Hotel and Grand Hotel.

They collectively gasped as the electric lights of Great Eastern Hotel came on. Raman talked about the wonders of electricity, the genie of lightning which could destroy but which now, thanks to science, could be put back in the bottle and controlled to make it work for society. The trams that trundled on the streets were once run by the energy of steam, but just two years ago had been converted to an electric traction, he said, and explained the way it worked.

At the end of Scott's Lane was a church. On their first Sunday they could hear the peal of the church organ, and Raman stood at the window and listened. The second Sunday, he took his wife and sisters to the church to listen to organ music. Meena and Sitalaxmi, totally unused to sitting in silence for so long, could not wait to return home. Lokam listened quietly.

On their return, Raman talked enthusiastically about how different the sound of the organ was from Indian musical instruments. Already his mind was working on the study of harmonics and acoustics. But the Brahmin cook, whom they had brought all the way from Madras, was not pleased. Indeed, he was extremely upset. Was this a Brahmin family at all? Maybe they were Christian converts who were maintaining their Brahmin façade while secretly attending Christian church services. He wanted none of it. He packed up his small steel trunk and left by the next train. Shortly after, Raman received a letter from a well-wisher in Madras seriously counselling him to think before giving up his ancient Brahmin faith to the rulers' religion; lower-caste people readily converted for material gains, but surely Raman was above that, he pleaded.

After a few days, Mother left with the sisters. She was heavy with her eighth child. (The child, Ramaswamy, was born on 20 August 1907.)

Raman's fascination with musical instruments had already charged him up. There was so much to be done. And no place to do anything. However, his new job was a challenge. It was not the job per se that he found daunting but the deference that he was accorded by everyone in the office. He realized that to appear like an officer, it would not do to be informally dressed; he had to tie his turban just so, he had to have his shoes polished to a shine and he had to behave with due authority. He was an Officer in His Majesty's government. He wished Paati was there to see him dressed for work.

Lokam had to run the house all on her own. Raman left for office in the morning at ten o'clock after breakfast. He had to walk a short distance to Bow Bazar Street and then take a tram to Dalhousie Square, where most government offices, including his, were situated. It would be past five when he returned.

Lokam was concerned about her husband. Her father-in-law had warned her that Raman was an easy prey to coughs and colds and that he did not take care of his health. Raman said he was in fine fettle, but he seldom had any lunch at the office canteen, and he refused to take a packed lunch. Rice and rasam were no doubt the world's tastiest food but not when cold. No, he could not be bothered toting a tiffin carrier to work. He shrugged off Lokam's concerns.

Lokam was on good terms with her landlady. Being quick to pick up new languages, Lokam spent time with Thakurma, who welcomed her as a daughter. Thakurma had already chided her for doing all the housework on her own, and now she got Lokam a manservant to sweep and clean the place. More importantly, he could deliver lunch to Raman. The servant enjoyed the tram ride for which Lokam provided him the fare, and he took his time coming back, but Lokam was pleased that Raman got the hot food he wanted and needed.

In the evenings, Raman would take Lokam to the Maidan, a huge open space in the heart of the city, one of the few green expanses that had survived the sudden expansion of the city in the last few years. He would talk about the day at office. He was all praise for the clerks, the way their fingers steadily clicked away at the keyboard of the Underwood typewriter, or the way they promptly brought out a pile of binders a foot high any time he asked about something. The shining brass buckle on the liveried peon's belt, he said with his characteristic loud laugh, made him the best-dressed man in the office.

Towards the end of July, ten-year-old Sundaram died after an acute attack of dysentery. Raman did not say much, but his little brother's death saddened him. Life was so fragile and death ever-present. One had to live each day to the full, and living, for him, meant working in a lab, reading in a library. But there was no lab or library in sight.

This death brought home to Lokam her own brother's death the previous year. Kalyanasankaran had been a well-grown, healthy young man of nineteen, a good student at college, a wonderful teacher who had taught her to enjoy the marvels of the seashore. She missed her home in Madurai and, to her own surprise, she missed her home in Madras, even Sivan's bossy voice, his sharp queries as to whether his bicycle had been wiped clean, his tennis shoes polished. To her, it was some relief that CS and Seetha would be joining them by the second week of August, CS having been appointed deputy accountant general in the accounts section of the public works department. It would be good to have Seetha to talk to during the long afternoons.

On his tram ride from office one day in early August, Raman saw a big board on a building that read: Indian Association for the Cultivation of Science (IACS). He jumped out at the next stop and walked back to the sign, at 210 Bow Bazar Street.[1]

Raman went into the building and was met by Asutosh Dey, the lab assistant and assistant secretary of the IACS, who was to become his staunch supporter for the next twenty-five years. Raman saw the vast empty rooms and wondered why no one was at work. He looked at the Vizianagaram Laboratory and gasped—here was a well-equipped lab just waiting for him; it must be a dream, he thought, a lab without anyone working in it! Ashu Babu talked sadly about how busy the place had been a few years ago and how desolate it was now. Raman said, 'It won't be desolate from now on. I am here.' His exile was over. He could return to his own land, of science.

He said as much with jubilation when he returned home and wondered why he had not seen the sign all these days.

'Because you close your eyes when you are thinking, and you are always thinking,' Lokam said.

Raman loved the way she said these things, with that mixture of shyness and sauciness that he had noticed at their first meeting. Yes, he had made a good choice. She would be the right companion for him, and a good wife when they came to that phase. There was a lot of time, they were young, and all those other pleasures and responsibilities could wait.

~

Amritalal Sircar sat back in his father's chair at his father's desk with closed eyes, as he sat every day at this time, between his day's work and his return home to his family. On the table lay a bundle of files that Ashu Babu had placed at his request some days ago. He did not remember what it was about, but knew he had to attend to it one of these days. The hour or two he spent here every day gave him both pleasure and pain. His father's presence hovered palpably in these premises, his energy and idealism emanating from every beam and pillar of the buildings. In front of him was a notebook he had just taken out of the locked drawer—one of his father's diaries. He did not need to open it; he had read most of it many times over: entries of all kinds, notes on individual cases and patients recorded with meticulous details, one-line jottings of appointments, lists of tasks to be done, and musings. It was the last that most saddened Amritalal. They revealed the idealist and tireless activist that his father had always been.

Build it and they will come. His father, Mahendralal Sircar had passionately believed it would happen, that if a centre of research were built, young men would come, knocking the door down in their enthusiasm to enter and work. Mahendralal Sircar (1833–1904) had come up the ladder the hard way. Losing his father at age five and his mother at nine, he had been brought up by his maternal uncles. He had received an English education at the well-known Hare School, where he was looked down upon by the rich schoolmates for being a 'free student'; *boreah* is what the rich brats called a scholarship boy. He was nearly thirty years old when he got his medical degree.

Mahendralal had straightaway got involved in activism. Noting that 'English' education in India laid emphasis on western philosophies and literatures, which aligned with the colonial agenda of civilizing India in Macaulay's sense of the word, he had spoken about the necessity of introducing more science courses in the curriculum. Science, the encouragement of the spirit of inquiry, was itself a force of liberation, and the imperialists would not want to promote that spirit, he could see. He had also noted how mired India was, steeped in rituals and beliefs that obfuscated ancient knowledge of philosophies and sciences. Build an interest in, and knowledge of, modern science and they will come, he had always held.

He was quickly accepted by his peers in medicine and became the vice president of the Bengal branch of the British Medical Association. He was as quickly thrown out when he presented a paper, in 1867, advocating that they should pay some attention to alternative schools of medicine, such as homeopathy. In his diary he noted how he had lost all his patients because of being ostracized by his peers, and how even when they did start trickling back, they wanted only allopathic treatments and not homeopathy. But he had persisted and his practice had grown. He built up credibility for homeopathy. People had sought him out, eager to be treated by him.

Don't depend on the government to start what needs to be done, he had said and started the *Calcutta Journal of Medicine* in 1868 as a forum for research and dialogue. In it, he published his essays on reforms in medical education and in medical practice, and records of diagnoses and treatments of various medical cases. The journal had received kudos from editors in Britain and Germany.

The Indian Association for the Cultivation of Science was formally inaugurated on 19 July 1876. It was his lectures, along with those of the co-founder Father Eugene Lafont (1837–1908) that had, over the next twenty years, drawn academic colleagues such as Jagadish Chandra Bose (botany), Ram Chandra Dutta (chemistry), Pramatha Nath Bose (geology) and Asutosh Mookerjee (mathematics) to join them in giving regular lectures, which had attracted two to three hundred listeners every week.

The Vizianagaram Laboratory, with instruments brought from Europe, was up and running by the early 1890s, with a generous donation of Rs 25,000 from the maharaja of Vizianagaram. The laboratory building was 141 feet long and 66 feet wide, with three large central rooms, flanked by five smaller rooms on each of the sides. There was a large lecture hall on one end and Raman, when he came, created a workshop where necessary instruments and tools could be made and repaired. The library was stocked with a fine acquisition of standard and recent texts. Sircar wanted to set up endowments for professorships but the funds never grew for lack of donors. Distinguished academics were ready to take classes, but no one wanted to work at the labs of the Science Association, as it was commonly called. They had their own college labs and student assistants.

Do it, and people will know it can be done, and they will step in to continue the work, his father had always said. But in the final count they hadn't, Amritalal thought, with some bitterness, feeling the emptiness of the labs around him. No one had come forward and his father had recorded his anguish in his diary and in the annual reports of the IACS. Had he made a mistake after all, he wrote in 1902, thinking he could build a science research centre run by Indians, for Indians, to show the country and the world that India could excel in the sciences?

'I have wasted a life,' Mahendralal wrote, 'in attempting to make it a national institution.'[2] In 1903, ill and dying, he was still certain that 'if our country is to advance at all and take rank and share her responsibilities with the civilized nations of the world, it can only be by means of science'.[3] He died on 23 February 1904, and Amritalal became the custodian of this ghost kingdom.

His father was always systematic in his research. He had instructed his homeopathy students to consider what the symptoms were, what was the prescription and how had the patient reacted. Especially if there had been no improvement, he asked them to go over it again and again, until the prescription was refined and the node located. These points dinned in Amritalal's head day after day as he sat there in the evenings: the absence of activities in the association, the malaise of non-dedication and non-interest, what else could be tried? How to invigorate the spirit of inquiry in young men too intent on more material gains?

One day, Ashu Babu knocked on the glass pane of the open door. He was leading in a young man, lanky and purposeful of gait, wearing a turban in the south-Indian style, awkwardly swinging his long arms as he walked towards him. Raman introduced himself as one who was looking for a place where he could pursue his scientific inquiries in the evenings and weekends. He worked in a government office all day, but he was a scientist in need of a home for his research, he said. He cited his papers in the *Philosophical Magazine*.

Overcome, Amritalal opened his arms and embraced him. You have come at last, he said. We have been waiting for you.

In his annual report on the year's activities, Amritalal Sircar recorded, 'In the month of August, Mr. C.V. Raman, M.A., came forward to carry on research work and has since been working steadily in the laboratory.' The annual report also recorded that C.V. Raman Esq. MA and Babu Amulya Ratan Dutt 'have subscribed Rs. 500 each to the Observatory Fund, and have thus become Life Members of the Association'.[4]

When CS, who had just arrived in Calcutta to join his position in the accounts service, heard about it, he was pleased to know Raman had found a place to pursue his interests in. As usual, he was worried about family debts. Raman had already put away 500 rupees on his obsession. He knew lab equipment cost money and he also knew Raman's priorities. They had a heated argument, and Raman assured him their father's debts would be paid, come hell or high water.[5]

Everything moved into place after that first visit to the IACS. At home, CS had got into his routine, Seetha's presence helped Lokam in more ways than the running of the kitchen, and Raman—if at all he had cared about such things as Lokam being on her own all day—could totally concentrate on his scientific research. Early morning he went to the IACS, returned home at 9.45 a.m. for a hasty meal before changing into his office attire. From work he went directly to the lab and returned home for a late dinner. Sundays were spent almost entirely at the association. Amritalal gave him whatever he asked for, ordered whichever lab equipment he needed (and he did not need much), and Ashu Babu, who lived on the premises, opened the door at any time of day or night when Raman knocked.

Raman went back to the note he had made about Newton's rings, completed the verifications and mailed it to *Nature*, proudly noting his new home base: 'Science Association Laboratory, Calcutta, dated 12th September, 1907'.

Chandrasekhara Aiyar visited them once every month. He had a great many extra-curricular responsibilities at the college. Eugene Sandow's body-developing equipment had just come out; he tried it out and encouraged students to do so. He was a scoutmaster as well. His own favourite pastime was tennis, and he played it at least four times a week. In spite of all this, he managed to steal away to his sons every month.

He was happy at the way things were turning out for them. He was delighted to know that Seetha was pregnant and that he would be a grandfather early next year. Each visit, he would bring packages of their favourite snacks. Once, he stayed for four days, and each day he came home with a basket of a different flower; he insisted that both young women braid each other's hair interwoven with the flowers. One day, it was jasmine, the next *taazhampu*, the next *mullai*, and then chrysanthemums. On one of his one-day visits, coming to know Seetha loved *tirattupal*—a milk sweet—he brought a whole kooja of it, and all four young people relished the treat. But after he left, try as they did neither Seetha nor Lokam could figure out where it was. Their husbands said they had no idea. The young women searched everywhere. On the third day, they saw the jug on the top of a very tall cupboard in one corner of the kitchen. Lokam climbed up on a chair and took it down. It was almost empty. The brothers had hidden the jug out of reach and by then had emptied it too. Confronted by their selfishness, they laughed their big hearty schoolboy laughs.

CS's daughter, Rajalakshmi, was born on 28 January 1908. CS had flouted tradition and insisted that the confinement not take place at Seetha's parental home in Pudukkottai but in his father's house in Vizagapatam, where modern medical facilities were available. Mother and child returned to Calcutta sooner than tradition decreed because CS did not want to miss out on his baby's first months. While Seetha's return with the baby brightened Lokam's life, it made barely an impact on Raman, who spent little time at home except during his father's visits.

When Father came by at Christmas time that year, he brought his violin and made CS practise the few songs he had already learnt. The evenings were spent at these lessons. Raman listened to them from his recliner while they sat on a mat on the floor. Father was teaching CS how to use the bow, and as Raman watched, ideas flitted through his head—what exactly was happening when he instructed CS how to hold and move the bow in order to avoid the wolf note? What vibrations were being caused by the hairs of the bow as they slipped over the string? How did the shape of the bridge affect the sounds that emanated?

At the end of his stay, Father gifted the violin to CS, saying he would get his good friend, Mr J.A. Yates, the inspector of schools, to arrange that a violin be bought and transported from England. CS practised whenever he could, and Raman listened if he happened to be at home. He asked himself many questions as he observed the effects of the forward and backward movements of the bow. He knew Helmholtz's idea that the bowed point of the string moves with the bow in a constant velocity up to a point and then moves back with constant velocity. But what happens when the change in movement and velocity takes place? What part did the bridge play in string instruments? The bridge in Lokam's veena was curved, and even the silk thread slipped between the bridge and the string was perhaps relevant to the differences in the sounds produced by the violin and the veena. There was much work to be done on the physics of acoustics. He was excited.

Raman got the workshop at the IACS in shape and had the equipment he needed made on site. The annual report of 1908 records that the workshop had turned out a variety of instruments and equipment, including a Hertz's circular wire resonator, heaters for the measuring of specific heat, conical brass vessels on stands to determine the freezing point of thermometers, a brass vessel to measure the boiling point, and two steel pulleys for Raman's work with Melde's experiment.

Raman planned to start a publication that would inform the world of their research. He knew that effective dissemination of research results was as important as the research itself. As soon as he settled into his research routine at IACS, he got plans for the *Bulletin* underway.

The first issue of the *Bulletin of the Indian Association for the Cultivation of Science* came out in 1909 and, along with other details, carried a reprint of Raman's paper on Huygens's secondary waves, one of the two papers that had been published earlier in the year in the *Philosophical Magazine*. But Raman could not be there in person to handle the issue as it rolled off the press.

5

Render unto Caesar what is his but not a paisa more

In Calcutta, life promised to be perfect: a well-paid job, a well-equipped laboratory—what more could one want? But with well-paid jobs in the government it was a given that one could be transferred frequently. Early in 1909, Raman got a hint that he might be transferred to Rangoon as currency officer, due to a promotion from his assistant accountant generalship. He did not at all like the idea of being sent to an unknown place, which probably did not have laboratory facilities that he could plug into. But it was a promotion, and he could do little to change any order that had been given. He tapped into the old boys' network of Presidency College and found that N.C. Krishna Iyer was teaching physics at Rangoon College. It was arranged that Raman would be met on arrival and helped in the settling-down process.

As March approached, his mother worried about his transfer to another country. To the British, Burma (now Myanmar) was just another part of the administrative entity but to his mother, it was a faraway, alien land. No one was in a position to help. Mangalam was pregnant. So was Seetha. She herself had her hands full with her own newborn. She suggested that Lokam should come to Vizagapatam. It was not right to make a woman cross the sea. Men had to go wherever the government sent them, but women would do well to wait for them within the country instead of taking a three-day voyage.

But Chandrasekhara Aiyar thought differently. He knew his son—he would forget about eating and sleeping at the appropriate times if left by himself. His health would deteriorate. He needed a restraining element in his life. Lokasundari would have to accompany him. True, she was a child, not yet sixteen, but she was level-headed, mature beyond her years, and had been trained very well. She could adapt herself quickly and as for learning new languages, there was none like her. Look how well she did with Bangla and English.

One fine April morning Raman and Lokam set sail. A pilot boat navigated them out of the Hooghly and into the sea. The next thing Lokam knew was that they were waiting at the mouth of the Irrawaddy for a pilot boat to take them up the river. All three days, she had been too seasick to know what was happening. Raman was fine. He enjoyed the sea breeze and the walks on the deck. He helped himself to the food that had been packed. He decided there was nothing that could be done for anyone's seasickness and so he did nothing.

They landed at Rangoon and were met by one Seetharama Iyer, a teacher at Rangoon College. He had been sent by Krishna Iyer, who could not come in person. Krishna Iyer met them later that day and took them to a house that he had fixed up for their temporary stay, until Raman got the quarters within the currency office.

When currency officers were transferred, the outgoing officer had to hand over charge of the currency by counting, weighing, packaging and sealing the currency in the government treasury. This took about a week. Then the outgoing officer would leave town and the incoming officer would move into his residence, which was on the second floor of the office building. The lockers and currency were in the basement. The currency officer had to be physically present in his suite of rooms every night, unless he made the necessary, elaborate preparations with a substitute government officer.

They moved into the temporary quarters next morning, and Raman went off to start counting out the money. But the queen was not in the parlour eating bread and honey. She was sitting in the kitchen, watching the grumbling cook who had come with them from Calcutta, and wondering how she was going to survive the next eight days until they moved to their own place.

Evening came, but not Raman. The sun set. The cook finished his cooking and sat in the kitchen, waiting. Lokam was in her room, waiting. Eight o'clock and still no master. The cook started to cry. He bemoaned his fate that had brought him to this wilderness. He vowed to take the first boat back instead of dying of fear in this godforsaken place. Lokam heard him crying, went to the kitchen and pacified him. She asked him to have his dinner and sent him off to bed.

Ten o'clock. Not a sound anywhere. She must have dozed off for she did not hear Raman coming in. He was happy and excited. He had gone off with Krishna Iyer to a place which sold scientific apparatus. Without a thought, they had taken a train to Insein, a town sixteen miles away, and ordered some essential apparatus for his experiments. He related all this happily, never for a moment realizing or apologizing for the worry he had caused.

They moved into their assigned quarters next week. Within two days, dragging a long table from downstairs, Raman set up an experiment in one of the rooms. That room was to be his laboratory.

For Lokam, living at the currency officer's residence was like living in a prison. The office floor and basement had security measures everywhere, which was reassuring. However, the currency officer was required to be at his residence sunset to sunrise. He could go anywhere, do anything, have anyone visit at any time, but he had to be physically present on the premises all night. This suited Raman very well, for with one stroke it absolved him of all social visits and allowed him to set up a lab in his quarters. But Lokam was lonely.

Every Sunday, Raman and Lokasundari took long walks, each time to a different destination. Once they went to a sawmill and watched elephants at work. The elephants pulled logs of teak, which had been sent downstream, out of the river. Other elephants pulled the logs to the power-saw. The power-saw sawed each log into planks. Men tied them into neat bundles and loaded the elephants, which carried them to waiting boats. It was fascinating to see logs floating down in such large quantities, because Lokam knew how much teak furniture cost back home in Madurai.

Their most favourite pastime was to go Dalhousie Park and take a boat across Royal Lake. At least once a month, they took a taxi to this large lake in the man-made park, 160 acres of water and 205 acres of well-laid-out parkland. The hansom-cab ride cost an exorbitant fifteen rupees, but the pleasure was worth it. But these walks and excursions depended on the vagaries of the weather. It rained a lot, the annual rainfall was over a hundred inches, Raman told her. He was always giving her little bits of information: of how drinking water was now being pumped from a new reservoir ten miles farther from Victoria Lake; or that in the old days all houses were made of wooden planks but now that bricks and masonry were used, the number of fires had gone down, and they would never have the kind of fires that destroyed the city in 1850 and again in 1855.

Social life at the official level was non-existent for them. Raman did not join any club and that ruled out the usual social rounds among civil servants. The lack of scientific equipment infuriated and depressed Raman by turn. Both Raman and Lokam, for different reasons, were marking time, waiting for the end of their exile. Towards the end of 1909, Raman suffered a serious bout of depression. He fell prey to insomnia. Evening after evening, he wore himself at his experiments, depressed that they could not be completed for the sheer lack of simple instruments. Night after night, he paced up and down, refusing to lie down, refusing to be still.

It had been a good year. He should have been pleased at the progress he had made in his research even at this outpost on the edge of nowhere. Two of his papers, on oscillations of stretched strings, had been accepted by *Nature* and one had appeared in the *Journal of the Indian Math Club*.

But all these results only added to his frustration. He had so many ideas and no place to carry out the experiments. It was ridiculous having to work on experiments using only the most basic apparatus, every single one of which he had to set up himself, with no help, except for Krishna Iyer, who himself was too busy with his work at the college and his growing family. It was frustrating to keep watch over His Majesty's coffers, literally counting money at times, to oversee the whole system. Night after night Raman paced up and down, his head ready to burst.

What deepened his dismay was the news that Halley's comet was soon to appear. Stars and the sky had always held a fascination for him. Here in Rangoon, the sky was resplendent on clear nights. If only he had a good telescope to map the movements of the stars, to see the effects of diffraction as the light floated through earth's atmosphere. News came slowly up this way but it did come—mid-September 1909, a comet was reported seen at Heidelberg. There were other claims to sightings through the next few months. In January 1910 there came a succession of reports, following the sighting from the Transvaal Observatory in South Africa—first observed by workmen at the diamond mine and confirmed on 17 January by Robert Innes, the director of the Transvaal Observatory—that a comet had been sighted which could be seen even during the day. Telegraphic messages went out all over the world that Drake's comet had been sighted. Only later it came to light that it was not Halley's comet but another great comet and that the telegraph operator had heard 'a great comet' as 'Drake's comet'!

All this excited Raman, who already had some ideas about the way a telescope would transmit stellar phenomena and how the light scattering could be studied. But here he was, far away from Calcutta, unable to pursue any experiment. He applied for long leave and knew even that would take a long time to be sanctioned. He needed his leave to come through by mid-April, which was when the perihelion of Halley's comet was expected.

A temporary reprieve came with the arrival of the Das brothers. Babu Bhagvan Das and Babu Govind Das, of Banaras, who were friends of Chandrasekhara Aiyar, wanted to visit Rangoon for a holiday. Raman received a letter from his father about their visit, asking him to extend his hospitality and help to them. Raman dropped his research for the duration of their stay and escorted them on sightseeing tours. Lokam got to see places that she would otherwise never have seen, and everyone had a wonderful time.

In the last week of February, Raman received a letter that Father was suffering from high fever. The Das brothers dismissed it, telling him not to worry. Their friend was a titan, an iron man with an iron body, and nothing could ever bother him, they said. That evening, they reminisced about their times in Waltair with Chandrasekhara Aiyar, his idealism that made him extend himself into so many initiatives—starting a Tamil association in Waltair, arranging theosophical society meetings, his dedication to his students and college. Next evening they spent an hour laughing over Chandrasekhara Aiyar's proverbial swimming schedule and Sunday baths. As a young man, he wouldn't have lunch until he had swum twice across the Kaveri, fair weather or foul. As for his Sunday baths when he was in Waltair, all the boys in the street would come to watch him being massaged by a professional masseur who served professional wrestlers.

The vacation, for it was as much a vacation for Lokam and Raman as for their visitors, was cut short by a telegram. Father had passed away on 27 February 1910, at 6.25 p.m. His pneumonia had escalated and he had succumbed. All three men were devastated. With deep sorrow, they reminisced the same details they had so happily relived that week. How could such a strong man succumb to any physical problem? How could fate take away such a man of action, ideals and energy?

The visitors sadly took leave. Raman's grief and frustration intensified because he could not get away. The whole red-tape procedure of handing over charge that he and his predecessor had gone through had to be gone through again with his successor. Every bill, every coin had to be counted, packaged, weighed and sealed. Raman and Lokam took a freighter and arrived in Vizagapatam on the eleventh day of Father's demise.

CS was already there, having rushed all the way from his post in Lahore, leaving his wife and two baby daughters. His wife was also pregnant with their third child. Sixteen-year-old Skandan had lighted the funeral pyre in the absence of the older brothers and was still dazed. CS had to take over the funeral ceremonies that would carry on for thirteen days. His grief was alarming. Even as he made arrangements for the rites, he wept and moaned. Father's last letter had said how happy he was that CS had given him grandchildren and that Raman was so engrossed in science. In that letter, he had made particular reference to the moral hazards of the positions his boys held and how well they were fortified against all temptations of bribes and black money—CS by his near-fanatic ideals of morality and ethics, and Raman by his mania for science. How short-lived was that happiness! He asked his mother about Father's last day, his last words. She said she had told him, 'You are leaving me alone!' and he had answered, 'I leave you under the protection of four lions.' And he had departed. Dead at the age of forty-four.

To Raman, this added a note of panic to his annoyance about the wasted time in Rangoon. There was no time, no time to waste on counting coins for the Crown. He had to get out of this miserable existence of serving the government night and day.

CS and Raman had been close as children and now they shared the weight of family commitments. CS worked hard at planning and executing how best to take care of the family, while Raman split the financial costs with him. In the early years, the brothers frequently argued and quarrelled, but they conscientiously performed their duty towards their mother and siblings. It was only after their siblings were well settled that the brothers went their separate ways. In time CS took early retirement so that he could pursue his musical interests and Raman went deeper and deeper into his world of science, building his own laboratory.

Raman was now on a six-month leave. CS had to go back to Lahore right away, but Raman had the time to help the family move to Madras. CS had rented a house with the aid of a friend. The family arrived in Madras and took up residence at 7 Neeliveeraswamy Chetty Road in Triplicane.

Raman and Skandan left for Presidency College early every morning, Skandan for his classes and Raman for the laboratory. Halley's comet was now in the daily newspapers. Excitement mounted in the third week of May, when the comet was suspected to brush the earth with its tail. It missed by about 3,22,000 kilometres, and the newspaper frenzy died down. Raman continued to work furiously at his experiments, not knowing to what backwaters his job would take him at the end of his leave.

At the end of Raman's leave, he was posted to Nagpur as deputy accountant general.[1] The region of Central Provinces and Berar was a large tract of land with virgin forests and tribal territory undiscovered by modern civilization. But Nagpur, as the provincial capital and former seat of the Bhonsles, was a flourishing town. The Bhonsles had ruled the region from mid-eighteenth century to mid-nineteenth century, at which time the British had taken it over under Dalhousie's Doctrine of Lapse. There were now two towns, the old and the new, in typical British style. Wherever the British went, they set up their administrative headquarters near an old city, building a new city next to it. The old city, with its narrow streets, lined with houses and shops, occasionally broken by the walls of some palace located farther inside, stood on the 'other side of the bridge'.

Across the bridge from Mahal and Itwari, was the new city, Civil Lines, with its wide roads and stately government buildings of stone or bricks, with domes and pillars; government offices and gardens that were maintained with grandeur; the high court and the general post office standing proudly with the flagpole where the Union Jack was mounted and taken down with due ceremony every day.

As one of the top-ranking administrators, Raman was allotted one of the houses in Civil Lines. These were similar to feudal manor houses, large houses in huge compounds, with two rows of servants' quarters to house the butler, the *khansama* (cook), the dhobi, the sweeper, the syce and as many other attendants as per custom. There was a separate stall for the horses and carriage, and the syce had his quarters close to it. A watchman stood at the gate of most of the houses. Civil Lines was still being expanded, to accommodate officials as the government base expanded.

Raman carefully considered the layout of the city. There were several colleges—Morris College, Hislop College and the Science College. The only really functional laboratory in town was housed at the Science College, a large brick building on one of the radial roads from Sitabaldi.

He had joined the civil service for one reason alone—so he would have time to pursue science. The job gave him enough money so he did not have to worry on that count; it challenged his intelligence just enough to keep his interest in the job, but not so much that he needed to fret over it; it demanded eight hours per day, five and a half days of the week of his time, and he gave it just that and not a minute more. He was scrupulous in rendering unto Caesar what was Caesar's, but he would not give Caesar any space in the rest of his life, not an extra minute, not an extra breath. The job did not tax his energy or time, and he was free to devote the remaining hours of each day to do whatever he wanted.

Raman spent every spare minute on his science. The first thing he did on coming to Nagpur was to get permission to use the laboratory facilities at Science College. Next, he selected a house close to the college as he was certain he did not want to live in Civil Lines. It was too far from Science College and there were no buses, trams, rickshaws, or even tongas to be found in Civil Lines. He toured the Sitabaldi area, which was within walking distance of Science College and had ready transportation at all times of the day.

The house he chose was the first one between Sitabaldi Square and Chota Dhantoli. Two hundred yards away lived Dr Gadre, who became their family doctor and helped them considerably. Opposite the house was a big maidan. Behind it was a huge garden that overlooked a bigger garden that belonged to a Buty (a family that owned large chunks of real estate) and stretched all the way to Buty Chawl. The house had large rooms, with a veranda in front, a central hall and an L-shaped veranda at the back. The walls and floor were of mud, but the outer walls were of brick. There was a large room upstairs. As in Rangoon, this room became Raman's laboratory, where he spread his instruments and equipment on large and small tables.

At the time, he was engaged in studying the wave motions of vibrating strings. Often he would take the help of neighbouring youngsters to hold the twine taut while he studied the vibrations.

Years later, a middle-aged woman came to see him in Bangalore. She was one of the youngsters who had often held the twine. She did not know then or later what those experiments were about, but she knew he was now a great man, respected by all in the world of science. Diffidently but eagerly, she came forty years later to visit him at 'Panchavati', his house in Malleswaram. On recognizing her, Raman warmly welcomed her and recalled various incidents of that time clearly and enthusiastically. She went away thrilled at the affectionate reception the Nobel laureate, Rajasabha Bhushana and Bharat Ratna awardee had accorded her.

It was August, the month of rains. It rained every day. Sometimes the rain came down in fine drizzles, like a pleasant spray. Sometimes it poured in sheets. The water rippled down the streets like a river and joined the Nag *nala* a few yards away at the turn of Sitabaldi Square. With the rain came mosquitoes and flies and carpenter ants; big black ants and tiny red ants. There were centipedes all over the courtyard and even snakes from time to time.

Soon after they came to Nagpur, Raman's sister Mangalam came with her family. Her husband had got a clerkship at a government office. Lokam, as at other times when the family suddenly expanded, was both pleased and not pleased; pleased at the company, not pleased with the added responsibilities. The house got crowded, and Raman retreated to his lab upstairs whenever he was home.

Then came the plague. A dead rat fell with a sickening thud on the floor of the central hall. Bihari, the manservant, knew it was a plague rat. He called in the neighbours who confirmed his suspicion and said the corporation office should be notified right away and the house evacuated. Raman promptly instructed Lokam to pack up necessities for a long stay outside the house. Next day, he arranged to have tents set up in his office compound. The corporation men came in the afternoon and clamped a quarantine order on the premises. They went from house to house in the area to see if any other house had to be vacated. The family moved out in several tongas—all but one person. The cook, who had been brought from Madras, quietly packed up his belongings and took a train back, telling Bihari to inform the mistress only after he had left, that he wanted nothing to do with a plague-infested house and city.

Life in the tents was another new experience. There was no water nearby. Faithful Bihari brought pails and pails of water from a tap in the office building. There were a great many tents in the compound and everywhere else, for many areas of the city had to be evacuated. Lokam, with some help from Mangalam who was getting bigger with child, did the cooking in one of the tents.

There were no residential areas near the office complex. But there were huts farther down the road and a toddy shop. At night, they could hear drunks walking home and the sounds of fighting and abusive language. The cloth door of the tent flapped in the breeze, and that would have been most welcome it if weren't for the prowling dogs, nuzzling at the cloth, trying to get in.

They lived in the tents for six weeks.

One day, Raman came home jubilant. He had got the longed-for posting—he was transferred to Calcutta. There was no promotion but he did not care; he was going home.

6

Star-gazing in Calcutta

By the time Lokam joined him, Raman had fixed up a house in Kalitola, the West End of Calcutta. Muktaram Babu Street, on which the house was located, was a row of manor houses. Lord Sinha, the first Indian to be made a baronet, lived in the house diagonally across from theirs. Another and even more famous neighbour was Raja Subodh Chandra Mullick (1879–1920). His manor was a palatial structure, with marble hallways and pillars, and stained glass windows from Italy and art treasures from all over Europe.[1]

The house Raman had rented was far from a manor. It was no bigger than the house in Nagpur, but the rent was high because of its location. The couple's needs were simple. Their furniture was minimal: chairs, tables and cupboards for the study, a couple of stools to reach the higher shelves and a well-equipped kitchen. They had always slept on the floor in the south, where the bedding was rolled away every morning and spread out every night, and in Nagpur they had rope-strung cots in the winter. Now they brought in regular bedsteads and mattresses.

As in his earlier stay in Calcutta, Raman would rise very early, take a tram to Bow Bazar Street and work for a couple of hours at the lab, return for a quick bite and then rush to work. Often he got late coming back from the lab and would take a phaeton-taxi, instead of the tram, so as to reach office on time.

That winter of 1911 saw the royal visit of King-Emperor George V and Queen Mary. Calcutta was their last stop, and they arrived on 30 December. Raman was not pleased at the various interruptions in traffic that preceded it. Roads were repaved, streets were cleaned, trees pruned, and all this came in the way of his routine of work at the IACS. The whole city had been turned upside down in preparation, and for a week, there were celebrations everywhere.

Now that he was back in Calcutta, work progressed at an accelerated pace. He had been interested in astronomy and meteorology from early on. Though he did not focus exclusively on these two fields at any time, he advocated their pursuits all his life. On his return from Nagpur, he promptly joined the Astronomical Society of India (ASI) that had been started the previous year[2] and gave several popular lectures at the ASI, which were published in the *Journal* of the society. Two of the longer talks were 'The diffraction of light and its relation to the performance of telescopes' and 'Astronomical Optics'.[3] He studied Saturn and gave two lectures on his observations. All these lectures were later published. These papers show that Raman was a fine lecturer from his earliest days. In 'Astronomical Optics', for instance, he clearly describes the apparatus he uses to study the fringes due to the interference of two light sources. It is such a simple one that any listener could have simulated the experiment for himself. Raman even gives a practical alternative to the use of electric light for the observation: 'the edge of the flat frame of a paraffin lamp'. His ambitions to encourage scientific pastimes are also evident from his earliest days in science. In one of these lectures written for the *JASI*, he says, 'There is no doubt that for us in India, we have in the Zodiacal Light and allied phenomena a splendid field for serious work by amateur astronomers who are situated away from the smoke and glare of the Calcutta sky, and the purpose of this note will be fulfilled if it encourages others to take up the subject.'[4]

He published a longer paper, 'Spectroscopic Notes', in the *Journal of the Astronomical Society of India* that made his name familiar to Gilbert T. Walker, director general of observatories in India. In this paper, Raman refers to an earlier theoretical investigation by Walker and says, 'It has occurred to me that it would be possible to give a somewhat shorter treatment of the case than that adopted by Dr. Walker,' and goes on to talk about his own experimental work on the subject. His work so impressed Walker that Raman had his support when he was nominated to the fellowship of the Royal Society ten years later.

With the help of the meteorological department a small wooden observatory had been set up on the roof of the IACS laboratory in 1906. The prince of Paikpara Raj (Mahendralal Sircar was born in a village in Paikpara) had gifted a seven-inch telescope some years earlier to the institute. Now, in 1912, Raman had the telescope mounted on the roof of the observatory. He studied Jupiter and, as he wrote in the annual report for 1913, 'made a series of 100 careful drawings of the surface of the planet . . . during the months of July–November' and posited, 'I think the problem of the scattering of light by a planetary body is not altogether an easy one and there may be room for further investigations here.'[5] This shows that his interest in light scattering started very early in his career and that astronomy was one of his great loves. Years later, in 1939, when asked what he would do if he could live his life again, he said, 'I would unhesitatingly choose that of an astronomer. Indeed, it has been one of my unfulfilled ambitions in life to be a star-gazer.'[6] In an essay he wrote for the *Annals of the American Academy of Political and Social Sciences* in 1944, he calls it 'the grandest of sciences'.

However, the only telescope that was available was not adequate for more meaningful studies and he dropped his experiments in astronomy, but he never lost his enthusiasm for 'star-gazing'. On his first visit to the United States, in 1924, he made it a point to visit Pasadena so he could spend some time at Mount Wilson Observatory. Founded in 1904 this observatory, situated in the San Gabriel Mountains of California at an altitude of 5715 feet, was the centre of astronomical research, and Raman was impressed with the huge 60-inch and 100-inch reflectors.

He advocated for observatories to be built in India. Astronomy was one of ancient India's fortes, Raman said, and the ancient writings 'of Aryabhatta, Varahamira, Brahmagupta and of Bhaskaracharya, which have come down to us, show that astronomy was actively studied in India at a time when the lamps of learning lighted by ancient Greeks had burnt out and Europe was passing through the dark ages'.[7]

Raman took vicarious pleasure in the achievements of his nephew, S. Chandrasekhar, eldest son of CS, whose work in astrophysics was to lead him to the Nobel Prize years later. They maintained a correspondence, and Chandrasekhar regularly sent him news of his early papers and presentations. Their letters, presented by S. Ramaseshan in an issue of *Current Science*, show how well Raman understood the implications of Chandrasekhar's work on white dwarfs and black holes, and the import of the paper he wrote from Copenhagen when he was just twenty-two. Years later, Raman's own son, Radhakrishnan, took to astronomy and Raman was very pleased about it.

In this period (1907–14) Raman worked alone, assisted by Ashu Babu when he was in Calcutta. Ashu Babu, whose education had stopped with high school, had the designation of a 'demonstrator', or lab assistant. But he soon became a research assistant, not only setting up the experiments but helping in carrying them out.

Raman's enthusiasm for his subject and the liveliness of his lectures attracted growing numbers of young men to spend time at the IACS laboratories. Within months of coming, he had charted out plans for lectures that kept the large lecture hall in use most evenings, and organized the three rooms of the laboratory so that anyone who wanted to work would have his own space.

He was on the managing committee of the IACS. His goal was to make it a national professional organization, along the lines of the Royal Society or the national science organizations of European countries. With that in mind, he initiated a new agenda for the annual meetings, namely, the reading of scientific papers. The 1913 annual meeting had a session for papers. D.N. Mallick gave a survey of optical theories; Raman followed with a more specific aspect, namely, 'On the Properties of the Synchronous Motor'. Within a short time, it was decided to have quarterly meetings of the association, where papers could be formally presented and discussed. IACS was on its way to becoming like European science associations. The annual science convention held along with the annual meeting of IACS became a gathering of scientists from all over the country.

These conferences were discontinued after a few years, once the Indian Science Congress Association took on the role of a national organization. Chemists J.L. Simonsen and P.S. MacMahon had initiated the establishment of the association, modelled on the British Association for the Advancement of Science, and it was founded in 1914. Soon, it became the main forum for annually bringing together researchers from all over the country to share their findings.

In the summer of 1914, Lokam went south for her brother's wedding and then spent a month in Madras with her mother-in-law. The family, now living at 2/11 Sydoji Lane in Triplicane, had converged again in sorrow. Early in January, Skandan had been diagnosed with intestinal tuberculosis. Mother had taken him to the T.B. Centre in Madanapalli (present-day Andhra Pradesh) and for a time he seemed to be recovering. He resumed going to college, where he was in the final year. But his condition worsened soon, and he was at home all summer. Now he lay dying in a darkened room, his body reduced to mere bones, his spirit resisting each onslaught as the disease galloped within him. CS was there, as he always was for the family, having taken long leave from work.

Sundaram's death in July 1907 was a blow but he had been a child of nine. Meena's death on 23 January 1912 had not been as shocking because she had been frail and anaemic all her short life of nine years. But Skandan was in his twentieth year, bright-eyed, darkly handsome and a promising student. And he was doomed not to live. Skandan died late in October 1914.

Skandan's death once again brought home the unpredictability of the future. There was so little time and so much to do. The association was already a beehive of activity. Raman increased his tempo. In the next three years, while his own research was in acoustics, he had students working on optics, some of whom were doing excellent work. The experiments of S.K. Banerjee, M.N. Basu, S.K. Mitra and T.K. Chinmayanandam were published in prestigious journals such as *Nature, Philosophical Magazine, Proceedings of the Royal Society* and *Physics Review*. A total of twenty-five papers came out in the years 1914–17. Raman wrote a monograph of 200 pages on *Acoustics of Musical Instruments in the Violin Family*, which was published in 1918 under a somewhat different title.

Work—his own and that of others—was moving well. One of the mechanics at the workshop, Bepin Chandra Mullick, was making instruments 'the finish and workmanship of which are in no way inferior to any English or American instruments'. There were applications from aspiring researchers from all over the country. Raman worked hard to acquire stipends for more researchers than were offered till then, even if many of those who came from different parts of the country were willing to bear their own costs in order to get an opportunity to work at the association laboratories.

During Lokam's absence, Raman had been having all his meals at a restaurant near the IACS office. The location suited him so well that it now irked him to have to return such a long way in the morning just to have his lunch and get dressed for office. He started looking for another house. About this time, his friend T.K. Rajagopalan was transferred back to Calcutta. He stayed with Raman for the first few days, house-hunting so he could bring his family to join him. Raman suggested that if they could find a house close to the association (210 Bow Bazar) he would be glad to swap houses. They went together to see several houses. Raman liked one; it was 54–55 Premchand Burral Street. This was a narrow street parallel to Bow Bazar Street. Raman decided to move into this house. Rajagopalan was very pleased to get the Kalitola house. He felt it was indeed a fine house, situated as it was in an elite locality.

The house on Premchand Burral Street, on the other hand, was in a crowded area, with slums nearby and an open sewer running behind the house. But Raman couldn't care less. It was within half a mile of the association and therefore worth its weight in gold. He could come home for lunch since his office too was much closer than before. He could work at the lab till late at night and not worry about when the last tram for the day was. He needed to take trams only to and from the office, and not twice over as he had been doing for the last three years. Moreover, trams were a lot more frequent on this route, and that meant he could indulge in his habit of starting late at less expense. Phaetons were readily available in Kalitola and it was a pleasure to ride in a carriage, the horses trotting briskly and rhythmically along Chowringhee to Dalhousie Square. But it cost much more than tram fare. Besides, one was never relaxed on one's way to office. It was so much better to hire a phaeton on weekends and savour the experience. They did that often, whenever Raman wanted to enjoy the colours of the flowering trees or the flowerbeds lining the main street, or when he wanted to think about his work amid the soothing trot of horses' hooves.

Lokam did all the work of moving again, from Kalitola to Premchand Burral Street. A year later, in 1915, Raman noticed a new block of four houses coming up further down the street, behind 210 Bow Bazar Street. Promptly, he arranged to rent one of the four houses.

The four houses 1/5/1A, 1/5/1B, 1/5/1C and 1/5/1D had common walls. Each house, like all houses in the area, had many rooms, all small, and it was three storeys high. In most houses each floor was rented out to a different tenant. But Raman had rented all three floors of one of the four houses—1/5/1B, which was sandwiched between two houses. To the right of the front landing on the ground floor was a room larger than the others, the farther end of which opened on to a veranda that ran on three sides of a small courtyard. On the other side were the stairs and the dining room, and on the third side were the kitchen, bathroom and lavatory, all opening off a narrow veranda and a small backyard. The other two floors were similar, except that on the second floor there was a terrace instead of a kitchen. The second floor had a guest room and Raman's bedroom. On the first floor, the front room was Lokam's and the rooms above the kitchen and dining room were Raman's study and dressing rooms. There was no need for setting up an experiments-table here and there wasn't any space for one either, the rooms being rather small. However, the open courtyard gave a good measure of sunlight and a feeling of space.

They lived in this house until they left for Bangalore in 1933. It was literally back to back with the IACS building. Raman could disappear into his magical kingdom in a matter of minutes because IACS agreed to make a door in the wall of their compound, and to give Raman a key.

Palit Professorship

The last decade of the nineteenth century was a period of growth everywhere, especially in the context of nationalism. The nationalistic resistance to British imperialism rose first in Bengal. Earlier in the nineteenth century, with Lord Macaulay's manifesto, the British had already set in place a national system of education that served them well by attracting their subjects to help in the administration of the country. The British were effectively using educational institutions to train generations of Indians to toe the imperial line through the way their minds were shaped by the curriculum's focus on European classical philosophy and English literature to honour the Western classical tradition, and to be grateful to the British for bringing this treasure house to them.

Calcutta, the seat of the Raj, was a centre of activities for every profession and business. The presence of the British had a strong influence on the thinkers of the city. Quick to absorb the literature and philosophies of the West, they were also quick to discern that India had to break free of the British and shape its own destiny. They realized education was one of the most powerful portals through which the masses could be awakened.

It was a case of each action being followed by a reaction. As with any sweeping movement, it is difficult to ascertain what came first, but an alternating cycle of action-reaction was set in motion which changed the face of education in Bengal.

In 1875 Sir Richard Temple, the governor of Bengal, wrote to the viceroy observing that the British focus on the humanities had encouraged the natives to dream of excellence and that in order to curb their growing self-confidence, 'We shall do more to direct their thought towards practical science, where they must inevitably feel their utter inferiority to us.'[1] Ironically, this promotion of the sciences in the curriculum whetted the intellectuals' appetite to excel on their own terms, as seen in Mahendralal Sircar and his circle.

The movement for nationalistic education spread after Satish Chandra Mukherjee founded the Bhagavat Chatuspathi in 1895. This institution mainly dealt with the cultural heritage of India, but soon Dawn Society set up the National Council of Education for the founding of private colleges to promote technical education. Donations poured in from patrons such as Brajendra Kishore Roy Chaudhuri of Gouripur and Raja Subodh Mullick.

Lord Curzon's education mission report of 1902 noted that educational centres were expanding young minds in what were considered 'improper' ways—instead of absorbing British values and accepting British superiority, youths were imbibing the airs of rebellion, dreaming of defying the British.

Noting this new phenomenon, the rulers sought to prevent the nationalists from impinging on the British hold on education by systematically controlling the curriculum so as to contain seditious inclinations. They enacted the Universities Act in 1904, ensuring that government-nominated British members controlled the senate and the syndicate of Calcutta University. One of the aims was to prevent any nationalist ideology from entering the administration and the curriculum of Calcutta University. They tried to sever from the Calcutta University the affiliation of many private colleges established by nationalistic individuals. But this only added fuel to the fire.

Meanwhile, Lord Curzon unveiled his plan to partition Bengal. Under the British until then, Bengal, Bihar and Orissa formed the province of Bengal. Curzon decided that this vast area of 4,89,508 square kilometres was too large to be effectively administered. He proposed to rearrange the political divisions by removing Dacca, Chittagong and Rajshahi from Bengal and create a new province called East Bengal and Assam, with Dacca as the capital. Protests erupted all over Bengal, for it was seen as an unjustified amputation of Bangla identity and culture. Curzon still went ahead and on 16 October 1905 established the division. It aroused deep anger among the populace. The poem 'Vande Mataram' became the battle cry and students joined the protest in great numbers. The fire now turned into a conflagration.

In the field of education, Bengal National College was started on 14 August 1906, with Aurobindo Ghosh as the first principal. The National Council of Education also started a number of schools all over the province. A sister-rival institution, Bengal Technical Institute, was started by the Society for the Promotion of Technical Education on 25 July 1906, with donations from Taraknath Palit and others. The two rival colleges ran into problems at first but continued to prosper once they divided the focus of studies between them, Bengal National College focusing on arts and humanities. This college drew a great many luminaries to join its faculty—Rabindranath Tagore, Ananda Coomaraswamy and Surendra Nath Banerjee among them.

In 1911 the partition of Bengal was annulled, but the increased swadeshi fervour that had been generated effected many changes in the life of the capital.

~

Sir Asutosh Mookerjee (1864–1924) was a key figure in the educational system of the time. Like his friend, Mahendralal Sircar, he was a visionary. As a student, he studied mathematics and physics and then took a degree in law. Between 1880 and 1890 he published nearly twenty papers on higher mathematics in learned journals. He was actively associated with the IACS and gave a series of lectures on mathematics between 1887 and 1891. He started the Calcutta Mathematical Society in 1908.

Sir Asutosh Mookerjee was a diplomat who knew how to achieve his goals within the system. He affirmed that a new university was not needed, and that he was for reform, not revolution. The British approved of his moderate stance, which was so different from the camp that clamoured for a new national university that would develop its own path towards nation-building. As a member of the university senate and syndicate (elected in 1889), Sir Asutosh quietly implemented a nationalistic agenda that seemed not to go against the values and returns that the British expected from their subjects. He maintained he was apolitical and that educational progress was his only goal, but he quietly advanced and implemented nationalistic changes.

After being appointed vice chancellor of Calcutta University in 1906, he set about changing the face of the university. Not satisfied with the emphasis on Western literatures and philosophies, he introduced a whole series of new courses that accomplished two objectives. One was to meet his goal of nation-building by including a strong Indian component even at the postgraduate level in areas such as Indian history, comparative literatures, anthropology, Islamic culture and mainly in Indian languages like Sanskrit, Hindi and Bangla. His effort to support the inclusion of Indian languages is reflected in his epitaph: 'His noblest achievement, surest of them all/ A place for his mother tongue—in stepmother's hall.'

To achieve his second objective, that India should take its place in the world of science, he expanded the offerings in science. His efforts galvanized his rich contemporaries such as Taraknath Palit, Rashbehari Ghosh, maharaja of Darbhanga and the raja of Khaira to donate enough to start the University College of Science (UCS), and to establish various chairs to be filled by distinguished Indian researchers.

The four Rashbehari Ghosh Professorships went to Ganesh Prasad, D.M. Bose, P.C. Mitra and S.P. Agharkar. For the chair in chemistry, Sir Asutosh chose P.C. Ray, inviting him in 1912 to accept the position. (Ray joined after his retirement in 1916.) From a letter Sir Asutosh wrote to the viceroy on 29 June 1912, we know he hoped 'to be able to secure Dr. J.C. Bose for the Chair of Physics'.[2] Jagadish Chandra Bose (1858–1937) was already a renowned scholar in physics and in botany. As early as 1885, he had demonstrated the existence of wireless waves. He had worked on the response of plant life to external stimuli.[3]

However, J.C. Bose declined. Some time later, after retiring from the university, on 30 November 1917, J.C. Bose opened his own centre—Bose Research Institute—which he had planned for long.

Sir Asutosh looked around for a suitable candidate. He noted that there was a young man, Raman, who had made the association his second home. His enthusiasm had brought the IACS back to life. Raman had attracted audiences to his popular lectures. Young men working in offices were inspired to try out their skills at the laboratories. Raman's approach was simple, logical: nature holds the key to all the mysteries of creation. Ask the right questions and nature will reveal her secrets. Observe nature and you will think of the right questions to ask. Experimental verification of possible answers is the key to science. Science can give you answers to the mysteries of creation. India can forge ahead if scientific research is supported and pursued.

Sir Asutosh could almost hear his old friend Mahendralal Sircar in the young man's voice and words. Moreover, his experiments were visual examples of his principles. Musical instruments were his favourite. The simple *ektara*—what could be a better example of the combination of experiment, mathematical relationships and aesthetics? When properly handled, this basic musical drone served to keep time to the vocalist as his voice moved up and down the notes. It was a practical example of the tuning fork experiments of Melde and Rayleigh on the phenomenon of maintained vibrations. Musicians may not even be aware that there are mathematical bases to the making of musical sounds that are aesthetically pleasing to the ear; that when the wire-string is plucked, its length increases and the tension varies at twice the frequency of the wire. Science explained everyday phenomena and in explaining, also opened doors to refining the applications that came of such knowledge. Above all, Raman inspired self-confidence in people—that they could achieve a lot despite scanty resources. Build it and they will come, Mahendralal Sircar had said, and Raman had not failed him.

Not only had he brought back activities to IACS, but had recognized the need to tell the world of what was going on. Again, so like Mahendralal who had started a journal to tell the world about his research practices with homeopathy and education. The *Bulletin* of IACS was being published on a regular basis. Scientific inquiry does not need a whole lot of money, and we have more than enough right here at IACS labs to do what we need to do to get started, Raman often said in his lectures. In private conversations, he was more explicit: We do not need to depend on governments to support us, for those funds will always have strings attached. It was like olden times when Mahendralal's declamations had inspired donors and audience.

This young man showed great promise. But he was an officer in the financial civil service and his salary was already far higher than the chair carried. Would he even be interested? Raman seemed perfectly happy to be conscientiously earning his salary and conscientiously working at the association the rest of the time.

But, and here Sir Asutosh smiled, Raman had a weakness—he loved to teach, to lecture, to stand in front of an audience and hold them spellbound. When he lectured, his small sharp eyes sparkled with pleasure, his long hands gestured articulately, his fingers ran equations and figures on the blackboard with broad flourishing sweeps. Standing behind the lectern, he was fully alive, as he could never be sitting behind his desk at his office, marble floors and salaaming chaprasis and clerks notwithstanding.

Sir Asutosh made the offer, and Raman was elated—this was exactly what he had dreamed of in his student days. His superiors and colleagues at work were shocked—surely he was not thinking of leaving! He was 'most useful in the Finance Department, being, in fact, one of our best men'.[4] They told him he had a bright future, now that the government was seriously considering moving towards 'Indianization'. Raman might even be made the education member of the Viceroy's Council, one of the highest positions in the entire Raj administration.

Raman, however, was not interested in administrative career opportunities. He was ready to resign right away, for monetary remuneration mattered little to him, now that his inherited responsibilities to family members were over. All debts had been paid in full, both his sisters were married, though they still needed financial support from time to time, and his own needs were modest. Travelling south was their only large expense and even that did not have to be as frequent as before, now that the family was settled. Lokam was a careful housekeeper and never complained about anything. She fully supported the idea of taking up the professorship.

There was one other requirement in the rules related to the endowed chair: the incumbent had to be trained abroad. Sir Asutosh did not consider this an issue as he was sure Raman could be sent to England for a short stint. But he had misjudged Raman on that count. Raman flatly refused. He had said often enough that no one needed to go abroad to prove himself and he had meant it. To be trained, indeed. As though he needed to be trained, in England at that. They could keep their chair.

Ever since Sir Asutosh was made a member of the university syndicate in 1889, he had been able to implement changes because he had kept his nationalism under the surface. But the swadeshi movement was all around them and Sir Asutosh had to fight those very forces, the British rulers, that had given him the wherewithal to change the face of education. In the second decade of the twentieth century, the movement to make higher education more relevant to the Indian context gained ground. There was a growing demand for courses related to technology and engineering and in the areas of science that would be more relevant to India's development as a nation. The British kept trying to look over Sir Asutosh's shoulder and resented when circumstances made them give in to certain demands.

Gestures—what would later be identified as satyagraha—flamed defiance among Indians, and gestures made by scientists were doubly dangerous. The fact that the British had succumbed to the pressure, when J.C. Bose protested against the inequality in pay vis-à-vis British-born colleagues by not drawing his salary, had become part of swadeshi folklore. J.C. Bose had gone further: he refused to patent his discoveries and to make money out of them, his philosophy being that knowledge was to be given freely just as the rishis of old had done. The swadeshi movement saw in this act a defiance of the European way of looking at things, a refusal to succumb to the Eurocentric order that considered itself superior to all others. The British had also gone along with P.C. Ray's hermit life and peasant clothing, and he had become another icon on the swadeshi altar. The British had thought promoting science education was safe but now they had to rethink in light of the attitudes and actions of Bose and Ray.

Now here was a young man, hardly twenty-six years old, who should feel honoured at the job that was being offered, with a stint of study in England to boot, but he was dismissing the offer out of hand, de facto stating that European academic training was worthless.

Sir Asutosh silently revelled in the young man's courage and diplomatically set about getting the syndicate to waive the requirement. Raman received a letter dated 26 March 1914 from the registrar: 'With reference to your letter of the 14th current I am directed to inform you that the Hon'ble the Vice Chancellor and Syndicate agree to the condition on which you are prepared to accept the appointment of Sir Taraknath Palit Professor of Physics, namely, that during your incumbency you will not be required to leave India and to proceed to any foreign country.'

At the foundation-stone-laying ceremony of the University College of Science (UCS), located at 92 Upper Circular Road in Calcutta, on 27 March 1914, Sir Asutosh announced, 'We have been fortunate enough to secure the services of Mr. Chandrasekhara Venkata Raman, who has greatly distinguished himself and acquired a European fame by his brilliant researches in the domain of Physical Science . . .'[5]

~

However, Raman could not join his new position immediately due to some problems related to the Palit endowment. The university needed funds to equip the laboratories so that the chair could function effectively. They asked the government for money and the government refused. The government did not like the clause in the endowment that said the professorship 'shall always be filled by Indians'.[6] The British government was funding the Tata Institute (Indian Institute of Science) in Bangalore because the professors were British. The British professors were paid much more in India than their counterparts were paid in Britain: the salary of the director of the National Physical Laboratory in England was 1200 pounds a year whereas the director in Bangalore was paid 4000 pounds a year. Yet, they were not prepared to fund chairs within India occupied by Indians. There were other problems regarding buildings too. Sir Asutosh finally worked out the problems and got the donors and the university to come forward with the required resources in three years' time.

During the time between the offer and the actual beginning of the incumbency in 1917, Raman's magnetic attraction of students had continued and his own research too had gone on full steam. His father's love of the violin had devolved on to him in another way: through his admiration for Helmholtz. Hermann Ludwig Ferdinand von Helmholtz (1821–94) was a versatile scientist whose work spanned mathematics, physics, physiology and the science of aesthetics—a combination that was to interest Raman all his life.

In 1947, when asked about the books that had influenced him, Raman had singled out three titles as nearest to his heart—Sir Edwin Arnold's *Light of Asia*, *The Elements of Euclid* and Helmholtz's *The Sensations of Tone*. Of Helmholtz's belief in the civilizing aspect of science and his approach to research, Raman said, 'For the first time, I understood from its perusal what scientific research really meant and how it can be undertaken. I also gathered from it a variety of problems for research which were later to occupy my attention and keep me busy for many years.'[7] Raman continues in this essay to express how he regretted not having been able to access Helmholtz's work *The Physiology of Vision* when he was a boy.[8]

The other scientist whose work tied in with Raman's interest was Lord Rayleigh (1842–1919), author of *The Theory of Sound* (1877). Rayleigh's work on how human beings perceive sound objects spatially, using the difference in the time delay of the sound and the difference in amplitude between the two ears, was taken up by Raman and applied to musical instruments such as the violin, the cello and the piano. Raman devised a mechanical

violin player where the bow was kept stationary and the violin was
made to move. As always, he used the simplest and most readily
available components to build it. Many of the parts came from
old bicycles—the chain, the hub, the ball-bearing of the axle of
a lever. He had the rest made at the workshop of the IACS. As he
described it, 'The apparatus was driven by a belt running over a
conical pulley of a shunt-wound electric motor controlled by a
rheostat' and the 'slide and cast-iron track were part of a disused
optical bench'.[9] The diagram and description make it seem a
cumbersome crude assortment of parts, but it was sophisticated
enough to perform all the experiments needed for the results,
which are today considered of utmost theoretical and practical
importance in the science of sound.

The pleasing effects of the vibrations produced by stringed
instruments had been mentioned as early as by Pythagoras;
Raman set about to study through experiments the mathematical
relationships that produced the pleasing effect of sounds. There
was also the question of the unpleasing effects of the bow playing
over strings, the wolf note in particular. He could remember his
father telling CS how to avoid the howl and the squeak of unwanted
resonances, that the E-string being plain metal with no winding
had to be bowed over gently so that the bow was always in contact
with the string. Father would tinker around with the sound post,
the bridge and the bow. Stringed instruments are hollow bodies
and any hollow body has a primary resonant frequency. The shape
of the violin too was important. Raman set about getting to know
all there was to know about the instrument.

This led him to think about other musical instruments—the
veena, which had a much bigger hollow body and whose strings
were plucked, not bowed; and the piano where sound was produced,
or 'excited' as the technical term goes, by the stroke of a hammer.
Helmholtz had regarded striking and plucking in the same category,
though he did recognize the difference. The main difference was

that only the single point that is struck is set in motion in the piano and produces abrupt discontinuities. Raman went further and calculated how exactly the force due to the hammer varied as a function of time and how the duration of contact of the hammer varied as a function of the strike position.

The differences between the piano and percussion instruments led him to other interesting observations. Of Western percussion instruments he said, 'All the instruments of percussion known to European physicists in which a circular drum-head is employed have therefore to be regarded more as noise producers introduced for marking rhythm than as musical instruments . . . Indian musical instruments of percussion however stand in an entirely different category [and] possess interesting acoustical properties.'[10] He went on to show how the construction of the *mridangam*, with its inner and outer rings, the long and the short conical parts combined in just the right ratios of length, was proof that the ancients had a method, which must have been a scientific one, to arrive at the precise construction that would make it emanate the notes with the richness it did. In the veena and the *tampura*, the right pitch is maintained by a simple device for the continuous adjustment of tension. Raman studied many aspects of percussion instruments and ends one of his essays with: 'All this may serve to give some idea of the extraordinary degree of development which the construction and use of percussion instruments has attained in India.'[11]

~

His papers on musical instruments sparked an interest in his work in Germany and he was invited in the mid-1920s to write a monograph on tones in musical instruments for the *Handbuch der Physik* series. In it, one can discern another trait in the way he approached his work. He does not repeat any of his earlier findings but includes instead an overview of basic terms and then goes on to the physical theory of musical instruments through quantitative

analysis of musical notes. Because he had already published so
much on the string instruments (violin, veena, tampura) and
the percussion instruments (mridangam and tabla), he spends
more time on the physics behind wind instruments: the flow of
air through the apertures, energy emission, the consequences of
vibrations on the variation of the cross section of the tubes, and
so on. He shows why instruments are shaped the way they are.
He talks about the *jaltarang* in great detail, probably because he
had not done so in earlier papers. The physics of this instrument
is close to his heart, namely, the influence of the liquid on
the vibrations of the elastic shell—a topic that had first been
investigated by Lord Rayleigh, who, like Helmholtz, was one of
teenage Raman's demigods.

In 1999 N.H. Fletcher, in an issue of *Reports of Progress in
Physics*, said: 'Musical instruments have been of interest to scientists
from the time of Pythagoras, 2500 years ago, and since then many
famous physicists, among them Helmholtz, Rayleigh and Raman,
have devoted at least some of their attention to them.'[12]

Between 1911 and 1918 Raman published thirteen short papers
on sound and vibrations in journals in England and in India,
most of the work being completed before he officially became a
Palit Professor.

While most of the papers were on vibrations and sound, one was
'On Intermittent Vision', which he published in 1915. He starts the
paper with, 'One of the most curious and interesting phenomena
met with in the borderland of physics and the physiology of vision
is the occasional appearance of intermittency . . .' and goes on to
explain what one sees when a disk with alternate white and black
sectors revolves in its own plane.

This shows one of the patterns of Raman's research approach.
He observed a great many phenomena and asked the right
questions that would lead to a significant conclusion; but he did
not always pursue them immediately. He often made a note or two,

which were sometimes sent for publication, and he often came back to the questions, sometimes years later, sometimes sooner. He came back to the study of vision in his last years.

Raman also wrote short notes on the experiments being carried out by him or under his direction. He realized the importance of prompt dissemination of results, the need to lay the findings on the table, as it were, so that further dialogue on the matter could take place. This was so with his experiments on the striations on mica. In a paper published in 1918, with P.N. Ghosh, he talks about their observations with diffuse reflected light on a sheet of mica. He gives full credit to his associate and explains the findings very succinctly, saying, 'The phenomenon is being investigated by one of us [P.N. Ghosh], but as to its general nature there appears to be little doubt. The striae are lines at which the thickness of the mica changes in a discontinuous manner, and the luminosity is due to the radiation from the discontinuity acting as a laminar diffracting boundary.' Colours were to fascinate him all his life—the seashells he had collected as a boy led him to study the formation of colours on them years later, in the 1930s; so also with the colours of the mica.

Often, however, he took up a topic, carefully carried out experiments, and came up with a series of short papers on different aspects of the same topic, as in the five years he spent on acoustics and musical instruments. Of the numerous papers in this period, three were on 'Discontinuous Wave-Motion'.

Two parts of this three-part paper that appeared in the *Philosophical Magazine* in 1916–17 bear the name of A. Dey as co-author. This tells us something very significant about Raman—his insistence on giving due credit to work done by others. Of the 465 papers he published in his lifetime, 324 were single authored and 138 others had another author besides him. In the co-authored papers, the main concept was his, as was the supervision of all details. There were about 1500 other papers that he directed, with around 200 students and associates working under his supervision, and he always let the student or associate take full credit even if the central concept and the overseeing were his.

This particular co-author, Asutosh Dey, was none other than Ashu Babu, who was a lab assistant at the IACS and had never enrolled in a college. But Raman fully acknowledged the invaluable help he had received from him. Raman even encouraged Ashu Babu to send off a paper on his own, titled 'A New Method for the Absolute Determination of Frequencies', which appeared in the prestigious *Proceedings of the Royal Society* (95, 533) in 1919, with Raman writing the foreword and appendix on the underlying concepts.

At the science convention of 1917 in Calcutta Raman could proudly say, 'I have had time to take on a large number of research workers and train them.' The proof that there now was a real scientific atmosphere in Calcutta, he said, was in 'the numerous requests that have been received from teachers and scholars in various parts of India and Burma to be permitted to work in my laboratory and to carry on research'.[13]

~

Meanwhile, the legal problems with the Palit endowment were close to being resolved. Raman did not pay much attention to what his salary was, but he was careful about his research. He wanted to be free, totally independent. As long as he did not owe anyone anything, nobody could have a hold over him. But whoever paid him would demand their pound of flesh. With his current job, it was easy—a certain number of hours every day, five and a half days each week—but a university job would have other constraints, other responsibilities. He carefully spelt out his needs. The incumbent was not required to teach, but he wanted to ensure that he would be given a teaching load comparable to that of a regular professor, cementing an inalienable right to the lectern. Indeed, Sir Asutosh was right on the mark about Raman's passion to lecture. Raman also wanted to be formally made the director of the Palit Physical Laboratory and wanted to have sole control in the running of the laboratory. Further, while he was at his list, he added that a house allowance of Rs 250 a month be added to his salary until he was provided a residence.

In his request for a residence, Raman shows a concern that he would fulfil for others in later life. To him it was a given that science was a 24/7 occupation, and that proximity of residence to the laboratory was a prerequisite for productivity so that one could easily move from domestic commitments to work commitments without loss of commuting time. Soon after he became Palit Professor, he wrote a monograph on *The Calcutta School of Physics*. In a section titled 'Our Most Urgent Needs' he lists that along with lab equipment and incentives to graduates to join educational and scientific services of the government is the need 'for residential accommodation in the premises of the University College of Science for the Professors and staff engaged in research work'. When he started his own research centre in 1948, there were specific plans for convenient and well-laid-out residences for students, staff and faculty, with dining facilities where healthy food was available at subsidized cost.

In a letter dated 11 May 1917 the syndicate agreed to all the conditions he had listed except that of giving total control of the laboratory. Soon after this, Raman joined his post as Palit Professor of Physics, with the right to use the laboratories at both the UCS and the IACS and a mandate to: (1) devote himself to original research in his field to extend the bounds of knowledge; (2) stimulate and guide research by students; and (3) supervise the laboratory in the College of Science.

Raman wished to take one more precautionary step. He wanted a year's leave from his job so that he could try out the Palit Chair, and return to his government job if things did not work out.

However, Sir Harcourt Butler, education member in the Viceroy's Council, decided that Raman would not be given leave and would have to resign his position if he wanted to take up any other job.

Raman resigned from his government position and took up the Palit Professorship late in July 1917. Immediately, he began to reorganize the laboratory and facilities for maximum productivity. Raman held that a good workshop was a prerequisite for good research, and in Calcutta he had got the support of everyone around him to build the IACS workshop according to his plans. However, in the UCS, in his forthright method of figuring out what was needed and then executing whatever had to be done, he unfortunately did not pay much heed to possible encroachment on others' territory. This led to some spates of bad blood between himself and some colleagues. But his actions were so clearly well meant that the spates were of short duration. For example, Rajinder Singh, an expert on Raman, mentions a letter from J.C. Bose to the vice chancellor dated 30 August 1917, where Bose complains of the visit of one of Raman's emissaries to 'invite my senior mechanic to transfer his services to the College of Science Physical Department, with [the] offer of increased salary above what he gets from me—even up to three times if necessary'.[14]

This is so typical of Raman's single-minded pursuit of his scientific interests that one need not doubt the veracity of the incident. But interpretations are usually varied in all such anecdotes pertaining to Raman, often attributing egotistical arrogance to him instead of a naïve directness of approach. There was at all times a childlike quality in Raman that those close to him could understand. He had a loud schoolboy laugh, a frank pleasure in viewing his own works, an exuberant appreciation when one of the students got results, an obliviousness to all extraneous matters, but also a deep power of observation of details that really mattered. However, in later life Raman paid dearly for such direct acts of pursuing his scientific goals which, though they had no malice or ulterior motives, were misconstrued by those who wanted to tar him.

Raman taught courses in the MSc programme: electricity and magnetism and physical optics. He was an inspiring teacher from day one. L.A. Ramdas, one of his first students, says of these courses: 'Both sets of M.Sc. students felt that they were indeed listening to a type of inspired teaching to which was brought all the original flavour and excitement of the great giants of the past.'[15] With Gandhi's message of non-cooperation in the students' ears, undergraduate students often staged protests and tried to bar everyone who wanted to enter the college. But Raman and his students never wanted to waste a single day and were always there. Sometimes his classes would go on for twice as long as the scheduled time.

Ramdas goes on to say how Raman would go straight to the IACS labs after his work at the UCS, or if he went after dinner he would often go to sleep on one of the tables in the lab. On most days, he would come to the IACS in informal clothes, work till 9.30 a.m., 'when he would remember his lecture engagement at the College of Science about four miles away'. He would rush home, have a quick bite, dress for work and rush back to the IACS, asking Ashu Babu to get a phaeton-taxi so as to be in time for class.

'Raman was a very special kind of a teacher. We learnt from him the excitement of scientific discovery, however small it is, and the role of intuition in the pursuit of science. He always told us not to be camp followers and to do something based on your own imagination and thinking. It was a great education to be with him, or to talk to him. We learnt from him to appreciate nature, to look at things in a simple way and above all self-confidence. By example, he showed us how to lecture and make it interesting to the audience.'

K.R. Ramanathan has reminisced about the atmosphere of the IACS laboratory as 'one of great informality and extreme cordiality.

All the workers lived either in the corner rooms of the Association or in rooms very near the Association, and work went on from morning seven till sunset with short intervals snatched for food and other personal requirements'.[16]

Raman's public lectures inspired young men in the regular workforce to join him at the laboratory after their day's work. Among the early researchers to commit themselves to regular research was T.K. Chinmayanandam, a clerk in a government office, with great potential for intellectual pursuits. He was young and single, a thin man with a passion for science. He would stay at the lab all evening and sometimes even sleep there, with no heed of eating at the proper times. Sometimes Raman would take him home for dinner, and Lokam usually sent extra portions of tiffin so Raman could share it with Chinmaya. But the young man's scientific career was short-lived as a few years later he succumbed to tuberculosis, to Raman's deep grief.

The flu pandemic of 1918 took a toll on the family. Raman's younger sister Mangalam died in November at the age of twenty-seven, leaving six children behind. The older children were taken care of by different members of her husband's family. Raman and Lokam took charge of the youngest, baby Dorai, for the next few years, until the father remarried and got all his children back with him. Mangalam and her family had lived with them for short periods in Madras and in Nagpur, and Raman had seen her go through her pregnancies. CS too already had six children. Mangalam's life story of perpetual pregnancies, as also his mother's and sister-in-law's, had a strong negative impact on Raman's views about starting a family. The children were healthy, the mothers seemed to cope well and others seemed to enjoy a full house, but whenever family visited, Raman extended his hours at the laboratory. Raman was not yet ready for such domestic responsibilities.

Blue of the Mediterranean

That India should make its mark in the international community of scholars was never far from Raman's mind. Raman was made a member of the university senate, and took his responsibility with utmost seriousness, turning his thoughts to the undergraduate scene with the same eye to detail that he had for postgraduate studies.

At senate meetings, he gave his views after full consideration of prevailing facts and needs. He pointed out that more postgraduate courses should be offered because of the superior qualifications of the faculty. He supported the proposal to start courses in psychology and anthropology because according to him India had an edge in these subjects; in psychology because 'the human mind, its power and processes form a subject which has always been of interest to Indian thinkers', and in anthropology because 'we in India have a field for work of the highest importance . . . we would soon find ourselves leading the rest of the world'.[1]

He took a stand on various matters with equal eloquence. He did not want a minimum age restriction for entrance into university—had he not himself benefited from the absence of such a restriction?[2] He supported the vernacularization of education, saying that an insistence on English would impact students' proficiency in their mother tongue. Moreover, taking lessons in their mother tongue would make subjects accessible to far more youngsters. He advocated for replacing Sanskrit with Bengali, again arguing that proficiency in one's mother tongue and regional culture was an education in itself.[3]

He supported the proposal for mandatory retirement, for which he became unpopular since many on the senate were over the age of sixty. But Raman drew examples from great scientists of the past to show that productivity declined after the age of fifty, and even the inspirational value of the presence of great scientists declined after the age of sixty.[4] On another occasion, Raman bluntly pointed out that funding for the universities came from the people. 'Everyone around this table and outside as well knows that the money is not the money of the government. It is the money of the people.'[5]

~

Raman's responsibilities within the association increased in 1919, when Amritalal Sircar died. Raman was elected to take his place as honorary secretary of the IACS. His administrative conscientiousness can be seen in the numerous details with which he filled the annual reports of the association. S.N. Sen, in his work on Raman, has gleaned little-known specifics from these reports, and has listed details such as the kind and number of equipment bought over the years and the titles and numbers of journals and books added to the library.

G. Venkataraman in *Journey into Light* speaks of the meticulousness with which the annual reports were written. They were in two parts. The first gave an exposition of the scientific work done during the year 'in language as free from technicalities as possible, of the scientific results obtained by investigations carried out under the general direction of your Honorary Secretary',[6] as Raman said, so as to keep a wide circle of readers informed of the progress of research at the IACS. The second part dealt with the administrative aspects of the association: a list of apparatus bought or repaired, a detailed account of what was done at the workshop and of the new acquisitions in the library, an update of the centres with which the publications of the IACS were exchanged and personal experiences in the discharge of his responsibilities. In one report, he narrates how he searched old iron shops for usable discarded material and equipment. Raman was always frugal and innovative, and when it came to lab equipment, he and his talented technicians made do with scraps and parts thrown away by others, and built most of the apparatus needed by the researchers who worked at the lab. As he said at the convocation address of Mysore University in 1929, 'We must learn to appreciate and use the products of Indian labour . . . We must acquire by labour and thought the secret of craftsmanship which lies in meticulous attention to detail and the continual striving after perfection.'[7]

His scientific research did not slow down, even though his teaching and administrative duties increased. This decade (1917–26) was extremely productive in every way. Raman loved to talk about his research and accepted many speaking engagements. He gave a series of six lectures on 'Recent Progress in Physics' at Madras University in January 1922. One was on musical instruments. His brother, CS, was in Madras at the time, and he records Raman's enthusiasm for their father's violin: 'When C.V.R. heard me play at home he got enthusiastic about it and was keen that I should demonstrate pure Carnatic ragas on father's violin, during the lecture . . . I suggested that Vidwan Sabesa Iyer [CS's teacher] might play . . . but he insisted on my recital.'[8]

Not much has been written on Raman's interest in and patronage of music. Over the years, he met many well-known musicians. There were several concerts in Calcutta in which he was the patron. CS records that on 11 December 1932, Raman was the patron of a concert by Palghat Rama Bhagavathar at Paddapakur Institute, and also records that Raman asked CS to play the violin at a private tea party early in 1933, hosted by Raman in honour of Sir Richard Gregory, editor of *Nature*. In May 1933, CS says, Raman happened to drop in when CS was entertaining a friend and after a piece, asked what emotions he had felt when playing the Kalyani ragam, and agreed that it was 'like the soft fall and calm of sunset, the oncoming of twilight'.

Most of the time, Raman was at one of the two laboratories, of University College, or of the association. However, he was already so well known that he had a great many visitors, many of whom had nothing to do with science and who came without any prior appointment. His office and laboratory doors were always open, and most who came to see him succeeded in meeting him, even if for a few minutes. Once a swami visited him at University College. Raman greeted him and asked him to take a seat while he completed what he was doing. But once he went back to his work, he forgot all about the visitor. When he came back, the swami was still patiently waiting. Raman apologized that he had only a few minutes to spare before a meeting that was coming up. The swami said Raman's concentration was admirable and then asked him for a donation. Raman gave him a generous amount and rushed off to his meeting. Later, when Raman was building his own institute in the late 1940s, he needed to go around asking for donations. When someone quipped that it was not becoming of a Nobel laureate to go begging, he said he was following in the footsteps of such beggars as the Buddha and Gandhi.

As a Palit Professor of Physics, the tempo of Raman's work increased. Even as he completed papers on sound and musical instruments, he planned to attract more students to the two laboratories. Several of his best students and associates joined him during the 1920s. K.R. Ramanathan (1893–1985) came to Calcutta in 1920 as a University of Madras research scholar. K.S. Krishnan (1898–1961) came to attend the University College and was promptly given a research assistantship by Raman.

While a list of published papers of the time would show that there were more than eighty students who worked with him during the momentous 1920s, photographs of the time highlight the names of those who worked with him for extended periods of time. A photograph taken in the early 1920s shows Raman with thirteen students and associates: D. Banerjee, S.K Banerjee, P. Das, G.L. Datta, A. Dey, L.A. Ramdas, K.S. Rao, B.B. Ray, N.K. Sethi, Sunderaraman, N.K. Sur, V.S. Tamma and Y. Venkataramayya. There is a photograph taken towards the end of the 1920s, in which Raman is seen with thirteen of those who were working at IACS with him at the time of the discovery of the Raman Effect. They are: A. Ananthakrishnan, S. Bhagavantam, A.S. Ganesan, K.S. Krishnan, K.R. Ramanathan, C. Ramaswamy, L.A. Ramdas, S.S.M. Rao, S. Paramasivan, S. Rao, N.S. Nagendra Nath, C.S. Venkateswaran and S. Venkateswaran.

Raman had an intuitive feel as to which candidate was made for research, and he directly and readily enlisted people to positions within the system. Many of those who were employed by him as students, associates or laboratory staff have similar stories of how they were inducted into his world. One of his students and biographers, A. Jayaraman, talks about a walk in the garden with Raman on 1 November 1949 in which Raman asked him about his interests and told him about his own plans for the new centre he was developing. After an hour and a half of this leisurely stroll, Raman told him that he was looking for an assistant, and Jayaraman jumped at the prospect of working with the Nobel laureate. S. Pancharatnam was recruited in a similar manner in 1954, when he happened to be on campus grounds on his way to meet his brother, who was Raman's student at the time. Raman never worried about paper qualifications; he himself had never bothered to get a PhD degree, and he held that people's potentials could be assessed through a personal interview more accurately than by their paper credentials. But then, like Sir Asutosh, he had that uncanny ability to find the right person for the jobs he needed done. So, by the early 1920s, Raman had a fine group of people working around him.

~

Raman's first trip abroad was in 1921, when he attended the University Congress, held 5 to 8 July at Oxford University, as a representative of Calcutta University. He was one of the members of a large delegation. But he made it a study tour as well, reaching England by mid-May and returning to India only in late September.

In England, even as he completed his role in the delegation, he was already thinking of new lines of research. As Raman went through St Paul's Cathedral in London, he was struck by the 'whispering gallery' phenomenon, that was a result of the curved shape of the dome. At certain points, a whisper can be clearly heard by a person at the far end of the dome, and at some points, a single footfall sounds as though an army is marching. Raman had already been studying, assisted by Bidhubhusan Ray, the curvilinear propagation of light along a curved reflecting surface. Raman now thought of the acoustical analogue of this phenomenon, and aided by Professor G.A. Sutherland, conducted experiments to show the radial fluctuations of intensity of sound waves. Raman also wrote two short notes in August that were duly published. One was on 'Conical Refraction in Biaxial Crystals' and the other on 'Smoky Quartz'.

On his way back from England, he thought about at least two problems, one of which was on how the visibility of distant objects could be improved by viewing through a Nicol prism, and he mailed a note about it from Aden to *Nature* on 18 September. The other was on why the sea is blue. The sea and sky had always caught his imagination, living as he had near the sea, both in Waltair and in Madras. But the blueness of the Mediterranean Sea and sky was breathtaking, and Raman was inspired as always by the wonder of nature's magnificence to seek answers.

He questioned Rayleigh's theory that it was due to the reflection of the sky and said that from his observations of the Mediterranean Sea, the Red Sea and the Arabian Sea, the colour was due to 'the diffraction effect arising from the passage of the light through the water' and that 'the diffracting particles, at least in part, may be the molecules of the water themselves'. The popular version of the story goes like this: Raman noticed the spectacular blue colour of the Mediterranean Sea on his voyage back to Bombay, figured out the answer, and immediately on landing at Bombay dashed off a paper, 'The Colour of the Sea', to *Nature* on his findings. That the paper he sent was dated 'S.S. *Narkunda*, Bombay Harbour, 26 September' might give credence to the story. It is likely that he always carried a Nicol prism with him, since it was basic to many of his experiments. This would explain the speed with which he wrote that note to *Nature* even before he disembarked.

As to why he did not observe the phenomenon on his way *to* Britain, a possible explanation is that he would have noticed it but did not concentrate on the question as he was too busy revising and editing a paper and thinking about his itinerary in England. We know that from England he mailed the *Philosophical Magazine* a long paper on 'Quetelet's Rings and Other Allied Phenomena', which he had written with his student G.L. Datta. The date on it is: 31 May 1921, 22 Oxford Road, Putney. We also know that he had already made several appointments with people he wanted to meet. He must have been busy planning and thinking about these meetings.

That he mailed the paper on the colour of the sea as soon as he got off the ship in Bombay is yet another example of what Ramdas talks about—that Raman would work at top speed to write up a paper and hire a taxi (phaeton) to the post office so it could be mailed without delay. Often he sent a paper by cable, for regular mail would take much longer. This was his process every time: to ask a question arising from his observation of natural phenomena, intimate others of his first thoughts on it through a short note in *Nature* or in another journal, then spend considerable time thinking of theoretical explanations, then carry out experiments to prove the hypothesis and very expeditiously write it up and send it for publication.

He followed up the short paper on the diffraction of light with a more detailed experimental verification. As soon as he returned to Calcutta, he spent several weeks collecting empirical data. On 15 October, he sent off another one-page paper to *Nature* that the scattering power of water is about 160 times that of air and stated that 'work is now in progress, testing the formula in the case of other liquids'. Then, after more experiments, he sent an eighteen-page paper in mid-November, which was published in the *Proceedings of the Royal Society* in 1922. This habit of staking his territory and keeping his colleagues informed was to prove most crucial later.

After completing that phase of work, he went to Coimbatore, to greet his firstborn, a son, born on 16 November 1921. Lokam had left for Coimbatore before his departure to England. Normally, as per custom she would have gone to her natal family only in the sixth or seventh month of her pregnancy, but since Raman was leaving on his trip, it was decided she would go to her sister Lakshmi's home before his departure. Sivan was now working at the Agricultural College in Coimbatore and by now he and Lakshmi had several children. Lokam had plenty of company and support. The child was named Chandrasekhar, after Raman's father, and was called Raja. In December 1921 Calcutta University conferred an honorary doctorate on Raman, a title he seldom used.

Raman followed up on his observations at St Paul's Cathedral and studied the whispering gallery phenomenon in several Indian monuments: the Gol Gumbaz at Bijapur (seventeenth century), which is larger than the Parthenon; the Victoria Memorial in Calcutta, which has two whispering galleries because of its inner and outer domes; the general post office in Calcutta; and the old government granary at Bankipore. Raman argued that the multiple sounds were due to the travelling of the sound waves along the circumference of the dome, which produced the effect at the end of each cycle, and not due to an echo, as had been assumed till then.

Jayaraman notes that his trips abroad changed some of Raman's work habits and that he began to take time to relax and to exercise. Jayaraman cites Ramdas, who speaks of how Raman—who had bought himself a phaeton in 1924—would go for a drive with Lokam every evening to the Maidan and do some physical exercise. If the trips abroad were the reason for his daily walk in the Maidan, there is an anecdote that Raman narrated in his convocation address at Banaras in 1926 that might reinforce it. While walking with Sir Ernest Rutherford through the campus of Cambridge University, they came upon students playing on the playfields. Jokingly Raman said Cambridge seemed to be a 'place for play and not for study'. Rutherford spiritedly replied, 'We do not try to grow bookworms here. We train men who can govern the Empire.'

But it was probably more a matter of health that made Raman change his work schedule. Lokam recalls that soon after he became a Palit Professor, he started spending all his time between the university and the IACS. Ramdas talks about it too; of how Raman would sometimes fall asleep in the IACS lab and be woken up by Ashu Babu in the morning. This overwork in a confined space for hours on end brought about a health crisis. Latently consumptive, he had bouts of breathing trouble, caught colds easily and developed digestive problems any time he ate anything other than home-cooked food. He consulted several doctors, but nothing seemed to help, mainly because Raman seldom followed through with the prescriptions.

Then appeared Dr Bidhan Chandra Roy. A massive man with a commanding personality, he made it clear he wanted implicit obedience or else . . . He prescribed medicines, gave a series of injections and, most importantly, he prescribed a two-hour walk every single day at the Maidan. Walking had been Raman's saviour even in adolescence and it came to his rescue again. Though he did not walk every day, at least several times a week Lokam and Raman would drive to the Maidan and walk for two hours. Sometimes he would play truant, walking into the enclosed air of New Market to browse the second-hand bookstalls. Lokam had to keep an eye on him and direct him away any time his feet turned towards New Market. Through strict diet, injections and regular walks, all signs of consumption disappeared with time. Throughout his life, he stuck to his habit of walking and had very few medical problems of a serious nature.

What next? The Nobel of course

The Royal Society was founded in 1660 as a community of scholars and a forum for discussion of the newest discoveries and theories in the world of science. Being elected a Fellow of the Royal Society is the top of the ladder. Having the right to append the three letters—FRS—to one's name 'was the ultimate mark of scientific distinction. Younger scientists lusted after it, older scientists lamented their lack of it'.[1]

In 1924 Raman was elected Fellow of the Royal Society. He was nominated in 1921 by G.T. Walker and seconded by George C. Simpson.

Only fellows could nominate a fellow scientist for this prestigious honour. The nominator is known as a proposer in the language of the Royal Society, and the nomination has to be supported by six other fellows. The whole process takes a considerable amount of time. Always keen to put India on the map of the scientific world, Raman proposed several scientists during the next few years: K.S. Krishnan in 1935 (elected in 1940); Homi Bhabha in 1940 (elected in 1941); and S. Chandrasekhar in 1941 (elected in 1944). He also nominated S. Bhagavantam and R.S. Krishnan, but they did not get elected.

~

The correspondence between Raman and his nephew Chandrasekhar has been written about by S. Ramaseshan in *Current Science*.[2] While they would have met often enough when Chandrasekhar was a child, the first significant meeting was in March 1928, when Raman briefly visited his brother CS in Madras, on his way to Bangalore where he was to give the momentous address of 16 March 1928, announcing his discovery.

Ramaseshan records Chandrasekhar's words: 'I remember well his showing slides of the first Raman spectra ever taken and of the state of euphoria he was in. On that occasion, someone drew attention to the discovery of the Compton Effect a few years earlier, and Raman responded with, "Ah but my Effect will play a great role for chemistry and molecular structure."'[3]

Chandrasekhar was not yet eighteen at the time. He spent two months that summer working in Calcutta at Raman's IACS laboratory and wrote a paper on 'The Thermodynamics of the Compton Effect with reference to the Interior of Stars'. It was published in the next issue of the *Indian Journal of Physics*, of which Raman was the founding editor. It is worth noting that both of them wrote their first published paper independently of outside supervision, while still in their teens.

Both got their most significant inspiration during the voyage from India to England. On the voyage, in August 1930, Chandrasekhar built on the work he had just completed, which had the conclusion that the density at the centre of a white dwarf star would be six times the average density.

Ramaseshan quotes from several of the letters, and the warmth that Raman had for his nephew is discernible. When Raman read Chandrasekhar's paper on 'The Compton Effect and the New Statistics' that was published in the *Proceedings of the Royal Society* in 1929, he realized its far-reaching implications and said, 'This young man shows all the signs of being a genius. He will leave an indelible mark on Physics.'[4]

For the first fifteen years after leaving India, in 1930, Chandrasekhar sent Raman a copy of every paper he published. When Raman received the paper 'Model Stellar Photospheres' that had been published in the *Monthly Notices of the Royal Astronomical Society* in January 1932, Raman was excited. Even eighteen years later, he could recall his excitement to Ramaseshan about Chandrasekhar's conclusion in that paper that in a star having a mass greater than a particular value, the perfect gas equation of state does not break down. He knew this was a groundbreaking concept and said as much.[5]

In 1941 Raman sent a cable to Chandrasekhar that he would like to propose his name for fellowship of the Royal Society and would like Chandrasekhar to send him the names of other fellows who could support the nomination. Chandrasekhar responded immediately, giving five names. Raman put together all the material needed for the nomination and Chandrasekhar was duly elected.

Such was Raman's faith in the significance of Chandrasekhar's work that he wanted to nominate him for the Nobel Prize as early as 1948. But the latter did not give permission, saying that astronomers did not qualify as candidates. Yet, Raman persisted and wrote again in 1949. Chandrasekhar, politely but firmly, refused again, saying that a nomination, if at all, should come from someone squarely within his field.[6] Raman was disappointed. He told Ramaseshan shortly after, in January 1950, that Chandrasekhar's early paper itself qualified him and that 'All his later papers completely vindicate his earlier stand. If this prediction turns out to be true, he is clearly opening up a new chapter in Physics'.[7] Thus, Raman knew the Nobel quality in his nephew all along, though the scientific world took another thirty-five years before it recognized Chandrasekhar's work.

In Raman's mind, the Nobel Prize was the highest award in the world. From the number of anecdotes we have, we can surmise Raman was obsessed with the Nobel. In 1924, when congratulated on being made FRS and asked 'What next?', he is said to have replied, 'The Nobel Prize, of course.' Sir Asutosh is said to have mentioned that Raman promised him to win the Nobel Prize in the next five years.[8]

Chandrasekhar too has an incident about Raman's aspiration for the Nobel. In 1924, when Raman was in California, he told Rosseland[9] that soon he would 'make a great discovery and receive the Nobel Prize'.[10]

In 1925 Raman wrote to G.D. Birla for a donation that would buy a spectograph. He wrote, 'If I have it, I think I can get the Nobel Prize for India.'[11] In 1927, when Krishnan came in to tell him that that A.H. Compton had been awarded the Nobel Prize, Raman enthusiastically told him, 'If this is true of X-rays, it must be true of light too . . . We must pursue it and we are on the right lines. It must and shall be found. The Nobel Prize must be won.'[12] Raman had already been working at the problem for six years.

While Raman's feelings for his nephew were always positive, the same could not be said for Chandrasekhar's attitude towards his uncle. When Raman invited him, in 1935, to take up an assistant professorship at the Indian Institute of Science, writing, 'I do not wish to make any rash promises but I have a feeling that at the end of your 5-year tenure, you can look forward to a full Professorship being created for you.' Chandrasekhar declined— seemingly influenced by a report he had heard that Raman had said an astrophysicist had no place in Bangalore.[13] Raman wanted Chandra to work in nuclear physics—just as he advised Sarabhai and Bhabha some years later—a field that Raman knew would grow rapidly. It was not the first time that a relationship had soured because of hearsay reports, and in Raman's case it was not the last either, his later estrangement from Krishnan being an example. Chandrasekhar declined the invitation, just as he declined several preliminary feelers from others in later years.

Though Chandrasekshar sent a copy of all his early papers accompanied by short letters, he was by nature never effusive. He was a very reserved, very private person whereas Raman wore his heart on his sleeve. Chandrasekhar strictly observed the protocol of what was accepted as proper, whether it was in the neat knotting of his tie or in using a measured, unemotional voice even when speaking of matters close to his heart.

Raman moved in another kind of world, where his casually tied turban often revealed the top of his head and his voice went through steep modulations that clearly calibrated his emotional temperature at any given moment. In short, in their personal value systems, as in appearance and behaviour, uncle and nephew were poles apart.

~

The years 1924 and 1925 were spent on long trips to North America and Europe. In August 1924 Raman was in Toronto, on an invitation to attend a meeting of the British Association for the Advancement of Science. He lectured on the phenomenon of light scattering being carried out in Calcutta. From Toronto, he proceeded to the Franklin Institute in Philadelphia for its centenary celebrations. There, R.A. Millikan[14] invited him to spend some months in California. Raman went to the California Institute of Technology in September and stayed there till mid-December. He visited a few other places in the United States and then travelled to Europe, visiting Norway, Denmark and Germany, and returned to Calcutta in March 1925.

Within months, in August, he was off again, this time to Russia, where he attended the Mendeleff Congress of Chemistry in Moscow, and then visited Georgia, Leningrad, Berlin and Paris. He also went to Switzerland and Italy, and observed light scattering on the snows of the Alps. He was back in Calcutta in November 1925.

The next two years (1926–27) involved many short trips within India. He was invited to speak at convocations and give public addresses, and he usually got a standing ovation for his speeches, which were often extemporaneous. He knew his subject so well and had such strong opinions on education and nationalism that he needed no preparation.

The tone and content of his convocation address[15] to the graduates of Banaras Hindu University in 1926 has the same passionate commitment to intellectual pursuits and to India and a direct appeal for his listeners that characterized many of his public lectures. He starts that address with his recent travels to Europe, the United States and Canada. He says of his speeches on India during his travels,

> Do you think I spoke about Madras or of Calcutta? No! I spoke of Kashi, of Benares, of the historic city on a ridge overlooking the Ganges which stands at the very heart of India, as the living centre of our ancient culture and learning. I spoke of the new University that has sprung up, so fitly, at this age-old seat of learning and is the living embodiment of the aspirations of new India.

He goes on to add,

> It is not the function of a university to grow bookworms. The function of a university is to train men to *serve their country* and above all to train those who can become leaders, leaders of science, leaders of industry, leaders in all other fields of activity . . . A bookworm consumes books but produces only dust. A true scholar does not merely consume knowledge but also produces knowledge [emphasis mine].

He redefines the paths of knowledge because we are 'not living in the age of the Vedas and the Upanishads'. Knowledge is that which constantly advances frontiers and research is the modern path for the modern world in which we live. He refers to two great minds that contributed to this striving for knowledge—Asutosh Mookerjee and Srinivasa Ramanujan.

He also defines the role of the professor as parallel to the gurus of the Upanishads, but adds that often professors failed to live up to the level of the ancient gurus. 'It is fatally easy for a scientific man who has reached eminence to reduce the workers in his laboratory to a position of complete intellectual subordination and in fact to turn them into mere mechanical assistants … [but] when professor and student are men of high calibre, the relations between them are of the happiest and are beneficial to both.' In view of the success of the chairs at Calcutta University, he advocates that more chairs be started at various parts of the country.

During this decade of intense activity, even as he published long papers that were written in great detail after due experimenting, he wrote numerous one-page papers. These usually served one or more of the following purposes: a) announced a new idea that Raman planned to follow through on; b) corrected or made an observation of someone else's theory or result; c) jotted down a path worth following later, while he was at work on some other idea; d) directed the reader to a longer paper that was in progress; and e) responded to someone else's response to a paper of his.

In short, the short notes served to keep the dialogue going. Often, he did not follow through with an idea that struck him, but it helped someone else to take up the concept and develop experiments.

The Raman Effect

'Bliss was it in that dawn to be alive, and to be young was very heaven,' said William Wordsworth of his excitement at the beginning of the French Revolution in the early 1790s.

Reading the reminiscences of Raman's students who were with him during the momentous 1920s, even at this distance in time, it is easy to get carried away by the exuberance and excitement that pervaded Raman's laboratories in Calcutta. During the 1920s researchers flocked to the riches of the IACS and the UCS laboratories from different parts of the country. From Trivandrum and Ajmer, Rangoon and Meerut, Lucknow and Bihar, Banaras and Madras, Vizagapatam and Amraoti they came, some as full-time researchers, some using their vacations and earned leave from regular jobs to work on specific experiments on each visit.

C. Mahadevan was a geologist, but Raman could always think of experimental assignments in different fields that intersected with physics. Mahadevan has recorded the atmosphere around Raman in the 1920s just as A. Jayaraman was to record the 1950s later on. Some, like S. Venkateswaran and T.K. Chinmayanandam, were in government jobs in Calcutta and they, as had their mentor in the earlier decade, spent every minute they could spare from their government job at the laboratory. Venkateswaran would 'be in the laboratory by 6 o'clock in the morning, work till 9:15, just have time to rush home, take food and go to his office, and be at the laboratory at about 5:30 in the evening to continue his work till late at night when he would go home for his food'.[1]

All shared a common passion for science but it was a diverse group: Panchanan Das usually with paan in his mouth, Ramdas full of jokes and songs, Vaidyanathan with his bag of anecdotes for every occasion, Krishnan working full steam until it was kick-off time at Mohun Bagan stadium to which he would hurry to watch football matches, C.M. Sogani painstakingly setting up apparatus from scratch, A.S. Ganesan, 'the most perfect gentleman we had at the Science Association', V.M. Dhabadghao who was a good head taller than the tallest of them, S.C. Sirkar whose main pastime was to listen to Vaishnava goswamis who were followers of Lord Krishna, Kedareswar Banerjee, shy but uninhibited in their small circle, S.K. Datta, J.M. Dasgupta and many others. In 1923 there were fifteen researchers and by 1927 there were thirty-two researchers, of whom twenty-three were full-time. During the year 1928 too, Raman had under him in the laboratories of the association thirty-two researchers, of whom eleven worked part-time.[2] Raman spent at least a few minutes with each of them almost every day, and all who have recorded their memories have talked about the individual attention and inspiration they received under his mentorship.

~

Raman often talked about science being a combination of observation of natural phenomena and experimentation with possible explanations. He did not speak as often about the role of intuition in scientific research although he referred to 'abstract thought' when he spoke of 'the originality of the Indian mind and its capacity for abstract thought' in a short essay on 'Scientific Researches'.[3] But it was intuition that led him to speculate that optical scattering would be accompanied by a change in colour.

Raman had long been attracted to the phenomenon of light scattering. During his short stint in astronomy, in the 1910s, he had talked about light scattering from Jupiter. His 1921 voyage had made him realize that this was one of nature's secrets that he had to unravel. He had published two short notes on his observations. Then, in 1922, he wrote a landmark monograph, 'On the Molecular Scattering of Light in Water and the Colour of the Sea', which was published by Calcutta University and dedicated to Asutosh Mookerjee. He intuitively concluded that the interaction of the photon with a molecule must reveal itself by a change of colour. During the next five years, he assigned several of his students to follow up on the monograph, with quantitative measurements of light scattering in liquids and transparent crystals. In September 1922, when one of his students, K.R. Ramanathan, was on his way to Rangoon, Raman instructed him to collect seawater from different areas of the sea. In 1923, back in Calcutta on vacation, Ramanathan found 'a trace of fluorescence' that could not be explained at the time. Ramanathan speculated that the colour was due to impurities in the liquid but Raman rejected that hypothesis since the track exhibited polarization.

Between 1921 and 1927, Raman pursued the phenomenon of light scattering in gases and liquids. His students were assigned various experiments that had to be repeated many times in order to confirm the conclusions. A.H. Compton's winning of the Nobel Prize in 1927 gave an impetus to the work in progress at Raman's laboratory. Compton (1892–1962) studied what happens when X-rays of a known frequency are fired into graphite. He noticed that X-rays enter the graphite at one wavelength and leave at a longer wavelength as they have transferred both momentum and kinetic energy to an electron. It is mainly through the Compton Effect that matter absorbs radiant energy. What Compton had proven with X-rays should surely be valid for liquids and gases, Raman argued. While on vacation in Vizagapatam a few weeks

after the Nobel announcement on Compton, he figured out that
the weak fluorescence, which he and Ramanathan had discussed
several years earlier without success, might be the incoherent
scattering with a change in wavelength, analogous to Compton's
concept of scattered radiation. On his return Raman worked at
a furious pace. He put Krishnan and Venkateswaran to work on
observing light scattering in liquids. Venkateswaran found that in
pure glycerine, the scattered light was greenish in colour instead
of the usual blue. About eighty different liquids were examined
and the effect observed in all cases.

Krishnan's diary entries record the steps. Early in February,
Raman asked Krishnan to stop his theoretical studies and start
experiments along the lines of what K.R. Ramanathan and
S. Venkateswaran had done under his direction. From 2 to 7
February, Krishnan experimented with liquids and observed
the polarization of fluorescence. On the morning of 8 February,
Raman and Krishnan set up the 'long telescope . . . for observing
the effect with vapours'. At that point, Raman had to leave for his
lecture at the Science College, and Krishnan continued with the
observation. For the next few days they experimented with other
gases and Krishnan records that on 16 February 1928 they sent a
short paper to *Nature*.

The paper, a short report of about five hundred words,
starts with the hypothesis that following Compton's study of
X-ray scattering,

> we should expect also in the case of ordinary light two types
> of scattering, one determined by the normal optical properties
> of the atoms or molecules and another representing the effect
> of their fluctuations from their normal state. [His experiments
> showed that] in every case in which light is scattered by the
> molecules in dust-free liquids or gases, the diffuse radiation of
> the ordinary kind, having the same wavelength as the incident

beam, is accompanied by a modified scattered radiation of degraded frequency.[4]

This, in essence, is the Raman Effect, and the lines (the weaker lines are called Raman lines) in the spectrum (called the Raman spectrum) proved the change of wavelength in scattering. Raman conclusively proved that molecular scattering is a universal phenomenon in solids, liquids and gases irrespective of the physical state of the scatterer.

Raman recognized the practical applications of his discovery:

> The study of light scattering enables us to photograph the whole infra-red spectrum with the same facility as the visible and ultra-violet spectra . . . The frequencies of the vibrations . . . can be determined with extraordinary precision, unapproachable by other methods.

His peers were prompt in recognizing Raman's work. R.W. Wood, renowned in the field of optical physics, wrote, '[T]his beautiful discovery . . . is one of the most convincing proofs of the quantum theory of light.' He also wrote, 'Raman's discovery makes it possible to investigate remote infra-red regions hitherto little explored.'[5]

Since no two compounds have the same Raman spectrum, and since the intensity of a Raman line of a substance is proportional to its concentration, Raman spectroscopy came to be used extensively in qualitative and quantitative chemical analyses. As Albert Einstein pointed out later, 'C.V. Raman was the first to recognize and demonstrate that the energy of a photon can undergo partial transformation within matter. I still vividly recall the deep impression that this discovery made on us all.'[6]

The datelines are very interesting in that they throw light on Raman's sequence of action. The final experiment that confirmed

Raman's theory on liquids was conducted on 8 February 1928. Within days they confirmed the results on gases. Raman and Krishnan sent a note on the discovery on 16 February and it was published in Nature on 31 March 1928. On 28 February, cognizant of the importance of the discovery, Raman contacted the local newspaper, the Statesman, and a note appeared on 29 February. On 8 March, Raman sent a further note to Nature, which was published on 21 April. On 16 March 1928, after establishing the presence of spectra through spectroscopic evidence, he presented his findings to the scientific community in Bangalore, concluding, 'We are obviously only at the fringe of a fascinating new region of experimental research which promises to throw light on diverse problems relating to radiation and wave theory, X-ray optics, atomic and molecular spectra, fluorescence and scattering, thermodynamics and chemistry. It all remains to be worked out.'[7] The lecture was published on 31 March in the Indian Journal of Physics, and about two thousand reprints were mailed out to laboratories around the world. Raman and Krishnan had already followed up on 22 March with yet another note on 'Optical Analogue of the Compton Effect' that was published on 5 May 1928 in Nature.

The succinct but clear summary in his first note to Nature was characteristic of Raman. He could explain the most complex concept in language that a non-specialist could understand, so much so that it made the listener think that either he or she is a genius to comprehend difficult concepts, or that Raman was making much of a trifle. The latter is what his aunt thought as in this oft-quoted anecdote: After he won the prize, one of his aunts asked him what all the commotion and excitement were about. He explained the Effect to her, in his characteristic lucid style. After listening to him with rapt attention, the old lady is said to have remarked, 'I didn't know it was so simple. I am surprised that such a simple thing should have merited international recognition!' Many who have listened to Raman's public lectures and demonstrations felt they understood exactly what was being explained.

Raman expected others to be as direct and clear in their presentations. Jayaraman records an anecdote of how Raman interrupted the talk of a high-energy physicist at the Indian Academy of Sciences conference in Baroda (1958) to say, 'My dear fellow, please try to explain what you have done in a few sentences. If you cannot do this, it is not worth knowing.' It became a habit with him to speak in a way that a lay person could follow the explanation. This endeared him to school students who became his main audience in his later years.

It can be said that Raman's habit of promptness in sending out his papers for publication and of talking about his work with colleagues within and outside the country gave him the Nobel Prize. It so happened that two scientists, Grigory Samuilovich Landsberg and Leonid Isaakovich Mandelstam in Russia, had got the same results about the same time while working on quartz, but Raman's cable of 16 February 1928 had established Raman's precedence over his fellow runners. Journals had the custom of recording the date on which the paper was received at their office and also often recorded the date which the writer entered as the date of mailing, so these too helped, even if the paper was published only weeks later (as was the case in this paper). Raman had also followed it up with another short paper on 8 March that was published in April.

An interesting story about this paper came to light in 1933 when the editor of *Nature*, Richard A. Gregory, came to India. He said that the referee had not recommended the 8 March paper for publication but that because Gregory knew that Raman always sent duly verified results, he disregarded the referee's verdict and published it. The longer note sent on 22 March with spectroscopic confirmation was published on 5 May. This gave Raman a distinct lead over the paper sent by Mandelstam and Landsberg on 6 May. Moreover, the choice of title for this paper—'Optical Analogue of the Compton Effect'—ensured that it would be noticed and read with care.

Mandelstam and Landsberg made the same discovery on 21 February, but they did not send in their paper until May, and it appeared only on 13 July. Also, the two Russians did not give an 'independent interpretation of their discovery', the Nobel committee that made the nomination noted. It also helped that Raman's paper was picked up almost instantly and used by several other scientists (A.S. Ganesan, one of Raman's students at the time, compiled a bibliography of 150 papers that had been published on the Raman Effect within a year of the discovery) and all of them gave full credit to Raman's note in *Nature*; one even referred to the phenomenon as the 'Raman Effect', and that is how it came to be called.

The seven-year saga of reaching the Nobel Prize illustrates Raman's concentration of effort in his own research, while at the same time directing a number of students in various fields of acoustics and optics, in addition to light scattering. Those who worked in his laboratories came from different parts of the country, and it was Raman's habit to meet researchers present in the laboratories on a daily basis and give them direction or celebrate their findings. Many have talked about the one-on-one conversations where he appreciated their progress or directed their experiments as needed. Ramanathan writes, 'The atmosphere of the Association, when I worked there, was one of great informality and extreme cordiality . . . and work went on from morning seven till sunset . . . Prof. Raman was the Central Sun round which the whole institution revolved and from which each part derived its energy.'[8]

The apparatus Raman had used consisted of a mercury lamp, a flask of benzene and a direct-vision spectroscope. In later years, especially when the Indian government was spending millions of rupees on imported equipment, Raman would often say how he had made a Nobel-winning discovery with apparatus that cost a mere Rs 200—a week's salary at that time.

The trip to Europe

The Raman Effect was hailed as a monumental contribution from day one, as it were. The first note on the Effect was published in *Nature* on 31 March 1928. In the very next issue, there was a note by F.A. Lindemann on the significance of Raman's work. Papers appeared in England, Germany, Austria, Italy, Russia and Japan. Recognition came swiftly on the heels of the discovery. The Italian Society of Science awarded Raman the Matteucci Medal for the year 1928. The University of Freiburg conferred an honorary PhD in 1929. The Physical Society of Switzerland admitted him with an honorary membership. The Royal Society awarded him the Hughes Medal in 1930.

The year 1929 solidified the recognition with the award of knighthood in June. Since then, Raman was usually referred to as Sir C.V. Raman, or Sir C.V., and Lokam as Lady Raman. There is a story that when an acquaintance, who wanted to address him on more personal terms, asked him for his first name, he answered, 'Sir.'

Sir C.V. Raman and Lady Raman took a four-month trip abroad in 1929 that has not been mentioned in any detail by earlier biographers. Jayaraman makes no mention of it, though he speaks at length of the 1924 trip to Canada and the United States. Keswani has only a line about the Faraday Society meeting and even

G. Venkataraman, the most comprehensive biographer of Raman's science, has only a line on it. It was the first trip abroad after the discovery and signalled that Indian science, through this Indian scientist, was being recognized worldwide.

Nineteen hundred twenty-nine was an important year for Raman. On the personal side, his second son, Radhakrishnan, was born, on 18 May.

The year started with the sixteenth session of the Indian Science Congress in Madras. Raman was the general president. Much of Raman's presidential address was devoted to his discovery. He listed the names of his associates and paid special tribute not only to Krishnan but also to Ramanathan, who had noticed as early as 1923 that when they filtered sunlight in order to see only the violet, they could notice a feeble green light as well. He once again talked about how they had first thought it could be due to impurities and that even though subsequent experiments had excluded that possible explanation, he had not quite figured out the reason at the time. Towards the end of 1927, he said, they made a breakthrough and then the results had followed quickly.

Invitations came from all over the country and the world. One was an invitation to deliver the opening address at a session devoted to the Raman Effect in connection with the meeting of the Faraday Society to be held on 25 September at the University of Bristol in England. He also set up several professional meetings after the Faraday Society conference, in Switzerland and Belgium, among other places.

He had already accepted to deliver the convocation address at Mysore University scheduled for 24 August. When he set about booking his travel, Raman found that the only ship that would help him reach Bristol in good time was due to set sail on the morning of 28 August. This was a tight fit, to travel from Calcutta to Mysore and then on to Bombay to board the ship, but there was no way out. Moreover, it meant they would arrive two weeks before the Faraday meeting. He decided to tour Europe before arriving in England.

Lokasundari Raman maintained diaries for many years. A few of them were book-size, about five inches by eight inches, but most of them were small, with pages that were about four inches by five inches, with two, sometimes three or four, days of the week to a page. Not much could be written in them, and the entries were usually in note form: snippets of information about appointments, names of visitors, some details about servants and cows and chores to be done. However, a few of them were bigger and had a lot of very interesting information. Once I knew of their existence, I talked to her about them and transcribed verbatim every diary that was in her almirah at the time. This was during my long visit with her in the summer of 1972 at 'Panchavati', their family home in Bangalore.

The following section is written taking the diaries for 1929 and 1930 as the source, and with information given to me by Lady Raman as I went through them. The first entry for the year 1929 is dated Tuesday, 20 August, and there is an entry for almost every following day.

The whole family left Calcutta on 20 August at 5 p.m. by train and arrived in Madras on the morning of 22 August at 7 a.m. The children—Raja and Radhakrishnan—and Lokam's widowed sister Meenakka went on to Coimbatore, to stay with Lokam's sister and brother-in-law, Ramaswami Sivan. Lokam was not worried about eight-year-old Raja but was loath to part with the three-month-old baby. The Ramans left for Bangalore that night by the mail train and then went on to Mysore, arriving at noon on the twenty-third. They were met by Raghavendra Rao, a close friend of Raman's and a classmate of Maharaja Krishnaraja Wodeyar, who escorted them to the guest house. Raman, who had been feeling unwell all along, now developed high malarial fever. He had a restless night, and was up early to get ready for the convocation that was to start at

9 a.m. Lokam too had contracted malaria; since her fever got worse, she spent the day in bed.

In the convocation address, Raman first spoke of his visit to Bangalore in 1917 for the Indian Science Congress and of the maharaja's hospitality. He then spoke of the applications of science in his characteristically accessible language: 'Remarkably enough . . . what interested me most in that visit to Bangalore was a little tube of glass six inches long . . . filled with glowing vapour of mercury emitting a dazzling white light . . . It opened my eyes to the immense power of the mercury arc as a tool of scientific research . . . It is no exaggeration to say that the quartz mercury arc is the veritable Aladdin's lamp of modern physics.'

He expressed his appreciation for that experience and said how a mercury lamp had helped him make his discovery. He went on to talk about the importance of scholarly pursuits for the nation's future, not only because of the numerous applications of science but because 'intellectual activity . . . leads to a quickening of the national life in all its aspects . . . The mainsprings of intellectual activity in every country are education and the spirit of enquiry, and its quality varies with the standard set by the thinkers and educators of the nation. Thus, in the last analysis, it is the leadership offered by the Universities that determines the level of intellectual activity in the country and therefore also the national efficiency'.

There is also a fatherly injunction: 'We must refrain from copying the vices and expensive habits of other countries and never forget that alcohol and nicotine are the deadliest of poisons known to humanity.' As always in his lectures, there was something about India's greatness: 'During the last few years, there has been a growing recognition that India is not a negligible factor in the advance of human knowledge. I will go further and say that the world outside has begun to learn that the Indian intellect can . . . march abreast, or perhaps even lead, in the onward march of scientific progress.'

The Ramans spent an extra day in Mysore as Lokam was still suffering from her malarial bout. They left on 26 August and arrived in Bombay at about 7 a.m. next morning. They were met by Sudanshukumar Banerjee, an old student, who was then working at Colaba Observatory. He was very keen to do them all the honours but Lokam was in no position to enjoy anything. She wanted only rice mixed with yogurt. Raman by then had totally bounced back from his bout of malaria and enjoyed the food and the company provided by their host.

~

They boarded the ship—Lloyd Triestino's SS *Cracovia*—at 11 a.m. on 28 August. The passenger list had a few familiar names, but there seemed to be only two whom they knew well enough to speak to—Raghaviah, father-in-law of S.V. Ramamurti of the Indian Civil Service and Sir C.P. Ramaswami Iyer. CP had been knighted three years earlier, in 1926. He was a well-known figure on India's national scene. Versatile and charismatic, he carried himself like an aristocrat and was a lawyer by profession. He had been joint secretary of the Indian National Congress in 1917–18 along with Jawaharlal Nehru. In 1919 he made news when he declined a judgeship in the Madras High Court. In 1920 he was made advocate general of Madras Presidency and passed several landmark laws. He had been India's delegate at the League of Nations in 1926–27. Later, one of his first acts as dewan of Travancore (1936–47) was to advise the king to introduce the Temple Entry Proclamation that allowed untouchables to enter temples.

Once the ship heaved anchor, Lokam was so seasick that she went straight to the three-berth cabin and stayed there for three days. As on her voyage to Rangoon, though she was excited to be on a ship with water all around her, she was too nauseous to enjoy the experience. She could not even have food. The porthole was open so they could get some fresh air, but this was worse because the Indian Ocean was rough and the spray lashed through the porthole; on the third day it completely wet the bed. Lokam had the berth next to the porthole and Raman the one near the door.

Raman, on the other hand, was fit and fine. He did not spend much time in the cabin during the day. He was on deck most of the time, going to the dining room for meals, and coming back to the cabin only at night. On the third day, CP asked Raman about Lokam as he had seen her on the first day but not since. Did she come only to bid farewell? Raman replied, Oh no, she is in bed, seasick.

CP was outraged. Didn't Raman know that lying in the cabin was the worst thing one could do when seasick? One should be on the deck, not cooped up in the cabin! And had she been given lemon juice? Raman did not know. CP was most upset. He rushed down to the cabin and met her. Then he called in a nurse and the doctor, who filled out a prescription. CP left after instructing the nurse to help Lokam out of her wet clothes and into dry ones, and then change the soaking bed linen. He created quite a fuss. He roundly scolded Raman for neglecting his wife for three days and that he should have told the doctor much earlier. What kind of man was he not to have realized that anyone who was in bed three days must be really ill?

That day, CP visited her every hour for a few minutes. As soon as she felt better, he had her carried to the deck. He told her to lie there all day and sleep there too, if necessary. He brought blankets for her. Thanks to him, the engineer came and assured him he would personally see to it that she was looked after. Lokam got better, thanks to CP's instruction that she was to spend a lot of time on the deck, lying in a deck chair if need be.

On 2 September the ship docked at Aden, and Lokam mailed a letter to her sister. She knew she herself would not be able to receive a letter about the children until they reached London.

On the seventh the ship sailed into Suez and everyone disembarked. Raman and Lokam hired a taxi and went to the

Pyramids. Raman enjoyed himself, explaining all the historical and local wonders to his wife. They went by train to Port Said, reaching at 10.30 p.m. and stayed at a hotel for the night. While Raman was busily engaged in writing, Lokam noted down the day's expenses in her diary: 190-8-0. Next morning they boarded the waiting ship and set sail into the Mediterranean.

Seeing how friendly CP and Raman were, the steward set them up at the same dining table, a table for three. CP was a brilliant raconteur and it was delightful for Lokam. It was at their first meal together that CP asked whether Raman had the insignia of knighthood with him. Raman did not. And it was only through this conversation that Lokam came to know what they were—the medals and robe that CP carried with him, which he showed to Lokam.

Raman, though proud of the honour, had never bothered to show these tokens to anyone, even to his wife. They lay untouched in an almirah at home. In contrast, he valued the shawl and decorated court costume given by the maharaja of Mysore in 1937 and always wore them at durbar events held by the maharaja. Talking to Lokam I gathered that though he was proud of the title of knighthood that he had won through his science, Raman had ambivalent feelings about the trappings of power and colonialism that went with the physical tokens of the British honour.

Lokam was in good spirits much of the time. Her weight, that had dropped sharply after Radhakrishnan's birth, now increased, just as the doctors had predicted. But there was intense ache and homesickness for her children. She wrote to Meenakka every day though she knew she could mail it only at the next port. Often, walking on the deck, or even in the middle of a conversation, her thoughts would fly to her sons. She would calculate what time it would be in Coimbatore and imagine what the children were doing. Often at night, she would surface to consciousness hearing infant cries. And sometimes she wondered if the trip was worthwhile—what worth were all the wonders of the world if she could not be there when the children needed her? She knew her fears were misplaced, for Raja was old enough to be busy with his school and play to miss her, and the baby was too young to remember her. Moreover, the children were in good hands, in her eldest sister's family of growing children, and with Meenakka ever-present to attend to them. Yet, when Raman pointed all this out to calm her, she bristled with anguish. How callous of him! What use being a world-renowned scientist if he were not human enough to be a father?

One day, Raman and Lokam shared a table with a friend they met on board. He was a good conversationalist and delighted them with stories of his earlier travels to Britain. He ordered non-vegetarian food. Lokam felt rather queasy looking at the meat on his plate and even more at the thought of a fellow south Indian Brahmin eating meat. He did so the next day as well. Lokam later asked Raman if it did not bother him. Raman told her he had not expected that their friend would eat meat, but it was not polite to talk about it. But Raman did ask the steward to give them their own table from then on. When they were invited to dine at the captain's table, Lokam kept her misgivings to herself, and with time learnt to mind only her plate rather than take interest in what others were eating.

Once her bout of seasickness was over, Lokam enjoyed the voyage. When she talked to me about it, forty-three years later, her voice still expressed wonder at the blueness of the sea. On the eleventh they landed at Brindisi at 11 a.m., walked about for two hours and then took the train to Naples at 2 p.m., arriving late at 1 a.m. The currency of the expenses is clearer in this entry: £20.

Next day was spent at the ruins of Pompeii and a walk along the foot of Mount Vesuvius. The following day they sailed to Capri and the Blue Grotto. From Naples they went to Rome and stayed at Esperia Hotel. After spending all of 15 September walking through St Peter's, the Forum, Coliseum, Museum and the Park to attend a war memorial event, they went to the cinema that night. Monday morning was spent at the Vatican. When Raman beheld the awesome beauty of the Sistine Chapel and Michelangelo's masterpieces on the ceiling, he stretched his arms upward and cried at the magnificence of art, tears streaming down his face. That afternoon they went to the science laboratory and Raman met the local researchers. The next day was spent on sightseeing: St Paul's, the catacomb and various cathedrals.

On the eighteenth they left for Geneva and arrived at 8 p.m. after a ten-hour train journey. It was late in the evening, but Raman loved to walk, and off they went along the harbour after checking in at Hotel Continental. Next morning they left by car for Monte Carlo. It was a ten-hour drive but on arriving, Raman would not forego listening to the band that played at the harbour from the beginning to the last note. The next morning was spent at the Aquarium. In the afternoon, they took a bus to Nice and returned in the evening, again in time for a music concert on the beach.

~

On 21 September 1929 they anchored at Marseilles and reached Paris at ten o'clock the next morning. They left for London the same day and reached at 8.30 in the evening. Lokam's diary entry is enigmatic: 'Arrived London 8.30 p.m. After 7 places got room. Grosvenor Hotel.'

Could it have been just an innocuous fact that there were no vacancies in the first seven 'places' and there was actually no room at the inns for these travellers from afar? I would hazard a guess that this was a case of racial discrimination. This was not Raman's first brush with racism. There is a story of how during Raman's trip to the United States, the maid at a house Raman was visiting was in shock at seeing a 'black man' coming for breakfast. But there seems to be some ambiguity as to when and where it happened. According to Wali, in *Chandra*, it happened during Raman's US visit in 'the late 1920s', in Ithaca, NY, when Sir William Bragg, who was a visiting professor at Cornell at the time, had invited Raman to stay with him. Venkataraman records that it happened during the 1924–25 visit to the US when Raman was invited for breakfast by A.H. Compton. Compton had moved from the University of Washington in Louisiana to the University of Chicago in 1923. The maid who opened the door for Raman is said to have screamed, 'Oh my God! It is a black man.'[1]

This is not the only recorded incident of racial insult during Raman's visit with Compton. Ramaseshan talks of it in his Raman Centenary lecture that was later printed in *Current Science* 57:22 (1988). Compton had invited Dean Gale to lunch to meet Raman, since Gale was also a specialist in optics. (Gale is also mentioned by S. Chandrasekhar as given to racism, in his own experience.) When Gale saw the dark complexion of the man he was supposed to lunch with, he 'just looked straight through them and walked away'. Compton was relieved that Raman had not noticed, but years later, Raman told Ramaseshan that he had indeed noticed the rebuff but did not want to embarrass Compton. Raman said to Ramaseshan, 'As in India, there are many stupid fools in every country.' Raman was very observant of small details though he often seemed to be in his own world.

They rested for a day in London so that Raman could prepare himself for the inaugural talk ahead and left on 24 September for Bristol, where they were warmly greeted by Professor and Mrs Travers. Morris William Travers (1872–1961) was a British chemist who worked with William Ramsay for about ten years (1894–1902) and first identified the inert gases krypton, xenon and radon. He was the first director of the Indian Institute of Science (1909–14). He was one of the members of the Faraday Society Council. As people who had been in India and had interacted with Raman whenever he visited Bangalore on duty, he and his wife were happy to play host to the Ramans.

In 1972, Lady Raman related two stories of her time in Bristol.

They retired early the first evening, and as she lay waiting for sleep, she heard the *clop clop* of horses' hooves on the street outside their window. This reminded her of Raja Mullick's horses. However, she found out that the sound was that of women's high heels as they walked on the cobbled pavement.

The other story is more relevant to Raman. While the men stayed back, Mrs Travers took Lokam on a long drive along the Gorges. Lokam said that during the drive, Mrs Travers told her to advise Raman against accepting any offer from the Indian Institute of Science (IISc). Lokam replied that Mrs Travers should herself give Raman that piece of advice since her words would carry more weight than Lokam's. This is indeed very intriguing. Had the wheels already started turning in the search for a new director? It was only in 1932 that Raman was offered the job.

Although there was no way to build a context around this tidbit, this remark seemed worth recording in light of what would happen more than a year after they returned to Calcutta. I followed this clue and found out more about Morris Travers's stay in Bangalore. He was a very talented scientist with a focused vision. However, he could not get along with Professor Chatterton, who was a member of the council that ran the institute. Travers wrote, 'Leave him [Chatterton] on the Council, and within a year the Institute will be a mere adjunct to the Department of Industries, Mysore.' He goes on to add, 'If Government had definitely laid down the policy of the Institute and decided whether we were to be Faculty of Pure and Applied Sciences, a School of Economics or a Medical School there would have been no trouble. While there is no definite policy, there will be endless trouble, unless the future Director is more of a humbug than he should be.'[2] This explains his advice that

Raman should not go anywhere near Bangalore, but it also tells us that perhaps the Bangalore directorship, unknown to Raman, was already on his horizon as early as 1929.

On 25 September Raman gave his lecture on 'Investigations of Molecular Structure by Light Scattering' to open the session that was devoted to the Raman Effect and was organized by W.E. Garner and J.E. Lennard-Jones, both local professors. The conference theme was 'Molecular Spectra and Molecular Structure' and it brought together many of those most active in these fields at that time, including F. Hund, R.S. Mulliken, V. Henri and G. Herzberg.

Dr Herzberg said of this session: 'It was a very memorable meeting largely because of the presence of Raman . . . He spoke clearly and lucidly in beautiful English . . . and his enthusiasm was certainly infectious.'[3]

The next day Lokam and Raman left at 11 a.m. and reached St Ives at 5 p.m., via Plymouth. They walked through the gardens and fields in St Ives. When talking about this trip, Lady Raman reminisced about a man they saw that evening. He was feeding pigs and fowls. 'I asked him why he left the bucketful of milk for the pig. He said it was no use; he had already taken the cream out of it. We [Indians] have no milk for our own poor children; there [in England] they feed the cattle and birds with milk.'

The Ramans went back to London on 1 October. Raman had arranged his schedule with various colleagues so that he could continue with his research visits. After breakfast, he would go off, leaving Lokam to herself. By now she knew she could not expect Raman to accompany her since he had a busy work schedule, so Lokam consulted the hotel concierge about tourist places and public transportation and decided to go sightseeing. She enjoyed the sights and sounds in the new city. Policemen and shopkeepers, she found, were very polite and helpful. It was the women who were haughty. There was an incident that proved this to her beyond a doubt.

Grosvenor Hotel was too expensive for a prolonged stay. And as they were thinking of where to move, students from the Indian hostel at Queensborough Terrace approached them and invited them to stay with them. They said they had a 'claim' to host the great man of science from their native country. So the Ramans moved and stayed there a few days.

The landlady was one Mrs King who had spent her childhood and younger days in India and was very sympathetic towards Indians. Lokam had heard of her even in Calcutta, and recalled that she was related to the editor of the *Statesman*. Mrs King loved her 'boys', mostly students studying for the bar. She told Lokam many useful things, one of which was to keep away from British women who had been to India. She said this when Lokam related an incident that had taken place in a bus. Lokam had found herself next to a woman whose face was extremely familiar. After concentrating a few minutes, she placed her: Mrs S. was the wife of a man who had worked with Raman for the Science Congress and the IACS. So she said, 'Excuse me, surely this is Mrs S.?' The woman stared right ahead, as though she hadn't heard her. Lokam felt very embarrassed, thinking the stranger was offended at being called by some other name. At the next stop, the lady got off the bus.

On hearing this, Mrs King replied that the woman was in all probability Mrs S., but, like most British women who had been in India, she was unwilling to publicly accept greetings from a 'coloured' woman. That was British arrogance, typical British arrogance, Mrs King said. Only in truly cultured people was it absent.

Raman too was fond of relating how Lord Rutherford called out to him in the Cavendish library to come up and sit in a cubicle on the upper level instead of down in the reading room. Rutherford was a scientist and a true gentleman and so made no distinction in skin colours, Lokam recounted in Raman's words.

After a few days, Raman wanted to move out of the students' hostel because it was too crowded. Mrs King suggested they go to her mother's boarding house in Putney. They did for a few days, but meanwhile students from the Birla hostel persuaded them to move to their place and so they did.

One evening there was a near crisis at the Birla hostel. The cook, who made every meal, took off in the afternoon with his wife, saying offhandedly that he might come back in the evening or he might not. He did not. So Lokam went down to the kitchen—it was the first time she had been to the cellar level—and with the help of the maid, made potato curry and chapattis, to the delight and gratitude of the students.

Every morning of their stay, Lokam took a bus or the underground tube and went sightseeing. Occasionally, Raman would join her. One day, when she was by herself, returning in the evening she missed the station—Bayswater—at which she should have alighted. She was nearly in tears. The ticket checker stopped and asked her if he could help. She told him she'd seen the name of the station only after the train had started. He laughed and told her not to worry and to just keep sitting. In another half hour, they'd be at Bayswater again, and he would see to it that she got down this time.

During her excursions, she'd lunch at one or other of Lyons' chain of restaurants. Usually she had an apple or banana, and a cup of cocoa.

One day Raman and Lokam went to the Tower of London. Innocently, she asked the sentry where the Peacock Throne was, and he bristled. Perhaps too many Indian visitors had asked that question accusingly. That evening Raman told her not to ask such questions and call trouble upon herself.

After lunch she would return to their room and spend the afternoon writing letters, washing clothes, reading the newspapers. They would go out in the evening, window-shopping or to the park. Hampstead Heath was one of her favourite spots when she went alone during the day.

In Lokam's diary entries, while her itinerary is known, it is not clear on which days her husband accompanied her. She refers to Raman as 'Prof.'

There is an intriguing entry dated 12 November [Wednesday]: 'Disappointed day. Still hope.' Could this be the day that the Nobel Prize for Physics was announced? That year the recipient was Prince Louis-Victor de Broglie. Raman knew his own name had been proposed for the prize that year, and it seems very likely that he had planned to stay on in England in the expectation that he would be awarded. Lady Raman said as much, telling me that Raman booked their return voyage from Europe to India almost immediately after the list of Nobel winners was announced.[4]

In 1929 and 1930 communication and transportation were not as fast as they are now. This leads us to interesting speculations about Raman's meticulous planning. It seems clear that he had planned the latter part of his trip after the Faraday meeting in Bristol so as to be close to Stockholm at the time of the announcement, knowing that the award ceremony is always on 10 December. D.A. Long, in an article about the Faraday meeting, mentions that A.C. Menzies said that Raman had 'regularly enquired' of the hotel porter if there was a cable for him from Stockholm. That the Nobel committee expected the recipients to arrive in Stockholm within days of the announcement might seem odd, but the prize seldom went to anyone outside the European or North American continents at that time, and the Nobel rules were that the announcements should be made before the middle of November, leaving enough time for any recipient from those areas to reach in time. Currently, the announcements are made by mid-October, and there have been many laureates from different parts of the world in the last thirty years.

Rabindranath Tagore (1913 recipient of the Literature Prize) was not present for the ceremony, and a telegram from him was read out instead.

The Nobel Prize and other honours

Raman had not been awarded the Nobel in 1929, but he had been nominated again, for the 1930 list. He made his reservation early. He had to book berths in a passenger ship—of which there were not many—that would leave after mid-November, when the awards would be announced. He would reach Europe the first week of December and could book the next phase of the journey in time to arrive in Stockholm for the 10 December ceremony, if he was indeed awarded the prize.

He barely made it, arriving in Stockholm on 9 December. The announcement for the 1930 prize was made on 13 November (early morning of 14 November in India) and his ship sailed from Bombay on 20 November 1930. There certainly would not have been enough time had he not made the booking much earlier. Ramaseshan, who has written extensively on Raman's life and science, says that Raman booked his berths as early as July 1930. Bhagavantam has said Raman booked his passage two months ahead of the announcement date. As Lokam's diary for 1930 shows, they left Calcutta for Madras (to leave the children with family) on 14 November, within hours of the announcement.

From Madras they went to Bangalore and on to Bombay, where Raman gave a talk on his discovery, and next morning they were aboard SS *California*. This time they did not stop anywhere except for two days in Berlin to book their journey to Stockholm and buy some winter clothing, while also visiting Professor Peter Pringsheim, one of the first to follow up on the Raman Effect.

There are several interesting points about the Ramans' stay in Stockholm. Lokam's article for the *Calcutta Municipal Gazette*[1] records their experience—the crowds of photographers and their blinding lights, the applause from those assembled, the pomp and splendour of the occasion and so on. In his speech at the dinner, as Lokam told me, Raman spoke about the Buddha and his philosophy of non-violence, showing that his boyhood admiration of Prince Siddhartha who sacrificed worldly pleasures so the 'light may break and all flesh learn the Law' had not diminished but had indeed become part of his core values. As Sir Edwin Arnold's *The Light of Asia* was one of the three books that had influenced him most, it is not surprising that Raman should have focused on the Buddha at this august ceremony where, as always, he was conscious of representing India and India's contribution to the world.

The other story worth recounting is that during the speech, Raman mentioned that he had received a telegram of congratulations from his very dear friend 'who is now in jail'. Lokam kept a copy of a letter written by the charge d'affaires of the US in Sweden to the US Secretary of State in Washington where he says,

Of all the prize winners, the day was easily carried, however, by Sir Venkata Raman the Indian prize winner, who upon returning to his seat on the platform after receiving the prize from the hands of the King, was visibly moved by his emotion and sat with tears streaming down his face.

He goes on to say,

> At the banquet that evening, Sir Venkata Raman's speech was a masterpiece of eloquence, which called forth tremendous applause from a banquet-weary gathering not noted for its responsiveness. Less appreciative was perhaps the British Ambassador, who sat one place removed from me, who was forced to listen with equanimity to Sir Venkata Raman's reference, brief though it was, in passing only, to the congratulatory telegram which he received 'from his dearest friend who is now in jail'.

This 'friend' was, of course, Mahatma Gandhi.

Years later, Raman said,

> When the Nobel award was announced I saw it as a personal triumph, an achievement for me and my collaborators—a recognition for a very remarkable discovery, for reaching the goal I had pursued for seven years. But when I sat in that crowded hall and I saw the sea of Western faces surrounding me, and I, the only Indian, in my turban and closed coat, it dawned on me that I was really representing my people and my country. I felt truly humble when I received the Prize from King Gustav; it was a moment of great emotion but I could restrain myself. Then I turned round and saw the British Union Jack under which I had been sitting and it was then that I realised that my poor country, India, did not even have a flag of her own—and it was this that triggered off my complete breakdown.'[2]

The third incident shows Raman's ready humour. When invited to drink a champagne toast at the banquet, he said, 'Sir, you have seen the Raman Effect on alcohol; please do not try to see the alcohol effect on Raman.'[3]

Raman delivered the Nobel lecture on 11 December. In it he traced the stages of the discovery from his first voyage on the Mediterranean in 1921, to 1923 when he and K.R. Ramanathan noticed the feeble efflorescence but could not explain it, to the experiments of 1927–28 on solids, liquids and gases, which confirmed the presence of the radiation. At every step, he also identified by name the associates who had worked with him:

The first observation of this phenomenon was made at Calcutta in April 1923 by Ramanathan . . .
   Liquid mixtures were investigated by Kameswara Rao;
   Srivastava studied the scattering of light in crystals in relation to the thermal fluctuations of density and their increase with temperature;
   Ramdas investigated the scattering of light by liquid surfaces due to thermal agitation;
   Sogani investigated X-ray diffraction in liquids;
   Krishnan examined a great many liquids, and by his work showed very clearly the dependence of the optical anisotropy of the molecule on its chemical constitution;
   Ramakrishna Rao studied the depolarization of scattered light in a very large number of gases and vapours . . .
   Venkateswaran studied the scattering of light in aqueous solutions to find the influence on it of electrolytic dissociation . . .
   Ramachandra Rao investigated liquids having highly elongated molecules and also highly polar substances over a wide range of temperatures . . .
   Krishnan and myself also published a series of investigations . . .
   I should also like to draw attention to the work of Krishnamurti, who has traced a remarkable dependence of the intensity of the spectral lines observed in scattering on the nature of the chemical bond . . .

Raman's scrupulous acknowledgement of his associates at that momentous occasion says something about him.

He was consistent through the years in this principle of giving full credit to those who worked with him. Some years later, there was discussion about Krishnan's role in the discovery and some talk of Krishnan being deprived of his due share. Much has been written on this issue. Rajinder Singh's carefully documented analysis of the work and Ramaseshan's article citing in detail Krishnan's own diary entries show that the concept for the discovery originated entirely with Raman as did the concepts worked on by his associates, and that Krishnan's careful observations certainly helped, but the credit for both concept and execution needs must go to Raman. Indeed Krishnan himself never disputed the issue and his diary records that Raman was always in charge, telling him what to do and doing the experiments himself when Krishnan was unavailable. But others, in the 1950s, added this to the litany of objections they had to Raman's way of handling science. Ramaseshan reports a long talk he had with Krishnan in 1953, when the rumour was spreading that Krishnan claimed to be the true discoverer of the Raman Effect. Krishnan said, 'It is a blatant misrepresentation. The best I can say is that I participated actively in the discovery.'[4] Later in the conversation, he said, 'I am convinced some evil-minded jealous person has gone and talked ill of me to Professor and he, in his childlike innocence, has believed these scurrilous statements made about me.'[5]

The habit of giving full credit to his students and associates has been affirmed by many. Jayaraman says, 'In his public lectures, Raman would refer to his students by name and talk about their work. All this was a thrilling experience to young students and a powerful incentive ...'

In 1930 Lokam and Raman met Nathan Söderblom, the winner of the Peace Prize that year. Tamil was one of the many languages that Söderblom knew well, and he asked Lokam to quote a few lines from a Tamil classic and to write her name in Tamil in the visitors' book. In Germany, they met a professor who recited from the Gita. The Munich museum had a beautiful statue of Nataraja.

Their visit to Egypt made a deep impression on Lokam, and she spoke about it for many years. In 1942 she wrote an article in *Kalki*, the leading Tamil weekly. One of the sights that impressed them, she says, was the difference in the landscape on either side of the Nile. 'In Egypt, heaven and hell seem to have come together; when you sit on the shores of the river, one side is an expanse of greenery; on the other side is a vast desert of sand' [translation mine].

Raman refers to this experience in poetic language that characterized many of his public lectures and also crept into some of his sentences in his scientific papers. In a lecture on 'The Elixir of Life', where he talks about water as *amrita*, he starts off with, 'I remember one day standing on the line which separates the Libyan Desert from the Valley of the Nile in Egypt. On one side was a sea of billowing sand without a speck of green or a single living thing anywhere visible on it while on the other side lay one of the greenest, most fertile and densely populated areas to be found anywhere on the earth, teeming with life and vegetation.'[6]

Raman responded with all his senses to nature's beauty, be it a barren desert or a snowbound mountain. The Alps so fascinated him, many have recalled him speaking about its magnificence. Jayaraman says Raman once told him he must go to Innsbruck where the view 'was one of the most spectacular sights'. Astrophysicist Chandrasekhar has said he got the same advice.

~

The Raman Effect rapidly impacted on different areas. In chemistry, for instance, by the late 1930s the Raman Effect had become the principal method of non-destructive chemical analysis for both organic and inorganic compounds. The unique spectrum of Raman scattered light for any particular substance served as a 'fingerprint' that could be used for qualitative analysis, even in a mixture of materials. Further, the intensity of the spectral lines was related to the amount of the substance. Raman spectroscopy could be applied not only to liquids but also to gases and solids. And unlike many other analytical methods, it could be applied easily to the analysis of aqueous solutions.

The euphoria of world recognition continued for a long time. Invitations came in from all parts of the country for the man who had brought honour to India. As Lokam's diary entries show, they were showered with garlands wherever they went. A story about Raman's ready wit is that when someone asked him why he wore a turban, he said, 'Oh, if I did not wear one, my head will swell. You all praise me so much. So I need the turban to contain my ego.'[7]

Of the many honours bestowed on him, one was by the Calcutta City Corporation. In a spectacle-filled ceremony, held on Friday, 26 June 1931, the mayor read an address; a copy of the address, printed on khaddar and embroidered with gold, was presented to Raman. It concluded with the words, 'May you, by your continued efforts, shed further lustre on this City, and bring greater glory to our Motherland, this ancient home of learning and knowledge.'[8]

Raman reciprocated with equal flourish and emotion, paying tribute to Calcutta's distinguished sons, Mahendralal Sircar and Asutosh Mookerjee, and added: 'It is my earnest hope that it will be possible in the near future to create opportunities in our own country for students to do the highest type of creative scientific work.' He ended his speech with his hope for the Indian Association for the Cultivation of Science, which had made it all possible for him. 'It is my earnest desire that its laboratory and library should be re-built and re-equipped so as to make their resources comparable with those of leading institutions abroad. If that desire were accomplished, not all the appointments in India joined together and offered to me as one gift would induce me to leave this great city.'[9]

House in Tiruvanaikkaval in Tamil
Nadu where Raman was born.
Courtesy: RRI archives.

Raman as a college
student, 1906.
Courtesy: RRI
archives.

Raman with Sir Mirza Ismail to his right
and Max Born to his left, in Bangalore,
1935 or 1936. Sir Mirza was the dewan
of the Maharaja of Mysore and Max
Born was a pre-eminent Jewish
scientist who received the Nobel after
the war in 1954. Both were close to
Raman. Courtesy: IAS archives.

Raman with his students at the Indian Institute of Science,
Bangalore, 1936. On either side of Raman are Max Born and
Hedi Born. Lokam is to Born's right. Courtesy: RRI archives.

Scientists at a conference of the Indian Academy of Sciences
at Annamalai, Tamil Nadu, 1959. Raman's brother,
Ramaswamy, is in the foreground, and A.S. Ganesan, in a
dark suit, further behind. Ramaswamy and Ganesan were
working with Raman at the Indian Association for the
Cultivation of Science, Calcutta, when he discovered the
Effect. Courtesy: IAS archives.

Raman with German theoretical physicist, Werner Heisenberg (in the foreground) at the Lindau Meeting of Nobel Laureates, 1956. Courtesy: IAS archives.

Raman with India's first prime minister, Jawaharlal Nehru, 1950s. Courtesy: IAS archives.

Raman and his nephew, the astrophysicist Chandrasekhar, circa 1952. Courtesy: RRI archives.

Three of Raman's sister Sitalaxmi's sons, who were Raman's students. From left to right: Pancharatnam, Ramaseshan and Chandrasekhar. Courtesy: Kausalya Ramaseshan.

Raman with children at the Raman Research Institute, Bangalore, 1960s. Kausalya Ramaseshan, Ramaseshan's wife, is in front of Raman. Courtesy: IAS archives.

This statement could have been made in the spirit of rhetoric. But it hints at invitations from one or more institutions. Banaras Hindu University had made overtures and would extend a formal invitation later.

In 1931, when Raman made the statement, he had no thoughts of leaving Calcutta. He had said, 'You, sir, have said that you desire my association with Calcutta to be a permanent one. Let me say at once that this is also my earnest desire. I consider it my great good fortune to have been a citizen of Calcutta for nearly 25 years.' The newspaper article above also printed within the main report a handwritten message to the citizens of Calcutta: 'For nearly a quarter of a century, it has been my privilege to live and work in this great City, and I have learnt to love it as my home.' Raman thought his work was going according to plan. He had been active not only in his research but in organizational activities. At the annual Indian Science Congress meeting of 1931, he was glad when the motion to start a scientific journal was passed. The first issue of *Current Science* came out in 1932, from the IISc, under the editorship of C. Narayana Rao. An editorial, written by Raman, for the May 1933 issue, called for 'an early establishment of a National Academy of Science' which would 'secure closer and better organized cooperation of activities among all research institutes in India'.[10] To stimulate discussion, scientists from all parts of the country were invited to give their views. Having seen the effectiveness of such national academies outside India, Raman wanted to make sure India kept in step with the rest of the world.

He had ambitious plans for the IACS as well. He wanted to bring it in line with international science organizations, as a centre for India to be proud of. He also wanted to improve on the structure of the IACS so that membership applications would be screened as in other science organizations, where membership was only for those who had proven their merit rather than being open to

anyone willing to pay the membership dues. He wanted to enlarge
the library holdings and laboratory facilities.

The finances of the IACS had improved greatly under Raman's
stewardship. Scholarships were offered to scholars who came from
all major provinces of the country, except for Bombay, which had
its own centres of higher education. Raman's annual report for
1932 (Raman as secretary presented meticulous details of every
aspect of the IACS) records that there were twenty-four full-time
research workers, and that approximately Rs 6700 were given
as scholarships to scholars from different parts of the country.
Raman also initiated the establishment of a Mahendralal Sircar
Professorship. Raman had taken Mahendralal's dream and made
it real—Calcutta was indeed a national hub of scientific activity,
and those who had worked at the IACS since he took charge were
now leading research at different institutions of the country.

Leaving Calcutta

'It is no longer necessary to look for directors in England when India has as distinguished a candidate as Raman.'[1] So said Lord Rutherford when the Tatas requested him to suggest names for the directorship of the IISc in Bangalore.

The director of the IISc, Martin Forster, was due to retire in April 1933. Since appointments at that level had to go through a long protocol, with names being considered by two committees, one in Britain and the other in India, the committees were set up as early as July 1931 and there might have been speculations even earlier about the next director. The council of the institute and the Tatas had also sent out requests for names to various institutions and individuals.

Sir William H. Bragg, the chair of the committee in England, wrote to his counterpart, Sir M. Visvesvarayya in India, about his committee's decision on the applications received in England. Dated 19 May 1932, the letter says that Bragg was enclosing the list of applicants, but that the committee had not considered them in any detail as yet. 'The English Committee does not think it necessary to amplify these details by the present mail because we are sending you a cable suggesting that Professor Sir C.V. Raman is obviously the best man for the post if he will accept. If you cable a reply that you agree and that Raman will accept then there seems to be no need to go further into the qualifications of the applicants. If Raman does not accept, then it will be necessary for us to go carefully through the applications.'[2]

The institute council in Bangalore passed a motion on 18 July 1932 to recommend that the viceroy appoint Raman as director.

Raman was surprised. He had not expected such a recommendation since he had not applied for the position.

Once again, Raman did not want to make a hasty decision. Calcutta was his home and the IACS his first and major commitment to the advancement of science in India. He wanted to make sure he could come home if he did not like Bangalore, so he asked for a fifteen-month leave of absence, without pay, starting 1 April 1933, and suggested that D.M. Bose could be the head during this time.

He made no alternative provisions for the running of the IACS and its publications, since he could serve on them even without being in Calcutta. Raman had probably assumed his request for leave would be granted and he could continue his associations with the city during his sojourn in Bangalore, but he was wrong.

Whether or not this negative decision on his request for leave was influenced by a movement that had started behind the scenes is difficult to assess, but there had been rumbles of discontent that Raman did not hear, or on hearing had dismissed as inconsequential. That is why he turned down the offer of a chair at Banaras Hindu University, even though it came with an assurance he valued above all else—a free hand to develop projects as he saw fit.

Towards the end of 1932 there were letters to the editor in the local newspaper against Raman's management of the IACS and the Palit Professorship. The accusations were that he had only south Indians around himself as scholars, and that physics was given too much prominence, to the exclusion of other sciences. The main grouse was that Bengalis were being sidelined in their own province.

It was no use to argue, as supporters like Professor C.M. Sogani did, that Bengalis had not been excluded and that those who worked with Raman were doing very well in different positions all over the country. It was no use arguing that Raman had set up an all-India centre of research, making Calcutta the country's main research centre, so naturally there had to be many non-Bengalis.

The annual reports showed that in 1928 there were researchers from every province except Bombay, which had its own major centre. The report for 1932 states there were twenty-four researchers from various provinces and that the number of scholarships too had increased, facilitating those from other provinces to live in Calcutta. But that did not convince the dissatisfied Bengalis. Calcutta was theirs, and they wanted to see more Bengalis, not so many 'Madrasis'. It did not matter that south India consisted of diverse languages and regions—anyone from the south of the Vindhyas was disparagingly called 'Madrasi'.

However, it was true that physics was far more developed than other sciences, and young scholars from the south were a majority in the inner circle of action in Raman's laboratories. They were keenly motivated and focused on their work, perhaps because they were outsiders in an unfamiliar land, with little else to distract them, whereas Bengali students and associates had their domestic and social obligations and distractions.

It was a time of political unrest in Bengal and the civil disobedience movement was in the air. In Bengal 'swadeshi' meant not just anti-British but pro-Bangla, and the fact was that the most recognized scientist in Bengal was not a Bengali.

In addition to Bangla nationalism, there were several academics who felt very strongly about Raman's dominance in the science stage in Calcutta. Whether or not it was a case of rivalry between Meghnad Saha and Raman, as many have speculated, we cannot know for sure though there are grounds for such conclusions.

Meghnad Saha (1893–1956) was a fine scientist, whose work opened up a new chapter in the study of stars. In 1919 he published a short note on selective radiation pressure in the *Astrophysical Journal*. In 1920 he postulated what came to be known as the Saha Ionization Equation, which concerned the thermal ionization of elements. This equation is one of the basic tools for interpretation of the spectra of stars in astrophysics. By studying the spectra of various stars, one can find their temperature; and one can determine the ionization state of the various elements making up the star by using the Saha Equation.

In the early 1920s itself Saha's supporters had hoped his work would be recognized and he would win the Nobel Prize. But Raman always seemed just a little ahead of him. While Raman was elected FRS in 1924, Saha was nominated to the Royal Society by Alfred Fowler in 1925. However, the competition was very stiff and the nomination, denied for that year, was automatically carried forward to the next year. Background investigation by the British revealed the swadeshi activities of Saha's student years, when he was a member of the Anushilan Samiti (Self-Culture Association). Today we record with pride that Saha was 'always an enthusiastic supporter of the freedom movement' and that he secretly gave financial support to 'political sufferers' and admired Subhash Chandra Bose. But these were considered definitely undesirable in the 1920s, especially by British institutions, and the home member of the Viceroy's Executive Council, A.P. Muddiman, advised against the nomination.[3]

Saha was finally elected to the Royal Society in 1927. We also know now that when the Nobel Committee sent their invitation for nominations to professors at Calcutta University for the 1930 Nobel award, professors Debendra M. Bose and Sisir K. Mitra did not nominate Raman but Meghnad Saha.[4]

We also know that Saha cautioned one of the PhD students to make sure that his examiners should not be 'Raman or Nicholson

. . . It is time that the Committee of Courses in Physics should insist on an internal man'.[5] Raman was considered an outsider, his twenty-five years of service to Calcutta brushed aside.

Outwardly, Saha's relationship with Raman was formally correct. In January 1933 Meghnad Saha wrote an appreciative newspaper article (from Allahabad) on Raman and ended it with the sentence that as he leaves Calcutta 'to shoulder the responsibilities of the Indian Institute of Science', he has 'the best wishes from the people of the land of his adoption'. He adds, a little smugly perhaps, 'though he is gradually passing into the afternoon of his life'.[6]

Raman was not fully aware of the growing antagonism from these different quarters. When he was denied leave of absence, he resigned and set his affairs at the IACS and the Palit Professorship in order. Raman recommended that Debendra Bose succeed him as he was the best person for the job of the head of the department at University College. For the newly established Mahendralal Sircar Professorship, Raman recommended K.S. Krishnan to be the best person. Unfortunately, he did not take into account the camp of regional politics and Bangla nationalism that favoured Saha. Saha, who was feeling exiled from the centre ever since he took up a professorship in Allahabad, wanted the new professorship so he could return to Calcutta. The salary in Allahabad was higher than he would get in Calcutta, but then Allahabad was far from the Calcutta school of scientists, which was active and productive. Even K.S. Krishnan had not been very happy when Raman recommended him to a position in Dacca in 1928, for it was like being exiled from the centre.

Though Raman had already left, Saha was likely disappointed to find that K.S. Krishnan had been offered the position as soon as the professorship was formally established, namely 20 May 1933. Krishnan, who was a reader at the University of Dacca at the time, joined only in December, but the die was already cast for

Saha once Krishnan was appointed. He could not hope to return to Calcutta.

Raman left for Bangalore in time to take up his position at IISc on 1 April 1933. The family took a steamer to Madras, the SS *Mulbera*, a British India Navigation Company ship which sailed the Calcutta–London route, with its first layover at Madras. They embarked on Friday, 24 March and arrived in Madras on 28 March. They drove by car from Madras to Bangalore, arriving on 30 March, and after a day with friends, moved into the director's bungalow on the first of April.[7]

But the politics of rivalry was to follow Raman to Bangalore, affecting his progress in more ways than one.

Since Raman had planned to continue his association with IACS, he did not give the editorship of the journal to anyone. He also had plans on improving the administration of the IACS and its charter by bringing its rules of membership in line with other international professional scientific bodies that were run by scientists, and non-scientists genuinely interested in scientific progress.

He wanted to make it an organization of peers where membership would be by nomination rather than open to all. The current IACS rule was that life membership was open to anyone who paid 500 rupees. He foresaw that the current system might very easily take away the role of scientists and open the door for management by a majority of non-scientists. But Shyama Prasad Mookerjee, who seemed to deeply resent Raman's success, was politically more astute. He ensured that a great many individuals, most of whom were non-scientists, became life members by paying the required amount. This helped Shyama Prasad become the kingpin in a banana democracy, and he was all set to oust Raman from his position at the IACS.

As the opponents' forces prepared to strike, Raman, now in Bangalore, made a move that further antagonized them. Raman was on the committee that had been set up to plan the establishment of a national academy of science, which had been proposed at the 1933 meeting of the Indian Science Congress. When it met early in 1934, Raman, who was a member of the committee, felt that there was too much discussion and that the committee had too many members to ever get anything done.

Mainly he was not happy with the number of non-Indians who were likely to be on the council of the proposed association that the committee was planning to start. 'How can Indian Science prosper under the tutelage of an academy which has on its council of 30, about 15 who are Britishers of whom only two or three are fit enough to be even its Fellows?'[8]

So on 24 April 1934 Raman registered the Indian Academy of Sciences in Bangalore and started inviting scientists to join. He got a surprising number of positive responses. Scientists from south India had felt ignored and excluded in the previous discussions and they readily joined him. Also, Raman already had a reputation for getting things done and there was immediate support from various parts of the country, not just the south. This upset many in Calcutta and increased opposition to his position within the IACS.

At the next annual general meeting of the IACS, towards the end of 1934, Raman was 'democratically' stripped of his secretaryship with the help of the new life members admitted by Shyama Prasad Mookerjee. The combined forces of Bangla nationalism and individual rivalries exiled Raman from the city he had thought of as his own. There would be no coming home for him, now or ever.

We know that when Lokasundari Raman went to take leave of P.C. Ray before leaving Calcutta forever after that annual meeting, he commiserated with her that there was so much bad blood but also said, 'My blood rises to fever pitch whenever Bangla nationalism is an issue. If it is so even for me, surely you can understand what it is for all those others when they think Bangla nationalism is being undermined.'[9]

Once Raman left Calcutta, the Calcutta School of Physics fell apart. All the main actors who had been at the IACS at the time of the discovery left. P. Krishnamurti, whose biographical sketch of Raman was published in 1938 records a list of eighty-five names of those who had worked under Raman's supervision and were now in jobs elsewhere. Of the twenty-three Bengalis on the list, sixteen stayed in Bengal, most of them in Calcutta. But of the inner circle that had worked with Raman over a longer period of time, only S.C. Sirkar continued in Calcutta. After the Second World War, when the IACS was reorganized, he became professor and some of the old fame of the physics school started growing again.

The directorship of IISc

Mahendralal Sircar (1833–1904) and Jamsetji Nusserwanji Tata (1839–1904) shared the same decades of life and the same vision regarding education. Both wanted to establish stellar centres of scientific research. Both died before their dream was actualized. Mahendralal Sircar's Indian Association for the Cultivation of Science was inaugurated on 19 July 1876, but it fell prey to inertia by 1904, and he died thinking his dream project had failed. Tata died before his dream centre was inaugurated in May 1909. As with the IACS, the Indian Institute of Science in Bangalore was on the brink of atrophy within twenty years of its founding.

Max Born noted in his memoirs, the institute was 'a sleepy little place where little was done by a number of well-paid people'.[1] Most of the professors were British scientists who drew a salary four times what they would have earned in Britain. Raman had revivified the IACS and made it all that Mahendralal Sircar had wanted it to be, but he could not work the same magic on the IISc. Raman's stint at both places ended the same way—despite his spectacular achievements in research and organization, he was driven out. Separated though the places were by hundreds of miles, the individuals who drove him out were the same. Such is the plague of political rancour.

The Indian Institute of Science was formally established in 1911, with a guarantee of Rs 1,25,000 per year coming from the Tatas and an initial 300 acres of land along with a pledge of Rs 50,000 per year from the maharaja of Mysore, and from the government an annual amount equal to half the income from the institute. The vision was to make it a centre of research—which would create a core of experts in various fields who could advise the government when necessary—and a place where development of industrial resources would be promoted.

The first director, Morris Travers, who had been recruited in 1909 before the formal opening, resigned in 1914, totally frustrated with the council's lack of direction. The next director, Alfred Bourne (1859–1940), served from 1915 until 1921, but no research of significance was done; it became another institution teaching at an average level. 'The Tata Institute has been a white elephant maintained for the comfort of a few Europeans and its record of work is a painful frustration of the noble aspirations of the famous Indian philanthropist whose benefactions helped to found it,' said the *Educational Review* of Madras as early as 1922. Matters worsened and the institute atrophied into a non-productive centre manned mainly by professors who enjoyed the sinecure.[2]

Martin O. Forster (1872–1945), who was director from 1922 to 1933, was more successful in getting a few projects underway. For example, he started *Current Science*, advocated at a special meeting of the Indian Science Congress in 1931. The April 1933 issue of the journal records his accomplishments and states that 400 students had passed through the institute during the last decade. The students in the department of electrical technology had increased from fifteen to fifty-three and faculty members from three to eight; the department of biochemistry from sixteen students to thirty-one, and the department of general and organic chemistry from fifty-two to fifty-eight and its faculty from four to eight. There was no department of physics and Raman's job description included the opening of one.[3]

The management was headed by the visitor (who was the viceroy) and a top-heavy bureaucracy called 'the court'. There was a review committee that reported from time to time; the final decisions were taken by the council, among whose members were representatives of the Tatas, several members from Calcutta and several British scientists.

In the early 1930s the institute was in financial straits. The Mysore government had reduced its annual contribution to 30,000 rupees and other sources of income too were decreasing. The review committee that advised the council pointed out that though this was a national institution with students from all over the country, only Mysore, Madras and the Central government were contributing financially. They were not satisfied with the amount of research being done either.

Industrial contributions would flow in only if there was applied research in progress. Raman was on record as saying in Calcutta as early as 1931 that if he were given a budget of ten lakh rupees at a research centre, he would not only work at half the salary but solve India's industrial problems in ten years, provided he was given a free hand. Much was expected of Raman and the council supported him during the first year. He was appointed with a mandate to start a physics department and to reorganize aspects that would help overcome the financial straits in which the institute found itself.

Raman rapidly set about his work. At the IACS, he could move forward rapidly because it had been utterly dormant and even when it had been active, the professors were volunteering their services without any monetary remuneration. But at the IISc he had to handle an institution that was half dormant with a great many salaried sleepers, and any move he made disgruntled them.

In order to accommodate the mandate about establishing a physics department within the budget, Raman proposed that there be a merger of the chemistry and new physics departments so as to save on duplicating office staff and lab facilities. The council fully supported him. Raman wanted an assistant professor of physics appointed and the council readily approved the position. However, the chemistry faculty was not happy with these decisions.

Nor was the Bengal school pleased when their candidate Prafulla Chandra Guha (1894–1962) was not appointed to the organic chemistry position. Meghnad Saha and Shyama Prasad Mookerjee soon joined the council of the IISc and carried old grievances to a new battleground. Administratively, Raman began to face great odds at every turn.

The head of the electrical technology department, F.N. Mowdawalla, resigned early in 1934, and his place was taken by Kenneth Aston, an Englishman. Though he was not Raman's choice, the Tatas wanted him there, and they had a strong say within the governing council. Aston arrived in mid-November, 1935. The *Hindu*, dated 18 November 1935, had a short piece on how Sir C.V. and Lady Raman had a pleasant at-home to welcome the newly arrived professor of electro-technology and also for Max Born who had arrived a few weeks earlier. Aston was to become one of Raman's bitterest foes.

~

Scientific production rose rapidly with Raman's coming. His presence drew researchers from all over the country and he encouraged them to publish their findings. In 1932–33, the year before he took charge, there had been thirty-two published papers running to a total of 210 pages whereas in the year 1935–36, there were 148 papers running to 1135 pages.[4]

Raman's first love was optics, and now he moved from the colour of the sea to the colour of birds' plumage. After describing the iridescence of the wings of a jay in language that Thoreau or

Audubon would have appreciated,[5] he makes his point. His own observations are different from the accepted theory of C.W. Mason, who noted, 'the non-iridescent blue colour exhibited by the feathers of numerous birds is a Tyndall effect due to the scattering of light by very fine air bubbles or cavities contained in the substance of the barbs'. Raman noted that the colouration was not due to a Tyndall effect but either due to diffraction by the cavities or interference from the surfaces of the cavities.[6]

His second paper, also in 1934, was on the iridescence of seashells. He also focused on the iridescence of the mother-of-pearl, noticing that Sir David Brewster's observation needed to be refined.

Many wanted to work with Raman, and he selected his students carefully. The way he selected N.S. Nagendra Nath was typical of Raman, and the faculty of the electrical technology department was expectedly unhappy.

Nagendra Nath had come to Bangalore from Bihar to join the institute. He did not think he would be accepted into the physics department since he had a degree in mathematics, but he wanted to meet the Nobel laureate and asked for an interview. Nath says of it, 'After a thorough interview lasting till evening, he stood up and patted me and said that I could join the department as his research scholar.' Nath told him he very much wanted to but was already enrolled in the electrical technology department. Raman thought nothing of it—Nath would just have to transfer!

Nagendra Nath rapidly entered the centre stage of research under Raman. At the time, Raman was focusing on the passage of waves through heterogeneous media. Another student, Parthasarathy, was trying to measure the velocity of sound in liquids by the technique of diffraction of light by ultrasonic waves. Every student had to make a presentation from time to time, which was attended by all students. When Parthasarathy made his presentation, Raman pointed out that perhaps Brillouin's theory was not adequate and that since light waves would move faster or slower depending on the compression or rarefaction of the medium, an analysis of a corrugated wave front might resolve the unexplained details.

Nath had a mathematical mind and the very next day produced a mathematical formulation. He also found an answer to a problem about the Raman line in diamond that Raman had mentioned in his Nobel address as an unsolved problem worth pursuing. Nath said the Raman line 'is to be attributed to the mutual vibration of the two face-centred lattices composing the diamond lattices'. Raman was overjoyed at this and insisted that Nath immediately write it as a paper. Raman promptly nominated him to the Indian Academy. Nath was only twenty-three years old.

Raman and Nath engaged in work that turned out to be almost as significant as the Raman Effect. In 1935 and 1936 they produced a series of five papers and Nath published two papers independently; two other students published two more papers on the topic. The Raman–Nath theory opened up the possibility of optical communication. It showed we can modulate light beams with speech and use light as a carrier for sound. Clearly, it is invaluable in a military context. The whole area of fibre-optic communication opened only in the 1970s, at which time the Raman–Nath theory led to diverse uses and innovations. Fibre-optic communication is a method of transmitting information from one place to another by sending pulses of light through an optical fibre. It is far less cumbersome than the electrical transmissions and copper wires that were being used. Raman and Nath pioneered in 1935–36 a concept that turned out to be of major significance in the 1970s.

Raman's own research and his overseeing of students continued to have spectacular results, but the administrative problems assumed dismal proportions.

~

There were several, mainly financial, problems that Raman inherited. But there were also problems that came from the class system that Raman wanted to dismantle, and the rapid pace at which he initiated changes upset the professoriate. The final blows, however, came from his antagonists in Calcutta, who were powerful on the council. They took every source of complaint and magnified it into a charge sheet against Raman. Many decisions taken or recommended by Raman met with resistance from some quarter of the professoriate, sometimes with outright hostility. Those on the council who were against him exploited every setback he encountered.

To work within the reduced budget, Raman reorganized the workshops for maximum efficiency and autonomy, reaffirming his faith in the expertise of Indian workers and to remove the need for imported instruments and equipment. A central workshop was built so that the stock and maintenance of all apparatus could be managed from one central location instead of each department having its own, thus saving money and centralizing local expertise. Some departments did not like this.

Along with this, Raman wanted to involve students with hands-on knowledge of how to make and repair apparatus. This upset many who were entrenched in the class system. They considered it below their status that faculty should be teaching technical skills and that students should be learning them—they held that technical skills were for the lower classes, for lab attendants and commercial traders and manufacturers, not for intellectuals. The council approved of Raman's plan, but some within the academic community were displeased.

Following the mandate that the institute should do all it can to attract renowned scientists, he wrote to several scientists. On the list of those with whom he corresponded or wished to correspond were world-famous scientists: Erwin Rudolf Schrödinger (1887–1961), an Austrian physicist known for the

Schrödinger Equation; Paul Peter Ewald (1888–1985), a German crystallographer and pioneer of X-ray diffraction methods; Sir Rudolf Ernst Peierls (1907–95), German-born British physicist; geochemist V.M. Goldschmidt (1888–1947); and George de Hevesy (1885–1966), a Hungarian radiochemist.

Jewish scientists were fleeing Germany and Raman wanted to persuade some of them to come to India. Raman invited Max Born (1882–1970) to occupy the new professorship that Raman was planning. Max Born was already a pre-eminent scientist. In 1912 he and Theodore Karman formulated the dynamics of a crystal lattice, which allowed the imposition of quantum rules and permitted thermal properties of a crystal to be calculated. He developed the concept of quantum mechanics for interpreting the behaviour of elementary particles and atoms which do not obey Newtonian mechanics. He was the founder of lattice dynamics, the theory of how atoms in solids stick together and vibrate. When Werner Heisenberg formulated his first laws of a new quantum theory of atoms in 1926, Born, who was his mentor, immediately developed the mathematical formulation that would describe it. Heisenberg was awarded the Nobel Prize in 1932 though Einstein had nominated Born, Heisenberg and Jordan, all of whom had worked together, to share the award. It is now generally believed that Born did not get the prize that year because he was Jewish.

Max Born was amenable to talk about the possibilities of a future in India and spent about six months in the country (November 1935 to May 1936), based in Bangalore. Budgetary restrictions were always a problem but Raman wanted to get a permanent position for him; he assumed Born's presence would make it easier to get the approval. But there was covert opposition from several quarters. It came to a head at the senate meeting where Raman's proposal to create a position for Born was discussed.

Aston, who had been made a member of the senate on his arrival, called Born a second-rate scientist who was thrown out of his own country and said he was not good enough for the institute. There seems to be a clear element of anti-semitism in Aston's actions. Max Born records his feelings in his memoirs. He says he was present at the meeting and was so overwhelmed by the open hostility that he went home and 'simply cried'. There is some irony in the fact that when the Astons came from England to join the IISc, they had stayed with the Borns for a few days until their own bungalow was ready. Aston's voice carried clout in the council and the offer that Raman had extended to Born was withdrawn because of council's opposition.[7]

Aston's arrogance was also aimed at Raman. As Max Born said in his memoirs, some of the British scientists at the institute resented being placed in a position of subordination to an Indian director.[8]

This whole episode sheds light on Raman's vision and values. He felt deeply for the plight of the German scientists who were fleeing the impending onslaught of the Nazis. He also had an instinctive feel for selecting talented scientists. Everyone on his list was brilliant in his field, many were already Nobel laureates; George Hevesy went on to win the Nobel Prize in 1943 and Max Born in 1954. Raman's objective was twofold. He wanted to help the scientists by offering what he considered the prime needs of a scientist—a place to work and a place to stay, with enough money to cover basic living expenses. He also wanted Indian students and scientists to interact with great minds in India itself instead of having to go abroad to an alien environment to get scientific training.

Denying Raman's proposal to get a position for Max Born was unfortunate for Raman in that a good scientist needs to be in the company of other good scientists to nurture his creative genius. Further interaction would have helped Raman to move into quantum theory, which would have helped him in the work he took up in the 1940s. But it was even more unfortunate for the cause of

science in India. Raman had drawn and would continue to draw
brilliant students from all over the country. He would continue to
send out well-trained scientists to occupy leading positions all over
India. But Born's presence would have helped attract an even larger
number of young minds to dedicate themselves to a life in science.
Raman always held that there needs to be a very broad grass-roots
base in order that some might rise to remarkable achievement. Max
Born and his wife Hedi left Bangalore in May 1936.

Correspondence between Raman and scientists such as
Rutherford and Born show that there was immense mutual respect
between them, as happens between truly great minds, far from the
rivalry seen in the lower echelons.

Women's education, Gandhi and God

In May 1936, Mahatma Gandhi was resting at Nandi Hills, near Bangalore. Raman had always held Gandhi in high esteem, and his later endowment of the Gandhi Memorial Lectures, to be given annually in October at the Raman Institute, is testimony to his faith in him. He did not always agree with some of Gandhi's precepts. For example, when the Second World War broke out, Raman had no patience with Gandhi's policy of non-violence. 'Force Can Be Vanquished Only By Greater Force' read the banner headlines of the *Hindu* that reported Raman's speech at a fundraising event on 22 July 1940. The report says, 'Sir C.V. Raman, in his remarks, pooh-poohed Mahatma Gandhi's theory of non-violence as a solution to the present crisis, and said force had to be vanquished only by greater force.' If only the people of India realized what motivated Germany and Italy, they would understand that 'they would get it in the neck from Germany'. Raman felt Indians were not ready for 'militarization' because the war was being fought far away. They would promptly arm themselves in full force if Germany were to bombard a few cities in India, he said.[1] Raman might have disagreed with Gandhi but he had deep respect for him.

In the 1920s whenever Gandhi came to Calcutta, Lokam would attend the rallies. Often Raman accompanied her. They would go to the Maidan to listen, sometimes along with Raman's students.

It was therefore natural that Raman would visit Gandhi when Gandhi was at Nandi Hills. Indeed, he seems to have met Gandhi at least three times during the months of May and June 1936, when Gandhi spent considerable time in and near Bangalore.

There is a detailed chronology of Gandhi's activities on www.gandhiserve.org, and the records for the year 1936 list that Gandhi met with Raman and Professor Rahm 'on or before 10 May', with Raman and Lady Raman 'before May 31' and 'visited Institute of Science' on 12 June.

Raman's visits have been recorded by two individuals. One is Mahadev Desai, Gandhi's close associate. He wrote a weekly column for *Harijan*, the publication through which Gandhi's message was propagated. The *Sunday Times* of 14 June 1936 quotes extensively from the column Desai wrote on a visit by Lady Raman. Students had asked her help in inviting Gandhi to the IISc. While speaking on their behalf, Lokam also talked about her efforts while in Calcutta to help spread the cause of spinning and the wearing of khadi. Desai records that Lokam said, 'My husband had no faith in the wheel then . . . He would put away my wheel, smash it and break it; but I am glad to tell you that in my own lifetime the day has come when he no longer ridicules the wheel. He too believes in it.'[2]

Even before the introductions were over, Gandhi said that if he accepted one invitation, he would be forced for the sake of fairness to accept others. But once he knew it was to visit the science institute, he readily accepted 'provided Sir C.V. Raman will show me some magic there'. He also wanted to use the visit to raise some money for his Kamala Nehru Memorial Fund.

Desai goes on to record, 'She was talking in Hindi as he [Sir C.V.] came in. "Now, is that Hindi any good?" he asked jocularly. "Certainly as good as your science," said Gandhiji.'

They then spoke about Lokam's knowledge of Bengali as well, and Raman said he too had lived in Calcutta but could not speak or understand Bengali. He understood Hindi well enough but did not speak it. 'It is that conceit, you know, that I am as full of as much as you.'

This is just an example both of Raman's ready humour and his personal relationship with Gandhi. A similar camaraderie was seen when Gandhi, on his visit to the institute on 12 June, greeted Raman with the words that he had actually come to see 'his old friend' Lady Raman, rather than Raman.

The other record is from an interview that Gandhi gave to Professor Rahm who had come with Raman. Rahm was introduced to Gandhi as a man who researched small organisms that can live for twelve years without food and water.[3] Gandhi was very interested.

When Rahm asked Gandhi what can be done to fight atheism, Raman, who had been quiet all along, joined in to say, 'If there is a God, we must look for him in the universe. If He is not there, he is not worth looking for. I am being looked upon in various quarters as an atheist, but I am not. . . . Science is nothing but a search of truth. . . . It proclaims from the housetops that there is no virtue in sticking to untruth . . . Salvation lies in the perfection of the biological instinct for the perpetuation of the race—the instinct to sacrifice . . . for the sake of the species.'[4]

Raman repeated innumerable times the idea of the divine power being within human beings and in nature. In 1950, giving the convocation address at Utkal University, he said, 'The more I pursue science, the more I am impressed with the infinite loveliness and wonders of the world. I have often gone further to give expression to this whenever I was asked whether I believed in God. I tell you, if there is a God, He is here in this world before us.'[5]

In November 1950, at the convocation of Agra University, he said, 'I study science not because anything is going to happen to me but because I feel it is a kind of worship of this great Goddess Nature of which we are a part.'

Speaking at a Bhoodan event in 1955, he said, 'God lives in us. See God in your own soul and heart. The human soul is the repository of the Divine.'

Elsewhere, writing about his vision for the Raman Institute, he said, 'It is my earnest desire to bring into existence a centre of scientific research worthy of our ancient country where the keenest intellects of our land can probe into the mysteries of the universe and by so doing help us to appreciate the transcendent Power that guides its activities. This aim can only be achieved if by His Divine Grace, all lovers of our country see their way to help the cause.'[6]

Raman did not participate in pujas and paid scant heed to the celebration of Hindu festivals or observances. However, it is on record in print and in photographs that when the Indian Academy annual meetings were held in Tirupati in 1957 and in Chidambaram in 1959, he visited the two famous temples and offered puja in traditional clothes and style, bare-torsoed and wearing the dhoti in formal *panchakachaam* style.

T.S. Satyan, the photographer who established a long-term rapport with Raman, talked about Raman's sixtieth birthday, when the *ayush homam* prayers for a long life were performed on Lokam's initiative at 'Panchavati', Raman's home. 'The whole house, filled with smoke emanating from the sacred fire, seemed to respond to the melodious chant of Vedic hymns,' he reminisced.

Raman wanted a clean simple cremation on his own property. As he lay dying in November 1970, ceaselessly talking about what needed to be done with his plans for his institute and for science, Lokam at one point reminded him to think of God, and Raman answered he had never met God but 'I have met a godly human being—Mahatma Gandhi'. And he went on to talk about Gandhi.

Raman was not an atheist. Rather, his faith seems to have been a combination of Advaita philosophy of the oneness of god and humans, and Vedantic transcendentalism that god is everywhere in nature. Essentially, the pursuit of science was a pursuit of truth through the study of nature.

~

This might be an appropriate moment to discuss Raman's attitude towards women's education and women scientists, for it was around this time that the Indian Institute of Science admitted its first woman student.

Mahadev Desai, writing in the *Harijan* about the meeting between Raman and Gandhi at Nandi Hills, says that Raman introduced to Gandhi a young woman who wanted to devote her time to science. Raman said to Gandhi, 'Try as much as I may, I cannot dissuade her from this pursuit, Mahatmaji.'

This young woman was in all likelihood Kamala Sohonie. Kamala Bhagwat (b. 1911) came from a family of chemists. She graduated from Bombay University and wished to pursue her studies in chemistry in Bangalore. However, she was refused admission because the institute did not admit women. She then wrote to the director, Raman. Having just joined his post, he took a quick look at precedence, which showed there was no provision for women students at the institute.

In true Gandhian fashion, she went to Bangalore in person and launched a satyagraha in front of his office. He accepted that the institute procedure was untenable, and admitted her on a one-year probation. She joined the chemistry department in 1933. In 1936, just about the time Raman met with Gandhi, she got her master's degree. Later, she went to Cambridge and returned to make herself a distinguished career in India as a biochemist.

Now that the injustice against women was brought to his attention, not only did Raman rectify the system and get the institute to start admitting women students, but he took it on himself to advocate women's education. Indeed, many renowned women scientists had their initial training at the IISc, thanks to Kamala Sohonie's pioneering efforts.

Raman, who could be extremely obstinate on some counts, was very supportive of this change, and spoke about the need for women's education at the convocation address of S.N.D.T. Women's University, Bombay, in July 1935, which was reported in the newspaper *Kaiser-i-Hind* (7 July 1935). How was it that India, with its culture and traditions venerating education, had been left out of step now, he asked, and gave his reply: because 'we have kept down our women, we have refused them their birthright, their birthright to knowledge . . . No country that keeps one half under suspension can ever hope to be a nation'. He believed in the ideals that had motivated the founder of the women's university, Maharishi Dhondo Keshav Karve (1858–1962), to promote and advocate women's education.

Karve had started the university in 1920, and the curriculum mainly focused on education for women's traditional role in society. There were courses in the fine arts, and the medium of instruction was not English but the local languages. It was a great step forward. Those who diminish its value today by questioning its emphasis on women's traditional roles are basically being unfair to Karve's idealism.

Raman, in 1935, seems to be in accord with Karve on separate educational institutions for men and women at the undergraduate level. 'We do not want to move straightaway into the vortex of sex conflict which has characterized Western civilization.'

Like Karve, Raman believed that women's education was one of the keys to India's progress, but unlike him Raman advocated women to take up the study of the sciences. Science needed patience, and since women were particularly rich in patience and perseverance, he urged them to take up scientific pursuits. There was no question, he said, that women were entitled to the same quality of education as men.

There were three women whom Raman took as students at this time. The best known was Anna Mani (1918–2001) who joined the Indian Institute early in 1940 and worked intensively for five years under Raman's supervision. She later made significant contributions in the field of meteorological instrumentation and pioneered research in the areas of solar radiation, ozone and wind energy measurements. Her five papers, while she was with Raman, on the luminescence of diamonds and rubies, are all single–authored, as was typical of Raman. She went abroad and returned to India in 1948.

It is also important to note that the doctoral thesis that Anna Mani wrote under Raman was submitted to Madras University but was not accepted on the grounds that she did not have an MSc degree. Like Raman, who rose to eminence without a PhD degree, she too rose to a high post, in the Indian Meteorological Department. Of her experience as a woman in her workplace, she said, 'I must say that at no time did I experience professional discrimination as a woman in what was considered largely a man's world. I did not feel I was either penalised or privileged because of being female.'[7]

Then there was Sunanda Bai. She was married early and she got her master's degree from Banaras Hindu University. She joined Raman's laboratory in 1939 and published excellent papers, completing her thesis around 1945. She was to proceed to Sweden for advanced work, but committed suicide a few days before her departure. Her research papers are available but her personal history seems to be a blank, except for the generally accepted theory that her suicide had nothing to do with her academic workplace but was caused by her personal relationship involving another woman. Her tragic end deeply disturbed Raman. A. Jayaraman, whom I talked to while writing this biography, thought this tragic incident might have affected Raman's decision not to seek women students when he started his own institute.

The third woman to study under Raman was Lalitha Doraiswamy (b. 1910). She was a graduate of Madras University and became a teacher and then the principal of a school in Karaikudi. She went to Bangalore as Raman's student. She was there only for a few months, for she got married in September 1936 to S. Chandrasekhar—the already eminent astrophysicist and Raman's nephew—and left for the United States. One wonders what might have happened had she continued for a while longer to work under Raman's supervision. Would she have been one of the trailblazers, like Kamala Sohonie and Anna Mani, instead of having her scientific abilities dormant for the rest of her life—of more than a hundred years—her major accomplishment being that she was a devoted helpmate to her famous husband? Would more time working in Raman's lab have given her the confidence and determination to be another Marie Curie, someone who worked alongside her husband rather than one who walked in her husband's shadow?

That Raman encouraged three women to work with him at a time when, as Anna Mani says, one could count all the women physicists in India on one's fingertips, is a comment on his faith in women's abilities to be scientists. Once he retired, however, he had only a handful of students, of whom none was a woman, although Anna Mani continued to be associated with his institute.

Raman was rather formal when it came to social interaction with women at his workplace—including the wives of those who worked there—and he expected the young men around him to keep the same formality and distance between themselves and the women who worked there. This gave rise to tales about his disapproval of social interaction. However, he valued what women brought to the laboratory: the virtues of patience and devotion. In 1941, speaking at Patna University, he said, 'I have a feeling that if the women of India take to science and interest themselves in the progress and advance of science as well, they will achieve what even men have failed to do . . . Let us therefore not imagine that intellect is a sole prerogative of males only in science.'[8]

His support of women's abilities is also shown in the fact that shortly after he founded the Indian Academy of Sciences, he invited E.K. Janaki Ammal (1897–1984) to be a member, and she was elected in 1935. Janaki Ammal was a botanist.

While he was formal with women in the workplace, he was more relaxed around women at other times, as with the woman mentioned earlier who had assisted him as a child in Nagpur. Vasanti Ram, one of CS's granddaughters, has an anecdote.

Vasanti was at 'Panchavati' one noon hour in 1956 when Raman had just had his meal and gone to his room for his usual rest. A jutka came trundling through the gates and on to the side of the house. A woman got off and came to the long veranda between the kitchen wing and the main house, where Lokam was standing. The woman was dressed in a rather gaudy and expensive sari, wearing heavy jewellery and a kumkum *pottu* on her forehead the size of a rupee coin. She said she had come to see the great scientist. The horse neighed loudly in support. Just as Lokam was about to say he was resting, Raman came out to see what the neighing was about. The woman beamed at him, went to the jutka and brought back a heavy, thickly woven rose garland and presented him with it, saying she was visiting the city from a long distance and had no intention of going back until she had seen the great one in person. Raman beamed back, accepted the garland, thanked her cordially and invited her in. But she declined. She was perfectly satisfied, having completed her mission. She spoke on for a few minutes about how happy she was to have her dream fulfilled, to greet in person one of the country's great men, and she left. Raman obviously enjoyed the visit. Indeed, he loved to receive garlands. It was his habit to wear any garlands he received at functions and to give them to Lokam on his return home. This time, he wore the garland to his room and hung it on his bedpost, enjoying its fragrance as he rested.

Had Raman known of Gandhi's later experiments in chastity with certain young women in his following, it is very likely that he would never have understood Gandhi's behaviour or rationale. Raman's moral codes were black and white, without shades of grey anywhere. That he endowed the Gandhi Memorial Lectures in 1959, and spoke about Gandhi even as he lay dying in November 1970, makes me speculate that it is likely he did not know of the experiments in chastity that Gandhi took up in the 1940s. After all, few knew of it until more recent times.

Ousted from directorship

Raman was in the habit of giving Lokam a diary on the first day of every year. In the 1937 diary, he wrote: 'Let the days roll by happily as the water flows in a river.' But it was to be worse than even Calcutta in 1933–34.

The events that led up to the turmoil had started almost as soon as Raman joined his post as director. It all boiled down to the fact that Raman moved too quickly according to his vision for the institute. The changes he made were many and rapid, just as he had with the IACS in Calcutta. What had worked then did not work now because the IACS had been totally dormant whereas the IISc was atrophied with sinecures. His rapid changes did not go down well with the establishment that had become slow and stagnant. For the professors, who had found a comfortable niche in the institute, all these rapid changes were extremely threatening. The chemistry department, in particular, felt most threatened.

On another front, frequent resignations and lack of replacement had been annoying the students. Between 1930 and 1932, three assistant professors in electrical technology had resigned and two lecturers were appointed in their place. Students were ready to rebel because for years they had suffered from the departure of several professors and the tardiness of the administration in replacing them. When Raman was appointed, Professor Watson, an Englishman, who had hoped to become the director, was not pleased at being passed over. He and Mowdawalla, his colleague from the electrical technology department, resigned within a year of Raman's joining. Seeing an opportunity in this, faculty members who were unhappy with Raman's direct approach to restructuring departments and workshops prodded the students to unite against him.

The students were divided when it came to rising against this particular director. But it sufficed for Raman's adversaries to get a handful of militant students who could be manipulated into throwing stones, literal and figurative.

In line with his firm belief that researchers should be given living space close to work, Raman converted one of the bungalows—that Max Born had occupied during his stay—as a student residence. This upset Professor Aston, who wanted that house for himself.

In short, there was opposition from most quarters to one or another of Raman's decisions and recommendations. The council majority supported many of his proposals the first year. But when Aston joined the council, several council members, Aston and Shyama Prasad Mookerjee in particular, who were against him managed to turn the tables. They were helped by Raman's attitude of concentrating on his plans to the point of running over people, as happened when he appropriated Nagendra Nath for himself or in persuading the council to merge the chemistry and physics departments. Raman's plans may have been sound, but he went about executing them in a forthright manner that many found abrasive.

A committee was set up to review his tenure. The members finally selected for the committee were not the scientists and administrators originally suggested by the viceroy but Sir James Irvine, A.H. Mackenzie and S.S. Bhatnagar, chosen by the council, where Aston and Shyama Prasad held sway. The Irvine Committee was announced on 20 January 1936 and submitted its report by

May—very rapidly for a slow-moving institution. Their report was that scientific production had gone up by leaps and bounds, but Raman's administration was far from satisfactory and he would have to go. The report blamed Raman for faulty administrative decisions, faulty use of funds and general lack of leadership. The invitation to Max Born had exacerbated matters.

By early 1937 Raman was increasingly isolated. His detailed response to the accusations and his charting of the many improvements that had been made by increasing the efficiency of the workshop and bettering fiscal management fell on deaf ears. As chairman of the Railway Board Committee on the Chemical Preservation of Timber, as adviser to the government of Hyderabad for the establishment of a research laboratory, as adviser in Mysore government's efforts to establish new industries and as a member of numerous committees on industrial development, Raman had promoted the applications of science in various ways. But the Irvine Committee did not take any of that into account.

Even as storm clouds gathered, Raman continued with his groundbreaking research with Nagendra Nath, and with his public lectures. Raman spoke forcefully as usual about his disapproval of mass-manufactured and imported goods, at the Mysore Chamber of Commerce on 18 April 1937. He condemned the 'cheap nasty, mass-produced materials which are made by machinery' and which have replaced 'the beautiful works of individual craftsmen'. He reaffirmed his faith in local craftsmen and spoke of the prudence required in using science. 'We must prohibit the import of articles that are not quite essential. . . . Science is used as a machine to kill the spirit of man. We live in a world where, unfortunately, science is abused or misused.' He reiterated what he had said six years earlier: if he were given a budget of ten lakh a year for ten years, and a free hand, 'I will solve all the problems connected with India's scientific and industrial development, and place India in a position to produce everything from a battleship to a pin.'[1]

One is reminded of another scientist, Benjamin Thompson, Count Rumford (1753–1814), who took charge of Bavaria and used the methods and knowledge of science to overhaul the army, transform beggars into workers, introduce universal education, change the nation's food habits and literally bring more light into people's daily lives with his invention of new types of lamps. Rumford also beautified Munich with a magnificent garden and park that were not only aesthetically pleasing but served many utilitarian purposes. But Rumford had a 'free hand' that Raman never got. He was hemmed in by people who did not want him doing anything, leave alone doing anything with a free hand.

When it was reported that Raman was being forced to sever his connections with the directorship, and was expected to leave by the end of June, the *Bombay Chronicle* called it a shame that someone who had accelerated scientific productivity of the institute so rapidly in three years should be driven out. It pointed out that Raman, to help trim the budget and show his sense of service, had agreed to have his salary slashed on condition that the amount go directly into the physics department facilities.

G. Venkataraman and Rajinder Singh have written in detail about the petty jealousies and rivalries that were at the base of the movement against Raman's directorship. They have listed the names of the 'informants' within the institute who passed on filtered information to the Irvine Committee that was set up to review Raman's tenure and to members from the Calcutta coterie of Raman's opponents. They show how students had been instigated to lodge complaints and print vicious pamphlets that reached even Max Born and other scientists in Britain, and how the plotters had set up baits and a slew of misinformation that would make the Irvine Committee come up with a damning report on Raman. The way the committee collected its data clearly made a farce of a fair process. Raman's habit of brushing aside interferences to his plans, his short-term expenditure for long-term benefits and his expeditious dealing with everyday problems without so-called due process were highlighted.

The final report of the Irvine Committee recorded that 'remarkable progress had been made' after the appointment of Raman, but in the final count it faulted Raman, accusing him of focusing on the physics department, of diverting funds to projects of his choice and of mismanaging the resources of the institute. Raman was not the only one axed; the committee recommended that the salary of clerks and peons be cut so as to save a mere Rs 8436. The committee was intent on saving pennies and losing out on the long-term benefits of Raman's vision for the institute.

Rajinder Singh has documented proof that Shyama Prasad Mookerjee, who was on the council of the IISc, had a hand in promoting antagonism against Raman. Singh passes no judgement but gives enough data for one to draw conclusions. He cites a letter from Mookerjee to Meghnad Saha where he wrote he had cancelled his trip to England so he could attend the special council meeting that was to look into Raman's directorship tenure. He wrote, 'The Irvine Report is now in our hands confidentially.... The report is most favourable. It is a fair and strong document and Raman has been painted in true colour[s] ... practically all that we urged in our joint memorandum has been accepted.... Naoroji, Chandavarkar and Ghandy [sic] feel I must not be away at this stage ... having worked at it so vigorously for a year and a half ...'

It clearly shows that a group of antagonists had been working for a year and a half to disgrace Raman. It is also on record that at one point Shyama Prasad Mookerjee wanted a 'no-confidence' motion passed against Raman but the final resolution which passed had been toned down to 'strong disapproval'.[2]

During and after the turmoil, voices were raised in support of Raman in the news media and elsewhere. A petition signed by a clear majority of twelve faculty members and ninety-eight students (there were 165 students at the institute) was sent in, and council member Bawa Kartar Singh formally submitted a Memorandum of Dissent. But, of course, the outcome was a foregone conclusion.

Max Born's letters to Rutherford, soon after he left Bangalore in October 1936, reveal the state of affairs. Born clearly shows that the cards were stacked against Raman from the very beginning. He explains this over a span of several letters. 'The English group resented an Indian director' as the resignation of Professor Watson proved. The Tatas were ready to drop a brick on Raman rather than offend their British partners, and they entrusted Professor Aston, newly appointed to the electrical technology department, with 'the definite mission to clear up the institute'. Aston had promptly become 'a centre for collecting ever so silly complaints against Raman'; 'it was evident to me from the beginning that they [the Irvine Committee] had received instructions beforehand . . . His enemies the Tatas and the Bengali members of the Council had made up their minds to get rid of Raman.' At some point in the second year of Raman's tenure, the Tatas seem to have withdrawn their support of Raman. They were pulled away by the complaints of the British professors. Born also speaks of the Irvine Commission as a kangaroo court. 'Instead of visiting the Institute and carefully studying the work done in the laboratories, they settled in a Government building some four miles away, where they behaved like a law-court . . . They examined chiefly Raman's opponents, even students. Men like Mr Jatkar of whose untrustworthiness I got personal proofs were allowed to "give evidence" . . . All the dirty affairs were treated in detail but no voice raised to take into account the good intentions of Raman or his achievements at the Institute.' Finally, Born zeroes in on Raman's shortcomings: 'He is rather an eternal and badly educated child, who does not realize when he is treading on people's toes.'[3]

Raman had no chance of a fair fight against the combined artillery of the 'Calcutta group', the Tatas and the Irvine Committee.

Even the viceroy, who suggested that Raman continue as director for another year, had no impact on the majority in the council. Raman was compelled to resign his directorship.

B. Venkatesechar was appointed acting director and J.C. Ghosh became director on 1 August 1939 and continued till 1947. The 'Bengali' group would have been happy, even though Ghosh himself was not in the group that opposed Raman.

The *Hindu* of 19 June 1937 reported that 'Sir C.V. Raman made a statement to the Governing Council, it is stated, agreeing to continue as Professor of Physics . . . he will continue to enjoy the same [academic] privileges he had while he was Director.'

~

But of course he did not get any privileges. Raman had been invited to attend the International Congress of Physics and Chemistry to be held in Paris at the end of September. He could afford to go because the conference organizers were paying for his passage. Lokam's diary entry of Thursday, 9 September 1937 reads: 'Sir Raman left for Bombay en route to Paris. A man came from Madras to keep him guard until Esavanthapur. I was badly disappointed by this incident. I have written this in a separate notebook. Students entertained him at the City Station.' We do not have that 'separate notebook' and this remains an intriguing entry.

Raman left for Bombay and 'At the City Railway Station last night, Dr. Raman was given a hearty send off by a large gathering.'[4] He sailed on the SS *Viceroy of India* on 11 September, and it was on this voyage that he first met Indira Gandhi. She recounted much later, in 1954, on the occasion of the award of the title Bharat Ratna to him, that she had called him a 'ratna'—a jewel—long before others had. 'I have been an ardent admirer of yours since that journey to England in 1937, and have regarded you as the Rathna of India.'[5] During the two-month trip he earned more accolades outside India. One such honour was his election to an honorary fellowship of the Hungarian Academy of Sciences in November 1937.

Raman returned via Colombo, landing in Madras on 23 November 1937. To the *Hindu* reporter who interviewed him that day, Raman talked about some of his observations and experiences. He admired the efficiency with which Bologna had rebuilt the university buildings and how houses for lower-income citizens were being constructed on a large scale. Of France he said that the Congress itself had been motivated by a desire that scientists should come together to promote international goodwill.

During his trip abroad in 1937, Raman was offered the professorship that Pieter Zeeman (1865–1943) was retiring from in Amsterdam. Raman noted in a letter to O.W. Richardson how pleasantly surprised he was and that he might consider it. However, the local government would not support a non-Dutch-speaking candidate and the offer was withdrawn; so Raman was spared making the decision. He was then invited to lead the physics department of Waltair University, but he said he did not want to stand in the way of his former student S. Bhagavantam, who was already there since 1932 and should be next in line for the job. Stoically, he decided Bangalore was to be his home base for the rest of his life.

The 1937 trip re-enthused Raman to wish to inform himself in person about scientific research in Europe, about work being done at various centres. It would be good, too, to get away from Bangalore for a while. So Raman planned a European sabbatical, but when he applied for a year's leave to spend at foreign laboratories, an extraordinary meeting of the council was held early in December 1937 and the request was denied. Raman's old opponents from Calcutta were still influential with the council. The council also decided that the physics department would be shifted to the central workshop, and the central workshop would be placed under the control of the electrical engineering (previously electro-technology) department. The majority on the council wanted to rub Raman's face in the mud and did so by reversing his stand about both the workshop and the electrical engineering department. They were also sore over their candidate Meghnad Saha not winning the Nobel that year, despite having been nominated for the third time. Despite all the politicking, Raman continued as professor of physics at the IISc for the next eleven years until his retirement, and concentrated on building up a strong centre of physics.

There was no dearth of excellence in Raman's own work and in the work of his students and associates even while all these administrative upheavals were going on. It is amazing to think that his creative genius continued full crest even during this time of intense conflict. He wrote a string of papers on diverse topics and, with his student Nagendra Nath, went on to another remarkable achievement—the Raman–Nath theory—in 1935–36.

The problem brings together the movements of light and sound waves. It was already postulated by Léon Brillouin (1889–1969) that when light is scattered in a liquid, the thermal agitation of atoms could be considered the equivalent of sound waves travelling in different directions. Scientists had observed the results of intentionally imposing sound waves on a liquid. Though the speed of light is always the same in vacuum, it varies when it travels in a medium, and the variation is dependent upon the refractive index of the medium. Raman and Nath studied the impact of ultrasonic sound waves on light in a liquid.

The Raman–Nath theory opened up an understanding of the philosophical foundations of quantum mechanics. Its applications grew in leaps and bounds after the 1960s, with advances in the use of fibre optics for storing digital information and for imaging.

Another student of Raman's, P.R. Pisharoty, was a man after Raman's heart. He was a lecturer at Loyola College in Madras and first came to Raman in 1932; he spent his summers in Bangalore working with Raman. About the year 1939, he gave up his lectureship and accepted a smaller research assistantship so he could spend all his time working under Raman's guidance. He left in 1941 with Raman's recommendation to accept a position with the Indian Meteorological Department, where he rose to prominence.

It is worth recounting an incident mentioned by Pisharoty in his biography of Raman. At 7 a.m. one morning, when Pisharoty was depressed about the slow progress of his experiment, Raman immediately noticed his despondency and asked what was bothering him. Pisharoty said that a distinguished scientist in Britain, who was working on the same problem, had a five-kilowatt X-ray tube at his disposal instead of the one-kilowatt tube they had at the Indian Institute. 'There is a very simple solution. Put a ten-kilowatt brain on the problem,' Raman said, smilingly.

Raman had the ability to recognize ten-kilowatt brains. Among other younger scientists whom he influenced at this time were two who went on to do remarkable work on their own—Homi J. Bhabha and Vikram Sarabhai. Both, like Raman, were brilliant scientists. And both, like Raman, loved music and museums and had a keen aesthetic sense. Both Bhabha and Sarabhai had financial resources and Raman wanted them to break new ground and lead India to another level, such as he never could with his limited financial resources and lack of industrial contacts.

Both, Bhabha and Sarabhai, were students at Cambridge, England, in 1939, at the advent of the Second World War. Both were born to wealthy families and had the best of early education. Indeed, the Sarabhai family had their own Montessori-type school for the eight children in the family.

Bhabha (1909–66) had got his PhD in 1934 from Cambridge and had already won recognition among physicists. He was on a holiday back in India when war broke out so he stayed on in India. He came to work with Raman in Bangalore in 1940 and was inspired by Raman, though he did not follow his suggestion that he should study neutron stars. Raman was also inspired by Bhabha, who had immersed himself in the newest scientific events of Britain and Europe. Bhabha had worked with Walter Heitler on the cascade theory of electron showers, which was of great importance for the understanding of cosmic radiation. Raman, as we have seen, had always been drawn to such new frontiers as astrophysics and nuclear research, but both involved more money than Raman ever had access to, so he had restricted himself to research that needed little funding.

Raman nominated Bhabha to the Indian Academy and to the fellowship of the Royal Society and to a readership at the Indian Institute. Raman's vision for India played a part in Bhabha's decision to remain in the country. Later, Bhabha was to say that though the work he did in India was less recognized on the international stage, it gave him far more satisfaction than anything he had done in England. Raman had great admiration for Bhabha, and at the Nagpur Indian Academy meeting in 1941, while introducing Bhabha, he said, 'Bhabha is a great lover of music, a gifted artiste, a brilliant engineer and an outstanding scientist . . . He is the modern equivalent of Leonardo da Vinci.'

Bhabha went on to build the Tata Institute of Fundamental Research and to be the chair of India's Atomic Energy Commission. But it all started in Bangalore. It was from Bangalore in 1944 that Bhabha wrote his historical letter to the Tata Trust for support in setting up a centre for research work in nuclear science, which would play a central role in the development of nuclear energy.

Vikram Sarabhai (1919–71) was a young man of twenty, working for his PhD in physics at Cambridge University, when the war broke out. He came back to his hometown of Ahmedabad and his father sent him to Bangalore to work under Raman. Sarabhai was interested in cosmic rays. Raman urged him to follow up on a paper that had recently appeared, on how cosmic rays were capable of leaving tracks on photographic plates. He told Sarabhai to pursue that line of investigation, studying cosmic rays at high altitudes with balloons, which could lead him to the Nobel Prize. This question did lead to a Nobel Prize, but not for Sarabhai, who took up some other topic. Cecil Powell of Bristol won the prize in 1950 for related work.[6]

Sarabhai did work on cosmic rays, however, revealing that cosmic rays are a stream of energy particles reaching the earth from outer space, being influenced on their way by the sun, the atmosphere and magnetism. Sarabhai published his first research paper, 'Time Distribution of Cosmic Rays', in the *Proceedings of Indian Academy of Sciences*. He worked with Raman between 1940 and 1945 and went back to England after the end of the war to complete his PhD. On his return, he went on to build India's space programme and succeeded Homi Bhabha as chair of the atomic energy programme when Bhabha died in an air crash in the Alps in 1966. Sarabhai also had a sudden death, in 1971. It is strange that the lives of India's two leading figures in nuclear development should have come to a sudden end.

Raman was a strong influence in the decision of both Sarabhai and Bhabha to stay on in India rather than return to the West after the war.

Standing alone

The acrimony of the unequal battles that Raman had to fight in Calcutta and in Bangalore left a core of bitterness. He seems to have made a decision never again to get involved in any situation where bureaucracy could trample on his individual insights and vision of what a scientific organization ought to be.

He declined to be a member of the National Planning Commission set up by the Indian National Congress. He declined to be on the board of Scientific and Industrial Research set up by the Government of India in 1940.[1] One wonders if the latter organization that later became the CSIR (Council of Scientific and Industrial Research) might have evolved differently if Raman had joined and participated in it from the very beginning. On the other hand, it is very possible that he would have clashed swords again with his adversary on the Irvine Commission, Shanti Swarup Bhatnagar, and emerged the loser once again, for Raman was not at all good at political manoeuvres and diplomatic negotiations. Bhatnagar went on to become the director of the CSIR (1942–54) and that probably reinforced Raman's decision to keep his distance from all government-initiated efforts at science planning for the country.

Many of the leaders in science-organization were unhappy with him, both for not joining them and for his criticism of their science policies. His detractors started a rumour discrediting not only his current research but his role in the discovery of the Raman Effect. They not only claimed that K.S. Krishnan was responsible for the discovery but that Krishnan himself claimed as much. Krishnan's diary and his talk with Ramaseshan that took place in 1953 (but published only in the 1990s), as noted earlier, show how false those rumours were. Nevertheless, during the 1950s, the Raman–Krishnan controversy as it was called caused a rupture in their personal relationship. This deeply affected both of them, and Raman felt he had been betrayed too often to trust anyone any more.

Raman decided to concentrate on his own science and his own vision for what needed to be done for science to progress in India. He focused on getting international recognition for the journals of the Indian Academy so that Indian scientists could be proud of publishing their work in India. He focused on building an appreciation for scientific pursuits at the grass-roots level by having the annual meetings of the Indian Academy in university towns, even small towns, across the country. Thus, through the Indian Academy, Raman practised what he had always advocated—that there should be an organization of peers to which membership was by nomination and election, that this organization should galvanize the younger generation towards a career in science and that scientists should work on the applications of science for the betterment of living conditions for all.

In the eleven years that he spent as professor of physics at the IISc, he moved into new fields. As far as feasible, he gave his students problems in fields that they were interested in, but in his own work, he pursued with single-minded diligence the problems that most interested him, regardless of what was in vogue.

His career can be seen in slots of ten years. The years 1910–19 were spent mainly on acoustics, 1920–29 on optics and light scattering and 1930–39 mainly on ultrasonic diffraction (that led to the Raman–Nath theory) and the application of Raman scattering to crystals. During the decade 1940–49, Raman focused on diamond and the vibration of crystals lattices. In the 1950s, optics, which was always one of the ongoing topics, came to the fore again. In the 1960s Raman came full circle, returning to his first fascination with Helmholtz's *Physiology of Vision*, and published a volume with the same title after exhaustive experiments on the physiology of the eye.

During each decade, except for the 1960s when he worked alone, Raman trained students who went on to continue their excellent research in different parts of the country. Most of Raman's students became renowned for their contributions to science.

Nature's beauty had an immense influence on him. He focused on the optical structures that produce the colours we see in nature. He studied the plumage of birds and the phenomenon of iridescence in seashells. Of the latter, he established that iridescent shells are essentially laminates of calcium carbonate in the aragonite form, cemented together by an organic substance, the so-called conchin.

During the time that he was professor of physics at IISc (1937–48), Raman studied glass, first the shards from glass factories that were readily available, then older samples of glass from excavations in Syria. He and V.S. Rajagopalan made some fascinating discoveries about the laminae consisting of shallow cups, which form into perfectly concentric arrangements of the interference rings.

He gave G.N. Ramachandran the task of working on the mathematical aspects of the configurations he had observed. Ramachandran, or GNR (1922–2001), as he was known, became one of the leading scientific minds in the country. He had a mathematical bent of mind that perfectly complemented Raman's intuitive concepts and experimental explorations. When he first came to the institute in 1942, GNR met Raman and longed to work with him but was registered with the electrical engineering department. Several times Raman requested the head of the department to allow GNR to transfer, but the head refused. One day Raman bluntly told him, 'I am admitting Ramachandran into my department as he is a bit too bright to be in yours,' and forthwith did the paperwork for the transfer.[2] GNR turned out to be one of his very best students. He went on to make a name for himself in molecular biophysics. He was one of the ten-kilowatt brains that Raman had spotted on sight and had drawn to himself from the electrical engineering section.

Raman's work on the optical effects of stratification in glass shows once again that his was a search inspired by beauty. The beauty of this phenomenon led Raman to museums in search of ancient glass. When he was in Paris in 1937 he had noticed a vase excavated from Syria. He got some of the flakes of this glass that had also been preserved in the museum, and he and Rajagopalan studied the differences between ancient and modern decomposed glass. They noticed that 'the development of colour occurs in antique glasses to a greater depth and in a more uniform manner than in the modern specimens.' The rest of the paper was on the characteristics of the ancient glass flakes, which they studied from different angles, noting its lamellar structure, what happens when it is seen through transmitted light, through reflected light, when dipped in liquids and so on. They concluded, 'The investigation makes it clear that Brewster's explanation of the iridescence as due to films of air separating thin layers of glass is definitely erroneous.'[3]

Raman also made a significant contribution to the area of coronae and speckles. The corona, the faintly coloured luminous ring that sometimes surrounds the sun or moon, had always attracted him. He had started studying this in Calcutta itself, in his astronomy phase, with his early students, Bidhubhusan Ray and M.N. Mitra. Now, in Bangalore, he took it up again, directing his students, Balakrishnan and Ramachandran, to make the observations. The lecture that he gave on the topic starts off with directly addressing the non-specialist listener even though it is a very technical paper: 'The well-known coronae or disks of light with marginal coloured rings seen surrounding the sun or the moon when viewed through thin clouds are amongst the most familiar phenomena of meteorological optics.' Once again, Raman was ahead of others, and the observations and conclusions he and his students made in the 1940s were used extensively, and were refined only when laser technology started developing two decades later. Laser technology allowed Raman spectroscopy to be developed for a wide range of uses.

The students with whom he wrote joint papers when he was at the IISc were not many. In addition to those mentioned already, there were P. Nilakantan, B.V. Raghavendra Rao, S. Ramaseshan and K. Subbaramiah, but he supervised a great number of students, as can be seen in the several hundred papers that were published from work done in his laboratory.

~

Even as he marched forward with his students to new areas of research, Raman knew he had to lose the shackles of external forces if he were to build the centre of his dreams. Even as he broke new ground in his own research, he set about laying the foundation for his own institute.

During his difficult years as director, Raman had found great support from the maharaja of Mysore and his dewan, Sir Mirza Ismail. Sir Mirza had been the maharaja's representative on the council and though in the minority, had managed to negotiate a better deal for Raman than Raman would have got without him. In 1935 the maharaja had conferred on him the kingdom's greatest honour—Rajasabha Bhushana, jewel of the king's court.

The maharaja, Krishnaraja Wodeyar IV (1884–1940), was an enlightened ruler who led Mysore into the modern age. Gandhi called him a Rajarishi, a saintly king. He was a philosopher in his own way and great patron of the arts. Plato has said, 'The world can only be saved if the kings become philosophers and philosophers become kings,' and this was true of Krishnaraja Wodeyar. He became king at the age of eleven and under him Mysore rapidly became a model kingdom. Raman and the maharaja shared a core of values and qualities. They were adept at choosing the right person for important positions. Krishnaraja had a stellar series of prime ministers—Sir K. Seshadri Iyer, Dewan Madhava Rao, Sir M. Visvesvarayya and Sir Mirza Ismail—and a stellar court of musicians, from both the Carnatic and the Hindustani schools. During his reign Mysore became the first Indian state to generate hydroelectric power and Bangalore was the first city to have street lights (in 1905).

The maharaja saw in Raman a man worth honouring and supporting. Raman saw in Krishnaraja all that a king should be—one who had a clear vision of what he wanted for his kingdom and the intellectual and intuitive skills to find the right individuals to actualize that vision. A king is one who is given much and has the power to give but must give wisely. Krishnaraja gave wisely and generously to Raman and Raman in turn gave wisely and generously to all who worked with or for him.

Krishnaraja donated eleven acres of land for Raman's vision of the Indian Academy of Sciences. It was close to one of the four Kempegowda towers. The Kempegowda towers were built around 1597 CE by a chieftain, Kempegowda, who predicted that the city of Bangalore would spread to all the space encompassed by the towers. At some point a legend grew that the city would fall if it ever spread beyond that space. The current boom of the city, that has grown way beyond the four towers, with consequent pollution and overcrowding, might well be considered its fall by some!

Raman now knew where his centre was going to be. He could already imagine the flower gardens and trees he would grow, the residences for the office staff and students and himself, the self-contained haven of research that no outside power could assail, for he would not accept funding from the government. He could work on his science, knowing he had a place to go to when his tenure at the IISc came to an end in 1948.

In this period, his great love came to be the colours of stones and gems. Anything that provided optical questions attracted him, and he had done some work on this even in Calcutta. There is an anecdote about Raman telling his younger brother, C. Ramaswamy, to do something worthwhile with the diamond ring Ramaswamy was wearing on his finger, a gift from his father-in-law. Ramaswamy took note, made a spectroscopic examination of the diamond and found that diamond exhibits a sharp Raman Line. Bhagavantam confirmed the experiment in Raman's laboratory in Calcutta and also found a complex luminescence spectrum. Raman was very interested and after that he began to collect diamonds. He borrowed a huge 140-carat diamond from a maharaja and Bhagavantam worked two days and nights. The paper Bhagavantam wrote was immediately published. Scientists abroad were more excited with the idea of a diamond that size than with the content of the paper and got an idea of the legendary wealth in the possession of Indians. Raman bought as many diamonds as he could afford.

At the investiture ceremony of the Rajasabha Bhushana title, the maharaja had presented him with a pendant studded with sixty-three diamonds. The diamonds promptly went into Raman's study collection.

The war years

When Raman's elder son, Raja, was seventeen years old, he wished to study in England. Cambridge had made a very good impression on Raman, and it was decided Raja should be sent to Cambridge to complete his undergraduate education. Raman had great regard for Lord Rutherford who was at Cambridge and so arranged to send his son there to study physics. Raja sailed on 26 August 1939. Lokam saw him off at Bombay with great misgivings. Germany's pact with the USSR that was signed two days earlier augured imminent war. Germany invaded Poland on 1 September. Lokam immediately sent her son a telegram asking him to return from Aden. But she missed him by a day. The ship had sailed on towards the Cape of Good Hope, avoiding the war zone. England declared war on Germany on 3 September.

Raja reached England on 10 October. He fell ill shortly after but recovered quickly and set about his studies. Lokam's diary notes the dates of the various letters from him and how two or three letters sometimes came together even though he had mailed them a week apart.

After a few months, Raja decided he wanted to study law and not physics. Raman disapproved and soon father and son were estranged. When the war escalated in England the next year, Raja returned home without completing the degree. He fell into

communist company and this widened the estrangement between
father and son. Raja was arrested for alleged political activities.
The freedom movement was on and the British tried to stem
the tide by imprisoning well-educated young people whom they
suspected might become potential leaders of rebellion. Raman
and Lokam went in person to Vellore Jail to stand guarantee
and bring Raja home. Later, Raja completed his law degree from
Madras University, but did not break away from his communist
connections. The chasm between father and son now became
unbridgeable.

Lokam, however, continued to support Raja all her life, sending a
monthly allowance to help him cover basic living expenses. It is very
likely that Raman knew about this, and though he did not interfere
he did not help her either. His monthly budget-money to her, which
was generous, did not take this large chunk of expense into account
and so Lokam became very thrifty, especially in her later life, just
so she would have ready extra cash if Raja came asking.

While the relationship between father and son became non-
existent by the late 1950s, it must have been extremely painful for
Lokam, from incidents I have heard from my mother and others.
I cite just two, both of which I have heard from more than one
source. Though ready to accept money from her, Raja treated her
very badly, often calling her names that no woman should ever be
called, least of all one's mother. This infuriated Raman though he
did not break up the mother–son relationship. Occasionally, when
he needed extra cash, Raja would come in person, usually late in
the evening. He never entered the house and Lokam would go out
into the garden to meet him. Once, she tripped into a shallow pit
and fell, and was severely bruised. When she stretched her hand so
he could pull her to her feet, he said he had sworn never to touch
any woman and would not help her up.

With her death in 1980, even this tenuous thread with the family
was broken, though she had made provisions for his monthly

allowance to be continued. Raja died sometime in the early 1990s, a recluse known only by a Muslim name that he had adopted. At the time of his death, he was living in a village where the villagers considered him a hermit who was content with a quiet life. Very little is known about his life once he broke away from the family. Lokam was perhaps the only one who knew of his whereabouts at all times and she kept it to herself. It is generally believed that he continued to be a card-carrying communist though he did not engage in any public commitments to his party or practise law.

During the war years, Raman travelled widely within India and Lokam's diary details his numerous travels in one-line entries, recording the city to which he went and the dates of his departure and return. He seems to have travelled at least twice every month. His destination was often Madras or Mysore, but he travelled all over the country, especially reaching out to towns and cities in south India, which did not involve long train journeys as trips to north India would.

In 1941 the Franklin Institute in Philadelphia awarded him the Franklin Medal of Merit. He was now in the company of other medallists such as Marie Curie, Einstein, Millikan, Compton and Hubble. Among science's highest honours, the Franklin Institute Awards identify individuals whose great innovation has benefited humanity, advanced science, launched new fields of inquiry and deepened our understanding of the universe. To receive it in person, Raman planned to go by the Pacific route since the war was in full progress in Europe, but his plan could not materialize. He received the medal next year from the Governor of Madras, who came in person to Bangalore for the occasion.

In 1943 Raman started Travancore Chemicals and Manufacturing Company with one of his early students, P. Krishnamurti. He saw this as an investment and it served him well, bringing in a steady annual income that he put into his institute. In later life, Raman was extra careful with his money, mainly because he did not

have business acumen. He had invested his Nobel money with a
financier who was fraudulent and most of the amount was lost.
But Raman had no time to brood over what might have been.
Always forward-looking, Raman wrote it off as a foolish mistake,
and when he happened to meet the financier some years later, he
is said to have told him he deserved a Nobel Prize for his cunning
in duping a Nobel laureate.

Whenever his trip took him to or through Madras, he would
drop by for a visit with his brother. In 1924 CS had built a house
named 'Chandra Vilas' after his father, on Lane 8 off Edward
Elliott Road, which is now called Radhakrishnan Salai. A base in
Madras helped his children continue their school studies without
interruption. Government service meant frequent transfers from
one city to another, and CS was invariably posted to cities in
north India.

'Chandra Vilas' was in the heart of Mylapore, the West End
of elites. Large houses with spacious compounds stood on either
side and on the lanes off this road. Kapaleeswar Temple was within
walking distance, as was the beach. The ocean breeze came through
the coconut, mango, banana and jackfruit trees that flourished
around every house. In the mid-1930s CS took early retirement
from the Indian Railways, where he had been auditor general, so
that he could he could pursue his passion for music in Madras.

Raman's visits with CS were usually very short, since he was
often on his way to someplace else. But he always made time to
see his brother. Once, during the early forties, he had a lecture to
deliver at Presidency College. He had communicated his schedule
to CS, saying he would spend the morning with him. CS sent his
car and driver to receive Raman at the station. As usual, he was to
arrive early in the morning by the overnight train. The driver came
back saying he had waited for half an hour after the arrival of the
train, but had not seen Raman anywhere. CS, as usual, fretted and
fumed, first at the driver, then at his brother. How could he say

he was coming by the overnight train and change his mind? How could he give his lecture if he was not in the city yet?

Raman walked in an hour or so later. He had got out of the station and seen a phaeton at the taxi stand. He was nostalgic for the old days, for phaeton-taxis were becoming a rarity, being rapidly replaced by automobiles, one-horse tongas and hand-pulled rickshaws. He felt a great urge to ride through the city in a stately carriage drawn by horses. So he did. He went to his old haunts and along the beach before heading to 'Chandra Vilas'.[1]

CS chided him for his irresponsible behaviour. Nobel laureate he might be, but still irresponsible, he raged. And then both laughed in their loud schoolboy manner and began to talk about what they had been doing since they last met. It had always been that way, and that is how it would always be. Raman did what he wanted and CS had no compunction acting out his role of the scolding elder brother. Their relationship was often stormy, but the storm always blew over. Though they were less than three years apart, Raman called him 'Anna', older brother. CS called him 'Thambi', younger brother, in his affectionate, imperious way. One of CS's grandsons reminisced that whenever Raman dropped by, he touched his older brother's feet in the traditional manner of greeting.[2] While this seems out of character for Raman, it may be seen as an example of the natural hold that traditional customs taught in childhood had on Raman.

During this decade of travel, Raman lectured at various centres and events. Since many of his popular talks were extempore, and there are no records of the notes he might have used, we have to rely on newspaper reports, which do give us an understanding of his central ideas and vision. During the war, he was staunchly on the side of Britain. Valuing as he did the sanctity of individual rights, he saw the danger the world faced from Hitler. However, when the war ended in the cataclysm of Nagasaki and Hiroshima, he was horrified at the potential destructive power unleashed by scientific knowledge. He had always advocated that science should be used for the benefit of humanity and he addressed this issue repeatedly in the years following the end of the war.

In his research Raman led his students into new fields. After the important Raman–Nath theory phase of ultrasonics and hypersonics, he spent a few years on the study of the acoustic spectrum of liquids, the scattering of light and fluid density.

Around 1940 he started focusing on the study of diamond from different perspectives. Raman's fascination with diamond started early, as has already been noted. Raman started spending a fortune buying diamonds on his travels to Europe and the United States.

In 1942 Raman bought a store of diamonds from the famous mines of Panna in central India. These diamonds have curved surfaces unlike the usual flat surfaces. Raman had visited the kingdom and got permission to look at the collection—there were hundreds—in the state treasury. A little later, he bought eleven small diamonds from Hyderabad that were very different from the Panna diamonds. He received sixteen diamonds as a gift from the famous de Beers firm that mined South African diamonds. The pendant presented by the maharaja of Mysore had sixty-three perfect diamonds.

Anna Mani has noted that Raman had a personal collection of about 310 diamonds and just about every student working with him during the 1940s was suggested a topic in this area of study. As Anna Mani said, it was 'an exhilarating time ... to see the pieces falling into place and meaning appear out of the most scattered and disconnected observation, when controlled and guided by the master's hand'. Later, Raman acquired more diamonds, and by the 1950s he had about 600 specimens.

Raman himself worked on why the Panna diamonds have a curved surface. He posited that 'It appears highly probable that diamond results from the solidification of carbon which has assumed the liquid state under conditions of high pressure and temperature.' Because of the thermal agitation, in smaller diamonds, 'it follows that the molten carbon would assume a rounded shape'.

Raman's work on diamonds followed the same sequence as his work on light scattering, namely, numerous experiments with careful observations and tabulations. However, in the final count, he was working ahead of the times and did not have the proper instruments. Later, when more refined results were obtained due to sophisticated instruments, it was found that many of the phenomena noted by him and his students were due to impurities in the diamond lattice. They were not intrinsic to the carbon atom as he had thought.

~

This period of his scientific life was marred by a dispute with one of his close friends, Max Born. Early in his career, Born had written a paper on lattice dynamics, where he had formulated a comprehensive theory of atomic phenomena in quantum mechanics, which was way ahead of its times. His theory was venerated but unstudied for a long time. When Born visited Bangalore in the mid-1930s, he gave a series of lectures on lattice dynamics and Raman and he had vehement arguments. The arguments continued even after Born left India. Both theories agreed as far as the first order of the Raman spectrum due to absorption or reflection of infrared range was concerned, but disagreed on the interpretation of the second-order Raman spectrum in crystals. The scientific disagreements escalated as more scientists joined the controversy, and soon Raman's arguments were refuted. Raman was conclusively shown to have erred. While his explanations held true for part of the spectrum, it did not take into consideration the whole spectrum.

The Born–Raman controversy became a battle as it were between theorists and experimentalists. The positive outcome of the controversy was that Born's theory on lattice dynamics that had been ignored for years came to the forefront again and its applications became far-reaching. The negative side of the final verdict was that Raman's correct data about the specific aspects of his experiments got swept over once his major mistake was discovered.

However, some years later, in 1955, Leon Van Hove (1924–90) showed that the frequencies predicted by Raman were indeed correct within the narrower parameters of the partial spectrum. In 1970 A.K. Ramdas, who had worked with Raman in the 1950s, and S.A. Solin showed once again that Raman was on the right track, and thanks to laser technology the prominences noticed by Raman could be seen with much clearer focus.

Though they disagreed in their science, and waged a long-drawn battle of ideas, Raman had a natural affection for Born. Born reminisces about their meeting in Bordeaux in 1953, some years after the battle. Raman effusively greeted Born, but then went on to argue over their divergent views on lattice vibrations. The second time was in 1956, at the Lindau meeting of Nobel laureates. Again, Raman talked effusively on the first day but kept his distance the next day. As Born noted in his memoir, 'He must have suddenly remembered that I was his "enemy".' In short, what came naturally and spontaneously to Raman was cordiality for Born and only then the matter of their bitter scientific differences.

'Panchavati'

While all who knew Raman knew he passionately loved his country, few knew about his love for particular plots of land. During his lifetime he bought several pieces of land, and it was not as rental property or investment. It is difficult to speculate his reasons.

Just before he joined as Palit Professor, perhaps because he was so sure Calcutta was going to be home for the rest of his life, he bought land near Shillong for Rs 40,000, undertaking a sizeable mortgage commitment. But a couple of years later he seems to have regretted the debt involved.

This was the time he was suffering from frequent coughs and colds, as noted previously, and the memory of the early deaths of family members was still haunting him. Two of his siblings had died in childhood. His brother Skandan had died in 1914 and now his sister Mangalam was dead at the age of twenty-seven. He knew the burden of saddling someone with one's own debts when his father, that man with a titan's body, had died in 1910 at the early age of forty-four. He decided he would relieve his older brother of any responsibility in the mortgage should he perchance die early. So he told CS that he wanted no share in the family property and that for all legal purposes, he would dissociate his own affairs from his inheritance by signing over his share to his younger brother, Ramaswamy. CS mistook this to mean Raman was severing himself from all their common family responsibilities and they had a huge verbal battle—a not infrequent happening, given their different perspectives. CS was totally committed to the concept of family, whereas Raman, though he contributed his fair share of money, had no time, and made no secret that in his opinion children and family commitments distracted one from higher pursuits of the intellect.

Raman gave away his inheritance but his emotional love for the ancestral land was great, and when he came to know in later years through a distant cousin that his younger brother Ramaswamy had sometime ago sold his portion of the land because of lean times, Raman was much grieved. He lamented that he would have helped out even as his father had helped out when Grandfather had thought of selling some of the land to help pay for growing expenses. He even asked the cousin to negotiate with the buyer to buy it back, but the land had already been partitioned off into four or five segments though the house was still standing. In 1969, already in the shadow of death, he thought again of his ancestral home and wanted to buy not only the ancestral house but the house at Porasakudi as well, where he was born. Lokam persuaded him not to worry unduly and that they would look into the purchase once he got stronger. After his death, a cousin, Dharmambal, initiated the idea that the house in which he was born, 8 Tiruvanaikoil Street in Tiruvanaikkaval, should be preserved as a national monument. Ramaswamy and even Kanchi Sankaracharya suggested the same and there was a lot of talk but nothing came of it.

In 1928 Raman bought land near Dakin Lake in Calcutta. This shows that he had expected to continue in Calcutta for years to come. But it was not to be. In the 1930s he bought land in Madras. Lokam speaks about it in her diaries as 'the garden'.

In the early 1940s Raman's desire for his own place consumed him. As professor of physics, he still had a house on campus, close to his laboratory just as he had always advocated for all scientists. But he also looked forward to being independent of the place that had treated him so shabbily. He had already got land from the maharaja for the academy. He now needed his own house. He looked for a suitable house in Malleswaram because the space around his future institute had nobody and nothing around it at the time, though he planned to have housing built in good time for himself and everyone who would work at the new institute.

Malleswaram had been developing in recent decades. Basavangudi and Chamrajpet had been the centres of Bangalore for a very long time. But towards the end of the nineteenth century, Venkataranga Iyengar, an influential officer in government administration, saw great potential in the undeveloped land around Malleswara Temple, and he suggested that it be developed for the elite of Bangalore. Well-established families such as those of Dewan Seshadri Iyer, Dewan Krishnamurthy, and the Patankars who were related to Dewan Madhava Rao, were persuaded to move there and build their manorial estates on vast acreage land. The Indian Institute of Science was started in 1909, and the area became a prime location for an elite community.

Between the institute and the railway station were four tanks: Sampige Tank, one behind the temple down 15th Cross, another in front of the mill and the last in what later became the exhibition grounds. Houses started being built around the tanks. In several of the manorial estates in Malleswaram, there were orchards, paddy fields, temples and houses for a whole entourage of hangers-on and employees. By the 1940s, the estate owners had sold off portions of their land, on which smaller houses were built. There were several stately houses on 8th Main, each compound spread out over two acres or more. At the four corners of 8th Main and 15th Cross were four lots, each with a fair-sized house.

Three of the houses were up for sale at the time Raman cast his eyes around for a place. The location seemed ideal. Fifteenth Cross sloped downwards and any of these houses would have a good view. Raman thought the only two-storeyed house of the three available houses would be good for them but Lokam thought otherwise. Where was the need for a two-storeyed house for one's retirement years, she said. Besides, she thought one of the two single-storeyed houses had a character and personality of its own, standing as it did towards the back of the large plot, with a beautiful space in front for a flower garden. At the time, there were no trees other than coconut palms, nor was there a flower garden, but Raman could see in his mind's eye trees and flowerbeds of his choice. The house was being sold due to the bankruptcy of a businessman in the cinema industry. There was also another story around the house that it was haunted, and Raman is said to have joked that he was a greater ghost and would soon drive away the resident ghost. Lokam's diary entry records that the papers were signed on 31 March 1942. The same diary also records that Edwards Estates in Madras was bought on 14 March.

During my conversations with her, she told me that the son of the man who had built the house had visited her in 1971/72 and told her the early history of the house. The son, Ambarisha, had come wanting to see the house in which he was born about sixty years before. He had been away for many years and had now returned to Bangalore and lived in Basavangudi. As she took him around the house, he pointed to what had been Raman's bedroom and said he was born in that room. His father, Kuppuswamy Arasu, had built it around 1911–12. Ambarisha's mother had died when he was four or five, and soon after that his father had sold the house and gone away. He knew the house had changed hands several times since the 1920s but did not know its later history.[1]

On the first day of their ownership, as they walked into the compound, Lokam suggested that they should name it 'Panchavati', after the hermitage where the epic characters Rama and Sita had spent the most peaceful time of their life. Raman liked the name and its association and went to the post office the same day to register the name. While they continued to live on the IISc campus, the 'Panchavati' compound was landscaped with trees selected by Raman and the house was later rented out on a short lease.

Raman also bought an estate of one hundred acres at Kengeri, a village about eight miles from Bangalore. It was his weekend retreat. Lokam's diaries show that they spent many weekends there, leaving on Saturday morning and returning on Sunday evening. They had a house at Kengeri, and it was a running household. For many years, Lokam's two widowed sisters, Meenakka and Parvathamakka, lived there, and it had servants to take care of the estate. They also had cows, and Lokam would always have one or two of the milking cows and their calves at 'Panchavati' while the other cows stayed at Kengeri. In Kengeri, Raman would walk several miles each day.

When Raman retired from the IISc, he moved from the campus to 'Panchavati'. He had wanted to renovate it a year ahead of his retirement, but those who had rented it from him to run a Harijan hostel would not leave and had to be legally evicted, and this took time. They moved into the unrenovated house. Their younger son, Radhakrishnan, helped with ideas on how to remodel the house, especially the kitchen wing so as to make it convenient for his mother.

'Panchavati' did indeed prove a haven of peace once they settled down. At first, Raman started to cycle from home to his new institute, which was still under construction but had basic equipment so that he could continue to research. He was a clumsy cyclist and paid scant heed to traffic. After a few months, Lokam persuaded him to use the car. The day paced itself to a more relaxed routine, with a more regular schedule of mealtimes and rest times. The driver had as long a day as his master—off to the institute around 6 a.m., back for breakfast a couple of hours later and then again to the laboratory, back at noon for two hours of lunch and rest, and then another two or three hours of work at the institute. Often, in the evening, Raman would go to Cubbon Park.

Lokam's diaries have a log of the cars they owned over the years. They had a Willys that had been bought on 19 October 1941 for Rs 5150. A second car was bought, for Lokam, in 1950, a DeSoto. Lokam's diary entry reads: 'Friday, May 5, 1950 DeSoto car arrived from Calcutta.' In 1957 they bought a two-tone, silver-grey Studebaker, which was Raman's favourite and most used car for the rest of his life. The Studebaker is still in existence and is, I believe, a treasured relic.

Other entries read: 'January 1961: bought an Ambassador for 15,000'; 'January 21, 1961—sold Willys for Rs. 1700.'

~

In the latter half of the 1950s, two of my siblings and I spent two summers at 'Panchavati'. In the 1960s, I was at 'Panchavati' during my college vacations, since my parents had moved there after the Ramans moved to the director's bungalow at the Raman Institute, and what follow are my memories.

'Panchavati' had a retinue of servants. Raman's driver, Parthasarathy, was a patient, stolid man who grew stouter with years in the service of his master. I remember being chauffeured in the mid-1960s by this faithful driver and I thought his driving was very jerky. But perhaps he never had an accident in all the years he was with Raman and Raman thought the world of him. Jayaraman, in his memoir of Raman, notes that Parthasarathy's watch had only the hour hand, but Raman relied on him to tell the time since he himself seldom wore a watch.

Everyone in Raman's employ was like the driver—patient, loyal and with him forever. There was Hyder, a watchman. He was a frail old man with a long white beard, who looked like he would drop to the ground if ever an intruder so much as touched him, but he was always there, walking his rounds several times each night, knock-knocking his staff on the ground.

And then there was Muthan. He swept the large compound, tended the flowerbeds and took care of the cows. Ramrod straight, with chiselled features and a perennial seven-day grey beard, he would do the chores around the garden much of the day, though the cows were his treasured charges. I remember him massaging a cow in labour, washing the newborn calf with expertise and love and smiling his toothless smile when it sprang up and away.

There was Abdul, sometimes slow to comprehend but always ready to serve and obey. Once Raman told him to buy *kudirai laddi* (horse manure), but he heard it as *kudirai vandi* (horse cart) and next morning there was a horse-drawn cart at their gate, with bells and ribbons for decoration, and the owner/driver extolling the qualities of the horse, much to Lokam's bewilderment as to what it was all about.

There was a live-in cook, Chakrapani, with a bald head and thick spectacles, whose culinary skills were mediocre, but he was regular and silent and dependable.

Raman had a huge personal library at 'Panchavati'. There were several glass-doored, floor-to-ceiling almirahs in the central hall and in his bedroom, stacked with beautifully bound sets of the English classics and the European classics in translation. Raman's library had an air of splendour, with its rows of uniform hardcover editions, not only of the usual classics but, in his bedroom, a whole wall-to-wall almirah of what would now be termed literature for adolescents. All the classical writers were there—Lewis Carroll, Robert Louis Stevenson, Arthur Conan Doyle, Jules Verne, et al.—but also volumes of Boys' Own Annuals, complete set of G.A. Henty's novels, James Hilton, Frank Richards (Charles Hamilton, creator of Billy Bunter stories), and omnibus volumes of tales of ghosts and the supernatural. I believe Raman read and re-read most of these volumes. To me it was a memorable experience to know the great scientist was steeped in such literature.

The main house of 'Panchavati' was spacious but not manorial in its dimensions, the way the director's bungalows at both the institutes were. There was a large hall with verandas at the front and back. The hall was about forty-five feet by twenty feet and we children used to pretend it was a badminton court especially since it had a wooden partition at the middle that was about five feet high. This central hall was flanked by three rooms and a bathroom on each side. Raman's bedroom was to the right as one faced the house, the small room behind it was his dressing room, and there was a bathroom between it and the farther room at the back that opened on to the back veranda. The other wing was Lady Raman's. Her bedroom was the room off the back veranda. Her mattress was cotton-filled and thin, whereas his was queen-size and deep. Her cot had a simple wooden headboard, his was an ornately carved bedstead with foot-posts and narrow mirrors on the headboard and footboard. There were woollen carpets worn with age in all the rooms, and the front portion of the hall had enormous sofas of dark green leather into which a teenager could disappear out of sight.

There was a long covered corridor at the back, open on both sides, that led to the kitchen wing of the house. The central room was the dining room, flanked by two rooms on either side, a puja room and storeroom on one side and the kitchens on the other. There were two kitchens, one where lunch was cooked on wood stoves, and the other where tiffin and dinner were cooked on electric and Primus stoves. All four side rooms had a *paran*, a loft where larger cooking vessels and boxes were stored. There was a small veranda at the front and a veranda at the back, which opened to the second kitchen on one side and the bathroom behind the wall of the puja room on the other. Lokam used the puja room every day, Raman never.

There was also a three-room cottage along the back wall on the right and numerous rooms by the rear and left walls, used as servants' quarters, cowsheds, etc.

The cottage was occupied much of the time by one or other guest from abroad or from outside Bangalore, people who wanted a place to stay for several weeks at a time. I remember some of those who stayed at the cottage for long periods of time over the fifteen years of my association with 'Panchavati', particularly a German lady, then two cousins of mine and then a young foreign couple, French as I recall, who wore orange robes and had found their guru in Kerala. The man was an artist, who presented me with a spirograph-looking tantric geometry design that he had painted; recent research shows he lived in the cottage for some time even a few years ago.

The Ramans moved to the director's bungalow on the RRI campus towards the end of the 1950s and some of the servants moved with them and some left. A few them stayed on, including Muthan, for 'Panchavati' was still a running household, with cows and calves, storage of the yearly stock of grain, etc., and its well-maintained garden of fruit trees and flowers.

In 1958 my father, A.S. Ganesan, one of Raman's early students, had taken up the editorship of *Current Science* after retiring from his professorship in Madhya Pradesh, and was allotted one of the quarters in the staff enclave close to RRI. Within a year or two, when the Ramans moved to the director's bungalow, he was moved into 'Panchavati' to make the staff quarter available to someone else. My mother was CS's eldest daughter, Rajalakshmi, and the arrangement of entrusting 'Panchavati' to my parents worked out well. The Child Welfare Office, where Lokam was the president, was located in one of the rooms of 'Panchavati', and so she came there every day. Raman, too, liked to visit and walk about the garden.

The loyal servants employed by my parents and by the Ramans continued to take care of the house after my mother's death in 1968. Among these was Devamma, who washed the vessels and cleaned the kitchen stoves, scrupulously thrifty with the thin stream of water from the backyard tap. There was Thimmamma, who seldom spoke perhaps because there was forever a wad of tobacco in her cheek, but she conscientiously swept the floor and washed the clothes.

When Lokam moved back to 'Panchavati' in 1971, after Raman's death, Parthasarathy had been pensioned off and there was a young driver, Raju. There was a Gurkha watchman, Pratap, who had lived at 'Panchavati' quarters even when he was night watchman at the institute. Like many Gurkha watchmen, Pratap went back to Nepal for six to eight weeks every year. One day, Lokam saw him knitting a baby bootee and only then discovered that he had got married on his last visit, and now had a baby girl whom he would soon be seeing for the first time. Lokam arranged for him to bring back his wife and baby, and soon Pratap had two more babies in quick succession. Mangala, the oldest, was Lokam's favourite and Lokam usually fed her from her own plate before having her meals.

I felt I should make this digression into the Ramans' servants to remember not only an age of retainers that has vanished but also the loyalty that Raman commanded not just from his students but from all who worked for him. He looked after their basic expenses and needs. He had the habit of going to the bank on the first working day of every month to withdraw money and would insist on getting sheaves of crisp new currency bills instead of grimy, tattered notes. He would come back and pay each employee in the office and the maintenance staff, drawing an aesthetic pleasure from handling and handing out fresh-from-the-mint currency notes.

Raman had great consideration not only for his students and associates but indeed for all who worked with him and for him. Jayaraman relates an anecdote from the time the Raman Institute was being built. Raman came across a labourer who was ailing but was still at work. Raman immediately ensured he got medical attention and that he would not have to forego his daily wages.

Raman Research Institute

Once Lady Raman, as asked by Raman, brought some British scientists from their hotel to the Raman Institute. Not seeing Raman at his office, she escorted them around the building, explaining various aspects of the institute. Since it was unusual for him to miss an appointment, she thought they would run into him in one of the rooms, but he was nowhere to be found. Nor did she see any one of the handful of students he had at the time. She continued showing the visitors around and they came to the Gem Room, a dark room in which Raman had his diamond and gem collection. She opened the door, said in a low tone, '*Idu enna koothu?* (What is this tamasha?)' and closed the door, telling the visitors, 'He doesn't seem to be here either.' She led them back to the office to wait for him. Raman was indeed in that room, with his students. All of them were stripped to their underwear. Raman had been explaining the experiments he wanted done, and one of the diamonds had disappeared. Everyone had stripped to see if it had slipped into their clothes, and so there they were, scientist and students, near naked and quite distraught.

This familiar episode is often repeated among the inner group when reminiscing about the early years of the Raman Institute.

~

Shortly after Raman started the Indian Academy of Sciences in 1934, the maharaja of Mysore gifted eleven acres of land for Raman's work. A few years later, at Raman's request, he gifted another four acres to the south side of the campus.

In 1943 Raman and the academy executed a formal agreement that a research institute would be built on the site, which would be independent of the academy and under Raman's management, with him providing the entire funding. Again, he was careful to retain control of the proposed centre and to be totally responsible both for its operation and its operating costs. Around the same time, in order to generate money for the institute he invested in a company, Travancore Chemicals.

He fenced in the area and planted flowering trees and shrubs and fast-growing trees. He had a grove of eucalyptus trees on the eastern side, so that he could block the view of the IISc whose towers could be been from his campus. Once the trees grew, he thought, the view would be perfect. The maharaja had several palaces in the city and each stood in a vast compound and garden. One of the palaces was close by. One would see Nandi Hills to the north, the Kempegowda tower adjoining his property, and green fields and palace gardens to the south and west. However, by the time the trees grew tall enough to block the institute towers, the area started developing fast, and the view was not as idyllic as Raman had hoped. But by then he had developed a sunken garden on the southern side, with a rose garden and flowering trees. The barbed-wire fence had been replaced by a stone wall, and he could walk in his own world, among his roses and hibiscus, eucalyptus and jacaranda.

~

At the time of his retirement in 1948, Raman's new institute was barely ready for occupation and construction was still on. As Raman did not believe in either the fanfare of a formal inauguration or the need for a religious ceremony, he continued his daily routine at the unfinished building, while planning and supervising all the details of construction and equipment-ordering.

The main building was an imposing two-storeyed structure, with large, airy rooms, granite staircases and floors and a stone-blocks exterior, and a veranda in front with ten pillars on each floor.

One of the first rooms to be furnished was the lecture theatre, with 100 extremely comfortable plush-upholstered chairs. The blackboard was of thick darkened plate glass, finely ground. Raman had purchased the latest models of microscopes, balances and spectrometers. But he also got a lot of used equipment. When the Second World War ended, the Deployable Ground Data Terminal (DGTD) of the US Army released all their surplus equipment to various educational and research centres in the region, and Raman applied for and got a good share for his institute. The equipment he selected consisted of aerial cameras, optical systems, infrared viewers and detectors, magnetrons, microwave generators, oscilloscopes, various electronic equipment, and also a large number of machine tools and lathes. Another good acquisition was a liquid oxygen/nitrogen plant. Few of the equipment were in working condition, but Raman had an ability to pick good technicians and mechanics who could repair them.

He moved his gems, other collections and library to the new building. Two of the rooms were the museum, in which was his collection of minerals, gemstones and crystals that he had expanded over the years. Mirror-backed, glass-shelved showcases displayed 'rocks and stones of every shade and colour, minerals of every hue and tint, crystals of every sheen and lustre, and gems of every form and fire'.[1] UV lights placed strategically, when switched on, made it a veritable Ali Baba's cave of gems. The other museum room had stuffed birds with colourful plumage, some of which Raman had studied in great detail.

He set up his experimental apparatus, but there was no electricity. This did not faze him a bit for there was nature's own sunlight. As always, he knew how to maximize on basics and devised means of harnessing sunlight for his experiments, with a heliostat that directed sunlight into his optics laboratory all day. He had a dark room on either side of his bright, airy laboratory and that was all he needed for what he was studying at the time. Filtered sunlight was excellent for the study of fluorescence in diamond and Raman could sit for hours in a darkened room observing a single beam of sunlight playing on a gem and recording the luminescence patterns.

His first office employee was a stenotypist, appointed in 1949. Towards the end of that summer, he appointed a technical assistant named J. Padmanabhan. Padmanabhan, like most of those who worked for Raman, was excellent at assimilating knowledge. Raman needed spheres of quartz for his research and Padmanabhan devised his own method that he perfected with time. Raman would go into raptures at his workmanship. One of Raman's qualities was his enthusiasm for admiring work that was well executed. Over the years that he worked with Raman, Padmanabhan himself became an expert at assessing the quality of diamonds.

The Raman spectrum enables one to know if the diamond is flawed or perfect. Perfect diamonds exhibit an absorption of infrared radiation in the spectral region of the fundamental atomic vibration frequencies. Simple tests will reveal their non-centrosymmetric structure. Padmanabhan was always in great demand during the wedding season when diamonds had to be bought for sons-in-laws' rings!

An hour of conversation with Padmanabhan was a most pleasurable and informative experience in itself for he worked with Raman for twenty years and was an excellent raconteur. He could give an insightful conducted tour of the gem collection as articulately as he could narrate anecdotes about Raman's idiosyncrasies, of which there were many.

Here is one example: One day Raman rang his wife from his office to immediately send two pillows. Perturbed at what might have happened, she sent pillows from the director's bungalow and sent for Padmanabhan to find out if Raman had perhaps fallen somewhere. Raman did not like to make a fuss about himself and so she was concerned that he might be minimizing his injury. But Padmanabhan reassured her that all was well, for he had seen what Raman had done with the pillows. He had piled them on the telephone, and placed the telephone directory on them to boot, to muffle the ring of the phone so that he could work in peace. If he heard the ring, he would feel a moral compunction to answer.

After employing Padmanabhan and the stenographer, Raman set about hand-picking students to work with him. Alongside, he equipped the laboratories with necessary apparatus and appointed very competent mechanics, concretizing one of his basic philosophies that a laboratory should have mechanics and technicians who could make and repair apparatus on site, to avoid undue dependence on imported equipment. Carpenters and bookbinders were also on his payroll.

The next five years were spent on continuing what he had started at the Indian Institute—the study of precious stones and crystallography. He worked with every precious stone one can think of, though diamond was perhaps his favourite because of the sheer beauty of its colours.

Colours held a fascination for him all his life. Just as the Maidan in Calcutta was his favourite space for his walks, Cubbon Park in Bangalore was his favourite destination. He would be chauffeured to Cubbon Park several times a week to spend two hours walking in the well-maintained gardens. One evening, Satish Dhawan (who later became director of the IISc) and Ramakrishna (a professor at the IISc) saw him bending over the ground and they approached him to join the search. It turned out that he had not lost anything but was merely collecting wings of dead moths. He took them to the street lamp and shared his excitement at the brilliant diffractive colours of the wings.[2]

Often Lokam would find seeds in his coat pockets. He never missed the horticultural shows for which Bangalore is famous. He loved the plumage of birds and had a collection of stuffed birds in his museum. For one of his projects, he bought a great many saris of different colours though he was studying only the types of silk. He is also said to have burnt a great many of them to show how artificial silks were a fire hazard since they were very flammable. I remember Lokam once telling us, when my sister and I were showing off our new, inexpensive Aurangabadi silk saris, that we had better not bring the saris to Raman's notice, else he would burn them to warn us of the risk of wearing them!

Alongside his regular schedule of work, Raman expanded the institute facilities. A workshop was built very early and then an observatory for he never gave up on his love of star-gazing. It was not developed in his lifetime, but in the 1980s the institute became a strong centre for astronomical research.

In the late 1950s Raman acquired another five acres of land on the eastern side, to house the library. As always, the first project was to landscape the area and plant trees.

He also spent a lot of thought and planning on the students' hostel within the campus and on the staff quarters on a plot of land within walking distance of the campus. When it came to building the director's bungalow, he planned every detail of the garden—the pergola of scented flowers in front, the stepped rose garden, the spacious curve of the veranda at the back that overlooked a flower garden. Knowing that Lokam did not at all look forward to moving from 'Panchavati'—or perhaps due to the attraction of getting a good sum as rent since funds for running the institute were always in short supply—when the bungalow was ready, Raman decided to rent it out to an American professor for two years. He very soon regretted it for he had always believed that a scientist's residence should be close to the laboratory. As soon as the period of contract ended, around 1959, he moved from 'Panchavati' to the director's bungalow, and his long workdays started again, though they were not as long as they had been in Calcutta, when he was much younger.

He was very proud of the institute and freely welcomed visitors even when they came unannounced. He would show them around, opening the museum door with one of the heavy bunch of keys that he carried around. In the early days of the institute, he had an elaborate system of locks and keys to the laboratory and steel cabinet; only he would open the safe, and ensure that he promptly got back any key that was taken from him to open any room. Later, he gave his students duplicate sets of keys for the laboratories. There were many renowned scientists who made a special visit to Bangalore after attending the annual conferences of the Indian Science Congress or the Indian Academy of Science. The Russian delegations were usually the largest. Much as Raman disliked communism, he welcomed them as scientists. However, in the mid-1950s, increasingly frustrated at the direction that science development was taking, he began to be more selective with visitors.

On 18 April 1955 Albert Einstein died in Princeton. When Raman heard the news, he promptly sent for a barber to have his head shaved—a Hindu ritual performed by a man on his father's death.[3]

In 1956 Raman bequeathed all of his assets, movable and immovable, to the academy with a trust that would provide for various expenses. Before doing so, he wrote to his two sons about his plan and asked if they needed anything for themselves. The elder son tersely replied that since he had cut himself off from all family ties, he did not care what Raman did with his property.

The younger son wrote back politely, saying that since Raman had dedicated his life to science, it was logical and right that he should give his material assets too to the cause of science. However, he added, he hoped that Raman would fully provide for his wife since his sons might not be able to give her the financial support she deserved.[4] He need not have worried, of course.

Raman was invited to conferences organized by the Nobel organization. In 1956 he attended the Lindau Conference of Nobel Prizemen in Physics. It was held at Lake Constance in Germany. But two years later, he declined an invitation to attend a dinner in New York in honour of Lester Pearson who had been awarded the Nobel Peace Prize in 1957. However, he sent a message about the great advances of modern science.

It is the saddest of thoughts that those very advances in knowledge threaten today to lead to an overwhelming catastrophe to humanity in the shape of a world-wide conflict. A special responsibility, therefore, rests today upon the leaders of science in every country to do their best to prevent such a conflict materialising. Fundamental thinking on the same high level that has resulted in the great scientific discoveries of the century needs to be devoted to the subject of human relationships between the large groups of human beings, which seem to be separated today from one another by differences in their way of life.[5]

The same year, he was invited to Russia to receive the Lenin Peace Prize. A reporter from *Pravda* interviewed him following the announcement. As in his Nobel speech, he was emotional about what the prize meant to India. He said, 'My heart filled with great joy and pride for my country and my people, for the Lenin Prize is more than a recognition of my efforts in defence of peace. It is a recognition of the peaceful policy of India.'[6]

Raman's dislike of communism was well known, but this honour, like the knighthood conferred by Britain, was for him beyond the lines of political ideology. On 9 May 1958 Raman, accompanied by Lokam, sailed from Bombay to Genoa on a three-month tour of European countries, at the invitation of the Russian Academy of Science Institutions, and to receive the Lenin Prize. Hungary had gone through political changes in the last two decades, as had the Hungarian Academy. That year Raman was re-elected to the fellowship of the Hungarian Academy of Sciences and invited to Hungary to be honoured. The Ramans went to Budapest to receive the honour.

Their younger son, Radhakrishnan, joined them and the three travelled together. At the time Radhakrishnan was working at the Chalmers University of Technology, Gothenburg, Sweden, as a research assistant. In the next decade he went on to become a renowned radio astronomer studying the polarization of radio waves, especially from the Van Allen-like belts surrounding Jupiter. He was also the first in systematic application of interferometry to polarized brightness distributions and an early study of the Zeeman Effect in the 21-cm line emitted by a hydrogen atom. His measurements of polarization of Vela Pulsar were decisive in establishing the picture of a magnetized rotating neutron star and led him to propose the paradigm of curvature radiation from polar caps of neutron stars, which has dominated the subject of pulsar emission mechanisms since that time.

The Ramans visited Czechoslovakia, Yugoslavia, Italy, Austria and Russia. In Russia, Raman was presented the Lenin Peace Prize for 'outstanding services in the struggle for the preservation and consolidation of peace'. Many times, including at the Nobel banquet speech, Raman had talked about the dangers of scientific knowledge. His speech this time too was a passionate plea to scientists and governments to promote peace and understanding, and not to escalate adversarial developments.

After thanking the presenters for recognizing India as 'a sincere champion of peace', he went on to say he regretted that advancements in physics were being used to manufacture weapons of destruction. He said, 'Japan had experienced the power of this weapon . . . but those who created this weapon failed to take note of the fact that other countries too could develop this weapon and that they themselves could fall victims to similar or more terrible trials.'[7]

Mister Prime Minister, all that glitters is not gold

When the annual academy meeting was held in Bangalore in 1948, Raman took Jawaharlal Nehru around the Crystallographic Exhibition that he had mounted. Raman showed one of his magician tricks. He placed a piece of copper and a piece of gold on Nehru's palm, switched off the overhead light and asked Nehru to identify which was the gold piece and which the copper. Nehru identified the brighter piece under the ultraviolet light as gold, and Raman laughed. 'Mister Prime Minister, all that glitters is not gold.'

The relationship between Raman and Nehru is material for drama. It was stormy on Raman's side and cordial on Nehru's side. It emerged from their different visions. Both wanted India to acquire an honoured place in the comity of nations, but each had different responsibilities that required different strategies. The autonomy that the scientist prized and relentlessly practised was totally impractical for the politician. The scientist's world was a hand-picked group of hard workers, all trained to get positive results, led by one man's vision of science. The politician's world was a huge democracy of disparate and chaotic groups, all of whom had to be given a measure of satisfaction whether the results warranted it or not, and the leader had perforce to rely on others who might not share his vision. Raman could afford to be independent and autocratic and uncorrupted. Nehru could not, tied down by the usual procedures followed in politics to keep the electorate on one's side.

As Raman prepared for retirement, Prime Minister Jawaharlal Nehru wanted to help fund the operating costs of the new Raman Research Institute and the announcement was to be made at the reception held on the occasion of Raman's retirement. There was just the usual condition, that the government be given an annual report accounting where the money was spent. When he was briefed about it, Raman flatly rejected any offer that came with strings attached, and the announcement was never made.

Given his careful accounting habits, Raman would have kept his own records where and when every rupee was spent, but he did not want to be answerable to a bureaucracy. He had suffered enough at the hands of those who had stabbed him under cover of 'due process'. However, Nehru apparently did not take offence, and went ahead with awarding him the first National Professorship, which was without any stipulations. Raman was India's first National Professor—a lifetime appointment. This came with a monthly income of Rs 2500.

Nehru and Raman had crossed paths several times before Independence and their friendship started off well enough. Nehru's commitment to science was clear. He made some choices that Raman did not approve of, but the field was still wide open and their relationship was cordial.

Nehru sent an autographed copy of the second edition of *The Discovery of India* to Raman with the handwritten inscription: 'To Sir Chandrashekhar [*sic*] Raman with all good wishes for the advancement of science in India. Jawaharlal Nehru. January 1, 1947.'

The thirty-sixth Indian Science Congress was held in the first week of January 1949, in Allahabad. Raman and Lokam flew to Bombay on 1 January and took the night train to Allahabad, arriving late at night. Sarojini Naidu welcomed them at Government House and next morning they went to Anand Bhavan and met with Nehru, his sister Vijayalakshmi Pandit and the rest of the family. The family had gathered for the wedding celebrations of Vijayalakshmi Pandit's daughter, Nayantara Sahgal. After the opening of the Science Congress at 2 p.m., they went to a garden party in connection with the wedding. On 5 January there was an event at Senate Hall, to celebrate Raman's sixtieth birthday (although his date of birth was actually 7 November, the Science Congress celebrated it during its session.) K.S. Krishnan, the president of the Science Congress, spoke on the occasion, as did Sarojini Naidu. Raman gave an extempore speech.

In October 1950 the Ramans were on their way to the Kanpur Sugar Factory Silver Jubilee celebrations at which Raman was to be chief guest. They first went to Delhi by plane. Lokam was airsick and rested after the flight, while Raman went to a party being hosted by Nehru.

There is a story that the government considered Raman for the vice-presidentship (*sic*) of India. He is said to have laughed it off with a 'What would I do with that ship?'

Once, when Nehru was in Bangalore with his daughter, Raman gave Indira Gandhi a conducted tour and told her, 'Tell your papa what you saw and ask him to visit my institute.'[1] Later that afternoon, he got a call from Nehru's secretary that Nehru would like to visit the institute the next morning!

On 15 August 1954 Raman was given India's highest honour— the Bharat Ratna. He was one of three recipients of the honour, given for the first time that year, the other two being President Radhakrishnan and veteran statesman C. Rajagopalachari. Oddly enough, Raman did not go to Delhi to receive the award. When President Rajendra Prasad sent a telegram on the evening of 19 January 1955 asking when he would be arriving so they could make 'reception arrangements', he sent a reply on the twentieth saying he would not be present because 'I am firmly tied down here to enable one of my students to complete his Doctorate thesis which the Regulations require him to submit to his University before the end of January. Thus my duty as a teacher has to take precedence over my own personal affairs'.

~

Nehru was certainly instrumental in awarding Raman the National Professorship and the Bharat Ratna. But, by now, Raman was of the firm opinion that the government policies being pursued would not benefit scientific progress but merely build façades run by the bureaucracy. The government was spending vast sums of money on establishing centres for the development and application of science. Millions were being spent on the import of equipment and on delegations that were sent to study how science was supported in other countries. National laboratories were being set up all over the country, but they were a world apart from places where foundational love for the sciences could be nurtured. These centres lured away the best minds in science from the universities, leaving them without any teaching responsibilities, which in turn prevented both them and the younger generation from inspiring each other. Soon the national laboratories became what the Indian Institute of Science had been before Raman shook it up—a place where sinecure scientists did little by way of innovation or discovery. This riled Raman no end.

   He held Nehru responsible. He felt Nehru had allowed Indian science to be hijacked by self-serving people who were given control of policy-making. Unlike Krishnaraja Wodeyar IV, Nehru was a 'king' with great powers but he had given those powers away to wastrels and opportunists. Raman could not accept that betrayal. He would not take into account the magnitude of the task before Nehru, or the pitfalls that perforce appear with a fledgling democracy, where opportunists can easily paint a veneer of democratic principles over their own incompetence or self-interest or both. Nehru trusted his advisers and Raman felt they were not worthy of that trust. Raman faulted Nehru for not having the knowledge, the intuition, what you will, to find the right people for the advancement of Indian science. All that glitters is not gold. Nehru had chosen the copper piece again and again, fooled by light that did not emerge from the natural light of wisdom. This seems to have been Raman's position.

Towards the end of his tenure at the IISc, Raman was appointed a member of the World Bank Advisory Board and twice he travelled abroad on delegation. He gave lectures in the United States while on delegation, once saying that the United States was making such spectacular progress in science because the government did not interfere in the running of research centres.

He was also invited to travel in the United States following his retirement, but he cancelled it because his priority had by then become the running costs of the new institute. He had to concentrate on getting donations, especially since he had lost a lot of his money by entrusting it to a banker who failed disastrously.

On one of Nehru's visits, Raman gave him a tour of the Raman Institute, and also a lecture on the need for an endowment of one million rupees so that the research base could expand. But Nehru would not commit himself and said instead, 'Raman, why do you worry about the future of your institute?' Raman shot back, 'I certainly don't want this institute to become another government laboratory.'

~

By mid-1950s there were many aspects of science planning that were against Raman's credo of self-reliance and hard work he wanted promoted at the personal and national levels. Raman blamed it all on Nehru, for his lack of wisdom or intuition to lead Indian science to self-sufficiency and research achievements.

There is a story of Raman entering his drawing room, picking up a bust of Nehru that stood on a shelf and hurling it to the ground, before going back to his room.[2] Several family members have narrated this story with slightly different variations. Sekhar dates it to the summer of 1955 and says he was actually sunk in one of the huge chairs in the room and was probably not noticed by Raman who came into the room, broke the bust and then bawled out 'LOGAM'. When she hurried in, Raman told her the bust had fallen and to have it cleaned up. When Sekhar told Lokam what he had seen and doubted it was an accident, she said with a laugh, 'You don't have to tell me that. I know it was intentional.'

There is an explanation given by a person close to him that it was about this time that—knowing Raman badly needed funds to run his institute—government representatives offered to provide funds if he would only provide the government with a certain kind of research, research that would be useful for India's defence ministry. This funding proposal that came with strings enraged Raman and reinforced his belief that taking government money was almost the same as selling one's soul.

When Raman's photographer friend T.S. Satyan was covering the 1960 All India Congress Committee session, and visited him with the journalist Donald S. Connery, Raman told them, 'While I admire Nehru personally, I dislike the cronies around him.' He referred to the AICC session as 'a big tamasha where they just talk, talk and talk from morning till night'.

I heard a story from my sister Vasanti of a motorcade in Bangalore where Raman accompanied Nehru, who was standing in the open-topped car, clearly beaming with pleasure as people waved and cheered from either side of the road. Raman said to him, 'Is that all it takes to make you happy?' However, we must remember that Raman himself loved to be feted and applauded.

In March 1962 the Ramans were in Delhi and were invited by Nehru for dinner on the fourteenth. They declined. So Nehru asked them to join a small lunch party the next day, and they could not refuse. There were only fifteen guests at the lunch, Indira Gandhi and Vijayalakshmi Pandit among them. Lokam has recorded in her diary that the meeting was pleasant.

Ila Chandrasekhar (wife of Raman's sister's son Chandrasekhar) relates a story of the time she visited him during his anti-Nehru phase. He was in a jolly mood and in the course of conversation told her with a loud laugh that he had got his first sliver of platinum when he smashed his Bharat Ratna medal with a hammer. This story is also said to have been used in one of his lectures where he talked about a series of experiments that required platinum; that in a rage at the government for their ill-conceived policies on science, he had taken a hammer to his Bharat Ratna medal, and when it broke, he had found the platinum.

In the mid-1960s, even after Nehru's death, Raman would not mince his words. Once, when my husband and I were visiting Bangalore, a senior person from All India Radio came for a visit, to request Raman to say something on Nehru's role in science planning for a special programme they were planning for Nehru's birthday. Raman told him half jokingly, half seriously, 'What? Do you want to lose your job? If you air what I have to say, you will surely be fired.'

Raman had no patience with the charades of politics. Many of the lighter parts of his speeches poked fun at the superficialities of the public masks put on by politicians. In his address in Madras at the IIT (Indian Institute of Technology) convocation of 1966, he recalled the occasion at which the collaboration between Germany and India for the creation of the IIT was initiated: in 1956 there was a lunch at the Rashtrapati Bhavan, attended by Nehru and

high-level representatives from both governments, and everything
that was said was translated into English or German as the case
warranted. Raman said he did not remember what was said, but 'I
presume it was the usual declarations of mutual love and affection
which are always made when dignitaries meet'.[3]

Since Raman made no secret of the contempt he felt for the
lip-service of politicians, it was not unnatural that politicians
were seldom on his side. Nehru, however, was above that. He
clearly thought very well of Raman, but Raman felt that newly
independent India was taking the wrong road in its science
planning and Nehru was responsible for it.

Raman was passionate about science policies in India and about
India's standing in the international community. Right from his
Calcutta days, he had emphasized the importance of making on
site the instruments needed for research. It irked him that the
government was bent on spending millions of rupees importing
instruments instead of encouraging Indian technicians and
craftsmen, in whose competence Raman had great faith.

He talked about India's potential many times, but his speech
at St Joseph's College in 1954 sums it up succinctly:

> There will be no science in India if we continue to rely on
> imported American and German equipment for research work.
> ... Do not buy such equipment but make your own. Science
> can and shall advance in simple ways. We often pay Rs. 50,000
> for something we can ourselves make for Rs. 5,000. ... There
> will be no salvation and no real advance at this rate.[4]

In Raman's opinion, science planning only got worse in the
1960s. The media loved to needle him into expressing his opinions
and they were seldom disappointed. Of the national laboratories,
which had atrophied during the previous decade, he said, 'Shah
Jehan built the Taj Mahal to bury one of his favourite women.

Bhatnagar built the national laboratories to bury scientific instruments.'[5] He zeroed in on one of the standard defences as to why the laboratories were not turning out good science—that when parts broke or became dysfunctional, it took a long time to import the replacements. India depended too heavily on other countries whereas he would have seen to it that India manufactured its own instruments.

Raman had strong opinions on non-scientific matters as well. Asked by the *Indian Express* to say a few words for the Independence Day of 1952, he said:

> Looking around and sizing the situation, it seems to me that the real danger before our country is the crushing down of individual freedom and initiative by the steamroller of government authority. Already we see indications of this in the . . . legislative measures having an expropriatory [sic] character and the passage of taxation and other bills calculated to kill private enterprise in the field of industrial development . . . . Democracy without freedom for the individual is a sham and a delusion.

Raman was always aware of the practical applications of science and talked about the need to explore scientific frontiers for the benefit of humanity. For example, in the 1950s he got interested in the science of meteorology. In 1951 he convened a symposium on the 'Physics of Thunderstorms'. He wanted scientists to find out more about the electrical aspects of thunderstorms and their bearing on the structure of aircraft. In 1962 and 1964 he invited oceanographers and meteorologists to organize symposia to give an impetus to the further development of the science in India. Even at the last meeting of the academy held in his lifetime, he made sure that there was a lecture on current developments.

In the decade that followed Independence, India sent thousands of students to be trained abroad, whereas like his wish to invite Jewish scientists in the 1930s, Raman felt experts should be invited to spend time in India so that interest in science would spread at the grass-roots level and inspire many to contemplate a life in science. He wanted originality in students and individual freedom for them, but the new system, he felt, encouraged aping the West and a certain subservience to the know-how of the Western world. He saw in anguish that the system not only throve on bureaucracy but that this monster was swallowing up even those scientists he knew well, like Bhabha and Krishnan, who sincerely believed they were serving the country by joining government initiatives. And then there were the many who left India for other countries. To him it seemed scientists had abandoned ship, 'Just for a handful of silver he left us, just for a riband to stick in his coat.'

22

The final decade

In the period 1949–50 Raman had selected seven research students to work with him at the RRI, but one of them left a little later because though Raman wanted a geologist to study the physics of minerals, the work did not develop. Then, in 1954, he recruited S. Pancharatnam almost the same way as he had Jayaraman—a brief courtesy visit to the great man that was to change their scientific lives for the better. Pancharatnam was his sister Sitalaxmi's son and was visiting his brother Chandrasekhar who was a student at the lab. By the end of the visit, Raman invited Pancharatnam to join his institute. Pancharatnam did some remarkable work under Raman in the area of light propagation, interference and the state of polarization of light in absorbing crystals. He formulated the Pancharatnam phase in 1956, a fundamental quantum optic effect which was rediscovered in 1984 by Sir Michael Berry and came to be known as the Berry phase.

Because they were all brilliant and dedicated, and had a strong mentor who motivated them to achieve, those who stayed with Raman for their training quickly got their doctorates from different universities. Raman gave them what he thought essential for a life in science: laboratory facilities, a residence, a salary that was enough for a comfortable though frugal life and freedom to pursue science without interference or interruption. They were welcome to continue at his lab, but they were young and the outside world beckoned with its promises.

They went their own ways. Chandrasekhar to Cambridge in 1954, A.K. Ramdas to Purdue in 1956, M.R. Bhat to Ohio State University; D. Krishnamurti, S. Venkateswaran and K.S. Viswanathan, all were ready to take on the world, and Raman helped them get positions they sought. That was the guru in him, to let the disciples make their choice. But there was no doubt he was anguished at the departures, especially at Jayaraman's departure for UCLA (University of California, Los Angeles) in 1960. Most anguishing was the departure of Pancharatnam, on whom he had pinned his hopes as a worthy successor to step into his shoes. But Pancharatnam wanted to leave, and Raman recommended him to a faculty position at Mysore University in 1960. Later, Pancharatnam left for Oxford in 1964. Raman refused to take any more students.

All the fledglings had taken wing and flown. The eagle brooded, paced the vast empty expanses of his laboratories, walked the vast empty gardens of his institute and pledged to continue entirely on his own, no students, no associates, just his ever-faithful technical assistants, Padmanabhan and Balakrishnan. Just two, but two were all he needed to work on his own. Padmanabhan had been the first to be appointed and Balakrishnan, an expert glass-blower, was appointed shortly after. Both remained with him for the rest of his life.

Over the next few years, he studied the physiology of the eye. He had started his studies earlier. The first Gandhi Memorial Lecture, given in 1959, was on 'Light, Colour and Vision'. He talked about how the human eye functions as an optical instrument. This led him to consider other aspects of the phenomenon of vision. The retina came under his scrutiny.

Raman devised a method whereby one could view one's own retina. One first looks steadily at a very brightly illuminated screen through a colour filter which completely absorbs one part of the spectrum and transmits the rest of the spectrum. When the filter is suddenly removed, one can see a highly enlarged view of one's own retina in full colour on the screen, displaying its response in different areas to the incident light. By using a series of filters transmitting different wavelengths, one could explore the behaviour of one's retina to various spectral excitations.[1]

Raman studied the eye as an optical instrument, and how it could discern colours with minute shades of difference. When he was in California, he had noted the Ring Nebula in Lyra exhibiting flaming colours and noted that the variegated colours in the nebula in Orion were determined by the line emission of the gases of which it is composed. Now he worked on those phenomena to measure the intensity at which colour perception is lost for different shades of each colour. After careful experimentation, he evolved many empirical theories to explain the perception of colour.

He enlisted from around him those who were willing to volunteer for his experiments. P.S. Jairam, a teenager on a college exchange programme from Madras to the Indian Institute, was curious to see the Raman Institute and walked into the RRI campus, hoping against hope that he might see the scientist in person. He not only ran into Raman, who was on one of his daily walks around the garden, but got to speak to him. In the course of the conversation, while Raman was explaining his study of the perception of colour, something led Jairam to respond that he himself was colour-blind. Raman was excited. He was experimenting with different types of colour blindness and here was someone who could help. Jairam was asked to volunteer as one of the subjects of the experiments, which of course he did readily. He recalls how cordial Raman was with all the volunteers and how carefully he carried out the observations. Jairam was thrilled when Raman not only gave him a cheque for his work but also invited him over to the director's bungalow for tea and biscuits.

Raman published his observations in a series of articles in *Current Science* through the 1960s and published the whole as a book, *The Physiology of Vision*. But Raman's theories and results on the physiology of vision did not receive much recognition, mainly because his simple methods of experimentation seemed primitive at a time when there were far more sophisticated measuring instruments and electronic tabulations for the investigation of the visual process.

Raman lived in and for the world he had built for himself. The Indian Academy of Sciences was manned by a small staff. The two journals, *Current Science* and *Proceedings*, were published with unfailing regularity. The annual meeting of the academy brought together a great many scientists from different disciplines, just as it was meant to. He also initiated an annual Gandhi Memorial Lecture. '[T]o enable the Institute to co-operate in the furtherance of the objects of the Gandhi Smarak Nidhi, an annual series of lectures on the subjects of "science and human values and/or any of its aspects" has been established at the Institute with the aid of the Nidhi.'

His Gandhi Memorial Lectures give an indication of how he sought to introduce complex ideas in simple diction. The titles were—Light, Colour and Vision; Eye and Vision; Earthquakes; The Diamond; Voice and Speech and Language; Perception of Sound: Mechanism in Human Ear; The Cochlea and the Perception of Sound; and so on.

Raman's scientific output continued with undiminished enthusiasm and concentration, and he found satisfaction in his pursuit of beauty. But as a person the politics of science in the country deeply troubled him and he gradually isolated himself from the world. He wanted nobody to disturb him. He placed a large board on the gate of his institute: 'No Visitors. Do Not Disturb.' He removed the telephone from his office table. The secretary was instructed not to make any appointments.

He shut himself up in his hermitage. In the early 1950s he had proudly shown visitors his sapling trees, saying that Hindu scriptures advocated a man to retire to the forest in his old age, but that he was making the forest come to him. Now the forest was his be-all and end-all, for he wanted nothing of the world. He had planted a grove of eucalyptus and now that the trees had grown, he walked in their scented shade every day. He had nurtured a gorgeous rose garden, with many different kinds of species, the details of each of which he knew by name and colour. The grounds of the institute were kept meticulously clean by a fleet of gardeners and sweepers. Raman lived in this world he had created, seeing hidden worlds of beauty such as we, average people, will never know.

23

Lokasundari Raman reopens the gates

In his isolation, he had one unwavering source of support, who had been by his side through his triumphs and trials—his wife Lokam. She had always been energetic, keeping his world stable and also living out her own potentials.[1] In Calcutta, thanks to her adeptness at learning languages and her outgoing temperament, she was active in women's groups and participated in Gandhi's movement. When their son Raja was a toddler, her sister Lakshmi had sent a cook, Hariharan, who turned out to be very reliable. She could then go out, knowing her children were in good hands. He stayed with her for ten years and even moved with them to Bangalore for a short time.

Soudamini Mehta, wife of a lawyer and daughter-in-law of a millionaire, was one of her acquaintances. Every Sunday, Soudamini and she would take bundles of khadi and visit rich Marwari houses to persuade the women in the houses to buy them. They would go to labourers' wives to talk about health and get doctors to volunteer for them. A dispensary was started at Ramakrishna Mutt and Lokam joined Soudamini in persuading women to come in for antenatal care.

They would go to Kali temples and campaign against animal sacrifices. Lokam had even written an article to the local newspapers about their campaign. The article concluded with the words:

A firm resolve on the part of my sisters in Bengal will achieve what either forced legislation, or a half-hearted support on the part of the legislator or the public fail to do. And I make bold to write this appeal to stop further the slaughter of the innocents; more so, for I am strengthened by the counsels of many of my Bengali friends here. It was more a request from them to appeal in the Press that prompted me to do so. Sadhus of the Belur Mutt have already promised their wholehearted support by way of volunteer service should others take initiative in this matter; they will induce the priests, at first, to give up the butcher's profession, cajole them to good acts, and suffer for them if necessary at all Kali temples where such sacrifices are made in the open and in public in the name of the goddess.

It rested, therefore, on me to write and I earnestly pray that my brothers and sisters in Bengal will rise to the occasion, as so many times before they did, to lessen greatly the number of such victims at least, if it cannot altogether be stopped.

Her motherless cousin, named Natesan, stayed with them in Calcutta for some time. She persuaded him to join Gandhi's movement. She was already sending yarn to Sabarmati Ashram and when she wrote to them about Natesan, they welcomed him. He stayed at Sabarmati for four years and even learnt to accept that cleaning toilets was a chore that had to be done by one and all.

When she came to Bangalore, she was appointed to various honorary positions connected with hospitals, social agencies, the jail and women's organizations, honours and responsibilities that came with being the wife of a distinguished citizen. For years, she was on the board of Vani Vilas Hospital and St Martha's Hospital; she had founded Seva Sadan in 1935 for the welfare of women and had been actively involved in orphanages and women's homes. She was the president of Bharat Scouts and Guides. She was also associated with the Red Cross.

She contributed to the Raman Institute in her own way over the years. There was no dispensary attached to the institute and often students came to her for help in cases of serious illness or emergency. She would ask her driver to drive the ailing student to the hospital and occasionally, would go with him. She campaigned for a dispensary and an on-site physician and for a women's hostel. When the women's hostel was finally opened, she was the warden for several years. She made friends easily and befriended those in need.

When they were living in the director's bungalow on campus, a Christian priest used to come from a nearby seminary in the evening and sit in the garden. Lokam used to be with her sons, and he would sit and talk of his Milan. The cypresses and the garden reminded him of his native town. Raman would come upon him occasionally and they would talk about music. The priest was building the seminary literally brick by brick—he would carry a few bricks at a time from a nearby kiln and a bricklayer would set them up. He asked Lokam how much the houses on campus cost and she did not know. They had pleasant conversations but he stopped coming at some point and she forgot about him. Years later she received a call from the seminary that Father would like to see her. He was in hospital. She went with flowers and he told her that after working in several places, he had come back to die at the seminary that he had built. He was now calling his old friends to bid them goodbye.

Another time, a group of ten or twelve nuns invited her to go on an excursion with them, and she packed idlis for all of them and set off. On the way back, their van stalled, and the old driver couldn't do anything. Lokam went to the side of the road but nobody stopped. So she stood bang in the middle and the driver of a car had to press the brakes. However, the man sitting at the back with his wife said he was in a hurry and would stop on the way back. A few minutes later, the car returned—they had probably come to buy eggs from the farm before it closed for the day—and the driver was rude but Lokam didn't care: she told him he had to help them. So he grudgingly helped push the van, and fortunately it started. Several days later, she and Raman were at a wedding reception and went to the dais to bless the couple. A lady came up to Lokam and with many apologies said she had been in that car. Her husband tried to hide but she called him up and asked him also to apologize, which he did sheepishly. But Lokam told them they had been of great help, and they recovered from their embarrassment.

Rich or poor, those who met her found in her a friend who was always ready to do what she could to help them. In 1955 she had founded the Mysore State Council for Child Welfare, later called Karnataka State Council for Child Welfare, and was its president. Soon, its office moved to one of the rooms of 'Panchavati'. There she had started a school for underprivileged children and had opened a library of Kannada and English books. The compound of 'Panchavati' was always open to children. After they moved to the Raman Institute campus, she would go to her office almost every day.

For over fifty years Lokam had provided Raman with what he needed at any given time, even in those times when he did not know what he needed. Now, in the 1960s, when the scientist-sage secluded himself from the outside world, she brought him exactly what he needed—she told him of children waiting at the gates, India's future waiting to be initiated into the wonders of science. Raman had lost much of his faith in India's future, having seen the grab-and-run mentality that had replaced the spirit of renunciation and perseverance, which had motivated Buddha and Ramana Maharishi and Gandhi, and which he himself had tried to follow.

Now, through Lokam's intercession, the world of children whom she served through the Child Welfare Council came dancing into his life, and he allowed them access to himself and all he had treasured in his world. Raman's old enthusiasm for educating young minds returned, and he welcomed meetings with children. Soon, there were busloads of school students coming by appointment to get a tour of the institute. Raman, to whom educational causes meant the world, threw open the gates of the institute to schoolchildren. Often he escorted them personally, talked about the colours of birds' wings and of seashells and gems. A stop at the gem-room was the finale of the tours—Raman would bring the children to the room, switch off the overhead lights, and exult in the gasps of astonishment and excitement that filled the room as the gems and rocks glowed and glittered and sparkled under special lamps. He invited small groups of children in the evening, and under the open sky in front of the main building, he talked to them about the wonders of astronomy. He gave many lectures, which were always geared to the understanding of the average listener, and with children, he seemed to know just how much of everyday experiences he should put into the scientific explanation. Children, like the adults, always returned with a feeling that they were more knowledgeable coming out of the rooms than when they had gone in. They might forget what they had thought they learnt but they never forgot the enthusiasm and passion for science that the great scientist had inspired in them.

Raman never lost faith in the capacity of the young to both absorb and accomplish. 'He disputed the statement that old age and wisdom went together. It is not wisdom, but the freshness of outlook, the indomitable desire to achieve something that matters and it is the characteristic of young people.'[2]

Do not go gentle

Raman might have shut himself off from the world but the world kept knocking on his door, and he sometimes agreed to give lectures. Every lecture repeated one or more of his favourite ideals—that India should carve its own scientific space, that Indians should stay in India, that India should manufacture its own scientific apparatus and equipment, that science should be applied to improve the quality of life in the country, that nature inspires at all times.

In October 1960, invited to open the graduate science department at Mysore University, he asked students to develop 'fanatic loyalty' and take pride in their own centres of learning. The local journalist reported, 'There was vast scope for research in India, he told them.'[1]

During the International Indian Ocean Expedition of 1962, Raman organized a symposium in Bombay on oceanographic research. In 1964 he followed it up with a symposium on meteorology in Pune, because Pune was the second most important centre for meteorological activities.

In 1966, addressing the graduating class of IIT, Madras, he said, 'We borrow money and expert know-how from abroad and forget to think for ourselves. We must shake this off and learn to stand on our own legs. It is better to work with the most inefficient and useless equipment than to stand on borrowed legs.'[2] Hyperbolic, but the meaning is clear.

In 1967, inaugurating a symposium of the mining industry in south India, he lamented that the principle of self-help and self-respect was lacking. 'Instead of trying to learn the real essence of science and to think independently, people leave for foreign countries to study. That should be discouraged.'

Raman went to Ahmedabad in December of 1968 at Vikram Sarabhai's invitation, to speak at the laying of the foundation stone for a Community Science Centre. The title of his talk was 'Why the Sky is Blue'. It is worthwhile quoting at length from this talk, for it reiterates what his science has said about nature and how nature at all times was his focus.

> I chose this subject for the simple reason that this is an example of something you do not have to go to the laboratory to see. . . . And I think it is also an example of the spirit of science. You learn science by keeping your eyes and ears open and looking around at this world. The real inspiration of science, at least to me, has been essentially the love of nature . . . To me, everything we see is incredible, absolutely incredible. We take it all for granted. But I think the essence of the scientific spirit is to look behind and beyond and to realise what a wonderful world we live in. And everything we see presents to us not a subject for curiosity, but a challenge, a challenge to the spirit of man to try to understand something of this vast mystery that surrounds us. . . .
>
> [M]y young friends, I want you to realise that the spirit of science is not finding short and quick answers. The spirit of science is to delve deeper—and that is what I want to bring home to my audience—and deeper. Don't be satisfied with the short and quick answers. You must never be content with that; you must look around and think and ask all sorts of questions.

... In the course of time you will find some of the truth, but you never reach the end....

I think dreams are the best part of life. It is not the realisation but the anticipation—I am going to make a discovery tomorrow—that makes the man of science work hard, whether he makes the discovery or not....

The greatest thing in life is not the achievement but the desire to achieve. It is the effort that we put in, that ultimately is the greatest satisfaction ...

Ultimately the aim of scientific knowledge is to benefit human life.

~

By 1968 Raman was not in good health but he still kept his work routine. One of his last projects was to study the geography and geology of the Krishna Valley, because in earlier times it had been a place where diamonds were mined. As with his ongoing interest in meteorology that spurred him to get scientists to work on patterns of thunderstorms in order to make air travel safer, his interest in diamonds had a very practical side—to mine diamonds from the Krishna Valley. He had studied the riverbed and the flow of the river, and established that the frequent flooding of the Krishna was because of underground high rock formation, which arrested its flow to the sea. He pointed to records of the presence of mining in the sixteenth and seventeenth centuries and said diamonds had been deposited along the rock formation, and that it was erroneous to assume that the entire supply had already been mined. In a two-page paper, written in his usual lucid style and published in September 1968, he argues that though an arduous project, it would be worthwhile trying to locate the veins of diamond that still lay in the valley.

~

Pancharatnam, who had left for Oxford in 1964, died there on 28 May 1969 of a respiratory disease, at the age of thirty-five. Raman was grief-stricken. Raman had a special bond with all his students, but for this youngest son of his favourite sister Sitalaxmi, he had deep love and respect. Raman had numerous brilliant students, but Pancharatnam was perhaps closest to his heart, and his death was a severe emotional blow. All his students had left him to pursue their own paths but he had hoped that Pancharatnam would be his heir, the one who would step into his shoes and carry on his legacy. It was not to be.

Though his health was failing, Raman went to Kanpur early in 1970 because he had given his word that he would. He spoke as he always did, saying what he wanted to say openly and bluntly, annoying many, inspiring others.

He then went to Delhi and delivered a talk at the National Physical Laboratory, on 'Fluorochromes'.[3] This is one of the few science-centred talks of which we have longer excerpts and it gives us an idea of his proverbial excellence at extemporaneous additions, a skill he maintained to the very end of his life. It is personal, humorous, and powerful. Though the main talk is on the colour and coloration of flowers, the conversational additions that characterized his public lectures come through very clearly. He spoke light-heartedly about his failing health: 'I told Lady Raman: I hope you see me coming back alive from Kanpur.' He talked about his visit to Kanpur and how he had fired them up saying, 'We must measure ourselves against the biggest man in the West and try not only to emulate them but to excel them. This is the sort of fiery stuff, revolutionary stuff, just as Bal Gangadhar Tilak did in the old days . . . he was not like Gandhiji . . . I think you must first rouse up a nation to fighting fury before you ask them to behave peacefully. It seems like a contradiction—to be in a fighting fury and then behave peacefully.' He ends the talk conversationally: 'I have spoken long enough. I lose count of time when I am on my feet and start speaking . . . I think I must have exhausted you. I have not exhausted my patience or energy . . . I don't say I am a volcano but I do say I get sort of worked up by continuing to talk . . . All that I say is this: that we in this country have to wake up and do something about it.'

Towards the end of May, he had an acute attack. Ramaseshan told me he had feared that Raman might die on the first anniversary of Pancharatnam's death. Raman knew he did not have much time. He had always kept his books in order, but it was time now to give the final directions. The academy usually had its annual meeting in December, but he decided to advance the meeting to September and decided it would be in Bangalore.

After conducting the academy meetings as always, there was one more public commitment—the annual Gandhi Memorial Lecture that he had delivered in the week of Gandhi's birthday every year. That year he spoke on 'The Cochlea and the Perception of Sound'. The only allowance he made to himself was that he would take the questions at the end of the lecture while seated, instead of on his feet as he had done for years.

Sivaraj Ramaseshan was never far from him during the last months.[4]

Shortly before his birthday, Raman was admitted to a private nursing home. He clearly stated that he did not want to be on life-support at any time, and indeed that he would like to die in his own home. On 3 November it seemed that the end was very near and Ramaseshan telegraphed Raman's son, Radhakrishnan, who was travelling in Europe. He sent telegrams to Radhakrishnan's contacts in both Paris and Cambridge.

On 6 November Ramaseshan went to visit him and stood at the closed door of the room before entering. He heard a soft voice and broke down, believing that the great bellowing voice had grown so weak, but then he heard a loud 'Hahaha' bellow of laughter, and realized the low voice had been the visitor's, not Raman's. The visitor was Raman's nephew, soft-spoken Balakrishnan, CS's third son. It was a comic interlude in the tragic drama of death.

Radhakrishnan arrived soon after.

Raman had his wish. He was moved back to his house. As he lay in his bedroom, he wished he had made the windows lower so he could have seen his flower beds and trees from the bed. His bed was then raised so that he could see the garden. His sister Sitalaxmi came from Madras to visit. She was herself ailing, her body bent with sciatica. As she walked about the room, Raman asked her to sit down, saying it pained him to see her in her weak condition. The bond between the two had always been strong. Sitalaxmi was nine at the time of their father's unexpected death, and Raman and CS had taken on the parental responsibilities of getting her married. Three of her five sons—Ramaseshan, Chandrasekhar and Pancharatnam—had been Raman's students, and each had made a mark in physics. And Ramaseshan was now more of a son and confidant to him than anyone else in the world.

Ramaseshan spent much of his time by Raman's bedside. He made sure Raman made all the decisions that had to be made, by asking him the necessary questions, and leading the conversation to the matters that required a decision.

Raman convened a meeting of the Raman Institute Board of Management for 19 November, to finalize and sign certain legal documents. Lokam was there, as was Ramaseshan. Bhagavantam arrived in good time for the meeting, but T.S. Sadasivan's plane was delayed, and the other members could not be there. Raman was impatient and angry at the delay. At last Sadasivan came in. Raman did not waste a minute. 'Sadasivan, you are late. I have no time. Now we have a quorum,' he said, 'read this over carefully and if you are agreeable, put your signature on it.' Sadasivan was in tears. He briefly scanned the document and signed it. Raman, particular and solicitous of such details, asked his secretary to give

Sadasivan the cheque for his travel allowance. Even as he glanced at the document that now had the necessary number of signatures, Raman noticed a typographical error. He had it corrected but was too weak to initial on the correction. 'Now go away, everyone,' he said. 'I have to rest.'

As he lay dying, Raman gave instructions on what he would like done by way of last rites—'no ritualistic mumbo jumbo' but only a simple cremation at the institute itself.

There was one big responsibility that was still pending—the choice of his successor. He had indirectly said several times that Ramaseshan should assume charge of the Raman Research Institute. That evening—19th of November—he asked Ramaseshan directly if he would take charge of the institute. To this, Ramaseshan responded, 'Sir, what about Radhakrishnan?' Raman answered, 'Yes, he has all the qualities one needs,' and he went on to talk about his son's sense of adventure in sailing around the world in a boat, enumerated the qualities of his son—perseverance, scientific acumen, originality, initiative, etc.—'but he would think of it as an inheritance and so refuse it, the stupid ass.'

Ramaseshan knew Radhakrishnan well and fully realized that, like Raman's nephew, the astrophysicist Chandrasekhar, his son too might decline any honour that might be perceived as nepotism, but Ramaseshan persisted. He asked Raman if he could make Radhakrishnan the offer anyway, and Raman said yes. That night, Ramaseshan typed up the conversation and thought he'd ask Raman to sign it next morning. However, by morning Raman was already losing control and coherence, and Ramaseshan did not want to be accused of having forced a dying man to sign something. But he showed it to Sadasivan.

On the 20th, Raman still had much to say, but he was getting unintelligible. When Lokam said he should be thinking of god and taking his name, he said, 'God? . . . I have heard of godly men,

Jesus, Buddha, and I have met a godly human being—Mahatma Gandhi.' And he went on to talk about Gandhi.

Raman passed away at 7.20 a.m. on Saturday, 21 November 1970. His death was first announced in the morning Kannada news of All India Radio. Politicians voiced their messages. The day was immediately declared a holiday. People came by the thousands to pay homage to the body as it lay in the central hall of the director's bungalow, and Lokam received them all with dignity and composure. Many busloads of school students, who cried openly, were on the institute grounds that day.

By special permission, Raman was cremated on the grounds of the institute, on the same day, early in the afternoon. Later, a tree was planted on the spot where he had been cremated. Its botanical name is *Cybistax donnell-smithii* and it is known as Prima Vera of Mexico. It has the unique quality of blossoming only once a decade. By some strange coincidence, it blossomed in 1988, the centenary of Raman's birth, on 28 February, the day designated as National Science Day, and again on 4 February 1999, towards the end of the year-long celebrations of the Golden Jubilee of the Raman Institute.

Epilogue

All of Raman's material assets passed on to the RRI Trust on Raman's demise.

In 1972 the institute came under the funding of the Department of Science and Technology of the Government of India.

Raman's son, Radhakrishnan, who had made a name for himself in the world of science as a radio astronomer, became the director of Raman Research Institute in 1972. He retired in 1994. Since then there have been other directors.

Lokasundari Raman died on 22 May 1980.

Sivaraj Ramaseshan, who did much to perpetuate the Raman legacy, died on 29 December 2003.

The Digital Repository of the RRI library has the *Complete Works* of Raman, edited by Ramaseshan. It also provides useful archival information on the life and works of C.V. Raman. One can access them, free of charge, as also many of the publications of the Indian Academy of Sciences.

Radhakrishnan passed away on 3 March 2011. He is survived by his wife Dominique (née Barnard), their son Vivek, his wife Namrata Kini, and their two daughters.

The institute is a busy place today, with researchers from all over the country and visitors from all over the world.

Milestones

7 November 1888	Birth in maternal grandparents' house in Tiruvanaikkaval near Tiruchi
1892	Family moves to Waltair (Vishakapatnam)
1900	Matriculated with top rank from Hindu High School in Vishakapatnam
January 1903	Joined Presidency College, Madras
December 1905	Earned BA degree
	Received Gold Medal for Physics; Elphinstone Medal and Jagirdar Memorial Gold Medal
1906	Published his first paper, in *Philosophical Magazine*
1907	First rank in Indian Financial Services recruitment examination
2 June 1907	Married Lokasundari, daughter of Mr and Mrs Krishnaswami Iyer
	Joined IFS as assistant accountant general at Calcutta
	Started research at Indian Association for the Cultivation of Science, Calcutta
End of July 1907	Brother Sundaram dies at age nine
	Brother Ramaswamy born on 20 August

1909	Posted to Rangoon
27 February 1910	Father dies at age forty-four
	Posted to Nagpur
1911	Posted back to Calcutta
23 July 1912	Sister Meena dies at age nine
1912	**Received Curzon Research Prize**
1913	**Awarded Woodburn Research Medal**
1914	Asutosh Mookerjee offers Palit Professorship in Physics, Calcutta University
	(October) Brother Skandan (Kumaraswamy) dies at age twenty
March 1916	Mother dies of small pox at approximate age of forty-seven
1917	**Resigns government job and joins as Palit Professor**
November 1918	Sister Mangalam dies in flu pandemic at age twenty-seven, leaving six children
1919	Elected secretary for IACS on the death of Amritalal Sircar
1921	Awarded honorary DSc degree by Calcutta University
	First trip abroad, as delegate of Calcutta University to the Congress of Universities of the British Empire, held at Oxford. Extended his trip to include research trips within England
	Observes blueness of the Mediterranean Sea and speculates it is not due to reflection of the blueness of the sky. Conducts experiments on return and publishes paper on the results
	First son, Raja (named Chandrasekhar after his father), born in November

1923	Grandmother Muthuchipi dies at Porasakudi
1924	**Elected Fellow of the Royal Society**
	Second trip abroad, to Canada and the United States
	Visiting Professor at California Institute of Technology at R.A. Millikan's invitation
1925	Visited Russia, invited by Russian Academy of Sciences for its bicentenary celebration
1927	Published a monograph on acoustics of musical instruments for *Handbuch der Physik*
1928	**(February) Discovery of Raman Effect**
	(August) Awarded Matteucci Medal by the Italian Society of Science
1929	Second son, Radhakrishnan, born 18 May
	Knighted by King-Emperor George V of England
	Invited by Faraday Society to open a discussion on Molecular Spectra and Structure at Bristol, England
	Awarded Hughes Medal of the Royal Society of London
	Honorary PhD from Freiburg University
	Honorary membership to Zurich Physical Society
1930	**Awarded the Nobel Prize for Physics**
	Awarded Honorary LLD from University of Glasgow
1932	**Honorary DSc of University of Paris**
1933	Joined Indian Institute of Science, Bangalore, as first Indian director
1934	Founded the Indian Academy of Sciences on 24 April

1935	**Awarded title of Rajasabha Bhushana by the Maharaja of Mysore**
1935	Invites Max Born to Bangalore
1936	Visits Gandhi at Nandi Hills. Gandhi visits IISc on 12 June
1936	Raman–Nath theory
1937	Resigns directorship of IISc. Continues as professor of physics
1939	Son Raja (Chandrasekhar) sent to Cambridge, England, to study physics
1941	**Awarded Franklin Medal by the Franklin Institute, Philadelphia**
	Elected member of the Optical Society of America
1948	Retires from IISc. Opens Raman Research Institute at Bangalore
	Appointed National Professor, the first person to be thus honoured
	Honorary doctorate from University of Bordeaux
1954	**Awarded Bharat Ratna—India's highest honour**
	Lenin Peace Prize
1960	(February) Elder brother CS dies in Madras
1968	Published *Physiology of Vision*
21 November 1970	Death at his home on RRI campus; cremation on RRI grounds by special permission

Within India, Raman received honorary doctorates from the universities of Allahabad, Banaras, Bombay, Calcutta, Dacca, Delhi, Kanpur, Madras, Mysore, Patna, Osmania and Sri Venkateswara.

Notes

The Man, the Scientist, the Legacy

1. Speech reported in *The Hindu*, 27 February 1940.
2. *The New Physics*, 1971, p. 141. Originally delivered in the 1940s as a series of nineteen radio talks, the lectures were printed by the Philosophical Library, New York in 1951 and reprinted in 1971.
3. S. Ramaseshan and C.R. Rao, eds, *C.V. Raman: A Pictorial Biography* (Bangalore: Indian Academy of Sciences, 1988), p. 15.
4. Agra University Convocation, 1950.
5. Rajinder Singh, *Nobel Laureate C.V. Raman's Work on Light Scattering: Historical Contributions to a Scientific Biography* (Berlin: Logos Verlag, 2004), p. 12, quoting from Raman's letter. The version used is a PDF copy of Singh's PhD dissertation that he kindly sent me early in the preparation of this biography.
6. Ramaseshan, in *Current Science* 40: 9.
7. Ibid.

Chapter 1: Family background and early years

1. Most of the family details in this chapter are taken from C.S. Ayyar's *Family History* (1946), a copy of which I inherited from my mother, Rajalakshmi, CS's eldest daughter. I got the name of Pethar Seshadry from Sunil Muthusami, who is also a descendant of Pethar Seshadry, through Muthuswami's brother. His family chart suggests that

Ayyamuthian's given name was 'Muthuswami' and that 'Ayya' is a common honorific.

Chapter 3: Marriage and government service

1. During the summer of 1972, when I spent a considerable amount of time talking to Lady Raman about her early life, she once referred to this friend as the son of Raghavendra, Sivan's family doctor. The identity, however, is not certain.

Chapter 4: 'You have come at last.'

1. Most other biographers say Raman saw the sign on his way *to* work and went to it on his way back. Lady Raman says that he saw it on his way *back from* work. This is corroborated in one of the earliest biographies, *Leaders of Modern India: Raman and J.C. Bose*, by the unnamed author of a textbook for Grade IV published by Oxford University Press in 1936. Given Raman's habit of immediately taking action on anything that interested him, I trust Lady Raman's version.
2. IACS Annual Report, 1902.
3. IACS Annual Report, 1903.
4. IACS Annual Report, 1907.
5. Between them, by the end of 1908, the brothers paid off all family debts, which had risen close to 4000 rupees.

Chapter 5: Render unto Caesar what is his but not a paisa more

1. In the summer of 1972 Lokasundari Raman provided me with details of their life in Nagpur and Rangoon.

Chapter 6: Star-gazing in Calcutta

1. In 1918 the National Congress was held in Calcutta. Annie Besant had just been elected president. In a procession held in her honour, she was seated in a carriage drawn by sixteen white horses that were

from Raja Mullick's stables. The 'charioteer' was none other than Rashbehari Ghosh, and he spent ten days polishing up his skills, coached by Raja Mullick.

2. After the citing of Halley's comet in 1910, enthusiasts started this society, with accountant general H.G. Tomkins (1869–1934) at the helm. The society was alive for a decade, when it published the *Journal of the Astronomical Society of India* (*JASI*), whose last issue is dated June 1920. This name was adopted by another society that was set up in post-Independence India in 1972, with its headquarters in Hyderabad. (Rajesh Kochhar and Jayant Narlikar, *Astronomy in India: A Perspective*, Indian National Science Academy, New Delhi, 1995, chapter 1.)

3. Optics is the study of the interaction of light with matter, and involves observation and tabulation of the behaviour and properties of light waves.

4. Raman's publications in the *JASI* are not included in the six-volume set, *Scientific Papers of C.V. Raman*, ed., S. Ramaseshan (Bangalore: Indian Academy of Science, 1988). I was curious about their absence and contacted Rajinder Singh, who responded that he had indeed been working on them. He kindly gave me the sources for these lectures and I traced them to volumes 2 (1911–12), 3 (1912–13) and 4 (1913–14) of the *JASI*. I am pleased to note that Singh's research on the subject has since been published in 2010 in *Current Science* 99:8, 1127–32.

5. *Report of Astronomical Society*, April 1913.

6. *Illustrated Weekly*, 23 April 1939.

7. *Current Science*, Vol. 12, 1943.

Chapter 7: Palit Professorship

1. Quoted in 'C.V. Raman and the Emergence of Modern Science' by M.V. Satyanarayana and M.D. Srinivas, in the *PPST Journal*, 17 December 1988.

2. Archives of Churchill College, Cambridge, quoted in Singh, *C.V. Raman's Work on Light Scattering*.

3. Bose started exploring the response in plants to external stimuli. He

was also able to establish a similarity in plant response. However, his theories met with stiff resistance from physiologists who feared that his new theories would upset the old ones and they persuaded the Royal Society to not publish his papers on the subject.

4. Quoted in G. Venkataraman, *Journey into Light: Life and Science of C.V. Raman* (Bangalore: Indian Academy of Sciences, 1988), p. 37.
5. Ibid., p. 38.
6. S.N. Sen, *Professor C.V. Raman: Scientific Work at Calcutta* (Calcutta: Indian Association for the Cultivation of Science, 1988).
7. C.V. Raman, 'Books that have Influenced Me: A Symposium' (Madras: G.A. Natesan, 1947), p. 29.
8. In the last phase of his life, Raman picked up this subject and wrote a book with the same title.
9. Venkataraman, *Journey into Light*, p. 94.
10. 'Acoustical Knowledge of the Ancient Hindus' (1922), in Ramaseshan, *Scientific Papers of C.V. Raman*, vol. 2.
11. *Sir Asutosh Mookerjee Silver Jubilee* (Calcutta University Press, 1922), vol. 2, p. 179.
12. N.H. Fletcher, 'The Non-linear Physics of Musical Instruments', *Reports of Progress in Physics* 62 (1999), pp. 723–64.
13. Quoted in A. Jayaraman, *C.V. Raman: A Memoir* (Madras: Affiliated East West Press, 1989), p. 145.
14. Singh, *C.V. Raman's Work on Light Scattering*, p. 17.
15. This and subsequent two quotes from L.A. Ramdas, 'Dr. C.V. Raman', in the *Journal of Physical Education* 1, 1971, pp. 2–18.
16. *Current Science* 47:6, 20 March 1978, p. 180.

Chapter 8: Blue of the Mediterranean

1. Quoted from the minutes of the university senate meetings, 16 May 1925.
2. Ibid., 29 September 1923.
3. Ibid., 26 June 1926.
4. Ibid., 26 March 1930.
5. Ibid., 16 May 1925.

6. Venkataraman, *Journey into Light*, pp. 49–50.
7. RRI [Raman Research Institute] Digital Repository.
8. C. Subrahmanya Ayyar, *My Musical Extravagance* (Madras, 1945), p. 2.

Chapter 9: What next? The Nobel of course

1. Robert Kanigel, *The Man Who Knew Infinity: A Life of the Genius Ramanujan* (New York: C. Scribner's, 1991), p. 291.
2. *Current Science* 70:1, 1996, p. 104.
3. *Current Science* 57:4, 1988, p. 171.
4. *Current Science* 70:1, 1996, p. 104.
5. Ibid., p. 106.
6. Ibid.
7. Ibid.
8. Cited in Singh's PhD dissertation, p. 71.
9. Svein Rosseland (1894–1985), a Norwegian astrophysicist and pioneer in the field of theoretical astrophysics.
10. Kameshwar C. Wali, *Chandra: A Biography of S. Chandrasekhar* (University of Chicago Press, 1990), p. 254. Wali cites this in an interview he had with Chandrasekhar, in which Chandrasekhar refers to a talk he had with Rosseland, where Rosseland told him Raman was disappointed that the audiences he addressed in California were so scanty, and that Raman vowed he would make a discovery that would make people sit up and take notice of him, as it were. There seems to be a slippage in this narrative, for Jayaraman quotes a long passage from the *Pasadena Star* of 19 December 1924: '[Y]esterday addressed an enthusiastic audience of more than 300 teachers, students and graduates . . . Interest in his subject here surprised him; attendance at scientific lectures in India he said being one of the much desired conditions that is sadly lacking.' (Jayaraman, *C.V. Raman: A Memoir*, p. 18)

    However, there is little doubt that Raman was aiming for the Nobel Prize, the only rung in the ladder that was higher than an FRS.

11. *Current Science* 57:22, p. 1210.

12. G.H. Keswani, *Raman and His Effect* (New Delhi, National Book Trust, 1980), p. 44.

13. This is reported in *Chandra* by Wali, as a hearsay report from an unnamed person and seems very inconsistent with Raman's letter of 8 August 1935 quoted on page 104. As Wali himself has pointed out, CS had great expectations of his son, and did not at all like the idea of his son being beholden to his uncle. So this probably influenced Chandrasekhar more, and the hearsay report gave him another reason to decline Raman's offer.

14. Robert A. Millikan was an American experimental physicist and received the Nobel Prize in 1923 for his work on the charge carried by electron, his experimental proof of Einstein's photoelectric equation.

15. Following quotes from the address as recorded in the RRI Digital Repository.

Chapter 10: The Raman Effect

1. C. Mahadevan, 'Some persons and personalities at Bow Bazar Science Association: 1925–1930', in *South India Club 26th Anniversary Number* (1952–53), pp. 65–71.

2. Sen, *Professor C.V. Raman*.

3. *Annals of the American Academy of Political and Social Sciences* 233, p. 39.

4. 'A New Type of Secondary Radiation', *Nature* 121, p. 501.

5. *Nature* 122, 1928, p. 349.

6. Cited in *Current Science* 75:1, p. 6.

7. *Indian Journal of Physics* 2, p. 398.

8. *Current Science* 47:6, 20 March 1978.

Chapter 11: The trip to Europe

1. Of the two versions, I would opt for Venkataraman's. Wali, who published much later, in 1991, could easily have checked that

Raman's visit to the US was not in the 'late 1920s' but mid-1920s. Venkataraman's story tallies with Ramaseshan's reference to Raman's visit with Compton in Chicago.

2. Singh, *C.V. Raman's Work on Light Scattering*, p. 98.
3. D.A. Long in *Raman Spectroscopy* 2000:39, p. 318.
4. While I had noticed that intriguing entry about 'disappointment', I had thought it was something wholly personal, not knowing at the time the significance of the date. During the research for this volume, the Archives Section of the Royal Swedish Academy confirmed to me the dates on which the announcements for the Nobel were made in 1929 and 1930—they were 12 and 13 November, respectively.

Chapter 12: The Nobel Prize and other honours

1. A special Raman number was published when Raman was honoured by the Calcutta Corporation in 1931. Cited in Jayaraman, *Memoir*, p. 116.
2. Ramaseshan and Rao, *Pictorial Biography*.
3. Jayaraman records another anecdote very like it in *Memoir*.
4. *Current Science* 75:11, p. 1271.
5. Ibid.
6. This is in an essay often included in school texts. It is available from an online text edited by D.K. Sebastian: *mission.akshaya.net/dpi/Textbook/Languages/English/chapter7.pdf*
7. Jayaraman records another similar incident. At his eightieth birthday felicitation event, after the encomia given by various scientists, Raman started his own talk by saying, 'You know, people may be wondering why I wear a turban in this day and age. I will tell you why. The turban is a bandage to prevent my getting a swollen head after hearing such speeches.' *Memoir*, p. 86. This, like the variation of the Raman Effect–alcohol-effect joke noted earlier, shows how Raman had a few favourite jokes which he repeated over the years.
8. Reported in full in the *Calcutta Municipal Gazette*, XIV:6, 4 July 1931, pp. 242–43, and cited in Sen, *Professor C.V. Raman*, pp. 266–70.

9. Ibid.
10. *Current Science* 1:11, May 1933, p. 335.

Chapter 13: Leaving Calcutta

1. Venkataraman, *Journey into Light*, p. 58.
2. IISc archives.
3. David DeVorkin, 'Quantum Physics and the Stars (IV): Meghnad Saha's Fate', *Journal for the History of Astronomy* 25, 1994, p. 163.
4. Singh, *C.V. Raman's Work on Light Scattering*, p. 80.
5. Cited from a letter dated 15 August 1927, addressed by Saha to Partap Kishan Kichlu. Singh, *C.V. Raman's Work on Light Scattering*, p. 18.
6. RRI newspaper clippings.
7. From Raman's son Raja's diary entry found among Lokam's diaries.
8. Ramaseshan, *Current Science* 57:22, 1988, p. 22.
9. Lokam used his Bengali words and translated them for me.

Chapter 14: The directorship of IISc

1. Max Born, *My Life: Recollections of a Nobel Laureate* (London: Taylor and Francis, 1978).
2. Cited from the *Educational Review*, May 1922, p. 662; in Sen, *Professor C.V. Raman*, p. 130.
3. 'Dr. M.O. Forster and the Indian Institute of Science', *Current Science* 1:10, p. 302.
4. Singh, *C.V. Raman's Work on Light Scattering*, p. 100.
5. 'Seen sitting with its wings folded up, *Coracias Indica* is not a particularly striking bird, though even in this posture its head, sides and tail show vivid colouration. It is when in flight that the gorgeous plumage of this bird is most strikingly seen ... The wings then exhibit a succession of bands of colours alternately a deep-indigo blue and a light greenish-blue; the tips of the wings show a delicate mixture of both colours. A remarkable feature is the striking

variation in the appearance of the wings with their position relative to the source of light and the observer ... When observed with the light behind the observer, they have a brilliant sheen, and at some angles an enamel-like lustre.' Cited in *Proceedings of IAS* A1-1-7, 1934, p. 101.

6. Ibid., pp. 101–07.

7. Already a few Jewish professionals had come to India and their presence stirred up a controversy. Newspapers made an issue of it, publishing the pros and cons of admitting refugees to India. Rajinder Singh quotes from the *Modern Review*: 'The Jews will never consent to assimilate with the Indians and help build the Indian nation. . . . We have a lot of unemployment existing among us due to being generous all these years in admitting various refugees from time to time.' Singh, *C.V. Raman's Work on Light Scattering*, p. 134.

8. Born quoted in Venkataraman, *Journey into Light*, p. 272. Of Watson he says: 'Certainly Watson did not like to continue as Professor under an Indian Director.'

Chapter 15: Women's education, Gandhi and God

1. *The Hindu*, 22 July 1940.

2. *Sunday Times*, 14 June 1936.

3. K.S. Gandhi. *Current Science* 57:24, 20 December 1988, pp. 1313–16.

4. Quoted in *Harijan*, 30 May 1936, and in *Collected Works of Mahatma Gandhi* (Publications Division, Government of India), vol. LXVIII.

5. This and subsequent quotes from speeches are from the RRI Digital Repository.

6. Facsimile of a handwritten letter (date not available), published in *Bhavan's Journal*, 27 December 1970.

7. Quoted in 'The Life and Times of a Pioneer', *The Hindu*, Sunday, 14 October 2001.

8. *The Hindu*, 30 November 1941.

Chapter 16: Ousted from directorship

1. Quoted from *Madras Mail* of 19 April 1937, which reported his speech in some detail.
2. Minutes of council meetings, 1937. My thanks to Malathi Ramanathan for sharing her copies with me.
3. Cited in Venkataraman, *Journey into Light*, p. 273.
4. Quoted from the *Hindu* dated 10 September 1937.
5. G. Venkataraman in 'The Spirit of a Giant', his Golden Jubilee Lecture delivered on 7 November 1998, stored in RRI Digital Repository.
6. S. Ramaseshan, 'The First Sixty Years: A Personal View', *Current Science,* 67:11, December 1994, p. 814.

Chapter 17: Standing alone

1. M.V. Satyanarayana and M.N. Srinivas, 'C.V. Raman and the Emergence of Modern Science', *PPST Journal*, 17 December 1988, p. 13 footnote.
2. Ramaseshan, *Current Science* 67:11, 1994, p. 808.
3. 'Colours of Stratified Media 1: Ancient Decomposed Glass', in *Proceedings of IAS* A11, pp. 469–82.

Chapter 18: The war years

1. Anecdote from Vidya Shankar, CS's fourth daughter.
2. As recounted by V. Chander, one of the sons of CS's second daughter, Balaparvati, who lived in 'Chandra Vilas' with her family after the death of CS's wife in 1931.

Chapter 19: 'Panchavati'

1. Lokam's story is somewhat different from a story that appeared on 3 August 2004 in the *Hindu*, written by Mala Kumar, which states: 'Sir C.V. Raman bought the house in 1942, and his love story with music continued here. The house was built in 1911–12 by the then Deputy Commissioner, Jagadeo Kumaraswamy

Naik. His wife Laxmammani was a revolutionary social worker, recall her granddaughters, Lakshmi Raju and Arundhati Verma Desai. She went on horseback carrying a leather whip and chased away dacoits!'

I was unable to find out if both stories are perhaps correct, in that perhaps the people referred to in the newspaper story bought the house from Ambarisha's father, and that the granddaughters might have been wrong as to who actually built the house but right about the later owners.

Chapter 20: Raman Research Institute

1. Ramaseshan, 'Raman Research Institute', *The Hindu*, 16 March 1953.
2. Jayaraman, *Memoir*, p. 140.
3. Related by CS's eldest daughter's son, G. Sekhar, who was visiting Raman at the time.
4. Quoted from conversation with S. Ramaseshan, summer of 1972.
5. 'Prevention of War Responsibility of Scientists', *The Hindu*, 11 January 1958.
6. *The Hindu*, 3 January 1958.
7. *Indian Express*, 15 June 1958.

Chapter 21: Mister Prime Minister, all that glitters is not gold

1. Jayaraman, *Memoir*, p. 115.
2. This anecdote is part of family lore and it is quite likely Raman had several such outbursts against Nehru during this period. Sekhar happened to be in that very room, but there were others in the house at the time, including his sister Vasanti, who thinks the incident might have taken place in 1956 rather than in 1955. Ramaseshan, who was not there that day, recalls that after breaking the bust, Raman swept up the pieces himself so that Lokam would not know!

3. RRI Digital Repository.
4. *Deccan Herald*, 15 August 1954.
5. Quoted from 'Raman Testament', a collection of Raman quotes, *Bhavan's Journal*, 27 December 1970, p. 75.

Chapter 22: The final decade

1. Ramaseshan, 'Introduction', in *Scientific Papers of C.V. Raman*, vol. 6.

Chapter 23: Lokasundari Raman reopens the gates

1. Details of Lokam's life and activities were gathered from conversations with her and from other sources during the 1970s, when I started writing a biography of her life.
2. Quoted from *The Hindu*, 31 July 1966.

Chapter 24: Do not go gentle

1. *Deccan Herald*, 25 October 1960.
2. Most of the quotations from or summaries of Raman's speeches are from the RRI Digital Repository.
3. What follows is from a report of his talk on 17 February 1970, published in the *NPL Techincal Bulletin* Special Issue, 7 November 1988, Raman Centenary.
4. Many of the details that follow are from a conversation I had with Ramaseshan on 1 October 1972.

Selected Bibliography

Bhagavantam, S. *Chandrasekhara Venkata Raman*. Biographical Memoirs of the Royal Society. London: Royal Society, 1971.

Bhavan's Journal. 27 December 1970 issue.

Current Science—relevant volumes.

DeVorkin, David. 'Quantum Physics and the Stars (IV): Meghnad Saha's Fate.' *Journal for the History of Astronomy* 25 (1994), pp. 155–88.

'The First Sixty Years: A Personal View.' *Current Science* 67: 11 December 1994.

Fletcher, N.H. 'The Non-linear Physics of Musical Instruments.' *Reports of Progress in Physics* 62 (1999).

Jayaraman, A. *C.V. Raman: A Memoir*. Madras: Affiliated East West Press, 1989.

Keswani, G.H. *Raman and His Effect*. New Delhi: National Book Trust, 1980.

Krishnamurti, P. *Sir C.V. Raman—A Short Biographical Sketch*. Bangalore: Bangalore Press, 1938.

Mahadevan, C. 'Some persons and personalities at Bow Bazar Science Association: 1925–1930.' *South India Club 26th Anniversary Number* (1952–53).

Pisharoty, P.R. *C.V. Raman*. New Delhi: Publications Division of Government of India, 1982.

Ramaseshan, S. and C.R. Rao. *C.V. Raman: A Pictorial Biography*. Bangalore: Indian Academy of Sciences, 1988.

Ramaseshan, S., ed. *Scientific Papers of C.V. Raman* (six volumes). Bangalore: Indian Academy of Science, 1988.

Ramdas, L.A. 'Dr. C.V. Raman.' *Journal of Physical Education* 1, 2–18 (1971).

Satyanarayana, M.V. and M.N. Srinivas. 'C.V. Raman and the Emergence of Modern Science.' *PPST Journal*, 17 December 1988.

Sen, S.N. *Professor C.V. Raman—Scientific Work at Calcutta*. Calcutta: Indian Association for the Cultivation of Science, 1988.

Singh, Rajinder. *Nobel Laureate C.V. Raman's Work on Light Scattering. Historical Contributions to a Scientific Biography*. Berlin: Logos Verlag, 2004.

Venkataraman, G. *Journey into Light: Life and Science of C.V. Raman*. Bangalore: Indian Academy of Sciences, 1988.

Index

263